VOLUME 3

...THAT THE WORLD MAY KNOW
that Thou hast sent Me, and hast
loved them, as Thou hast loved Me.

John 17:23

THAT THE WORLD MAY KNOW

Volume 3

THE CHALLENGE OF INDIA

The Challenge of India

By
FREDK. A. TATFORD, Litt.D.

*in association with
the Editors of Echoes of Service*

with Appendix by

DR. STEPHEN S. SHORT, B.D., M.B., Ch.B.

1983
ECHOES OF SERVICE
1 WIDCOMBE CRESCENT, BATH, AVON, BA2 6AQ

ISBN 0 946 214 02 6

Photoset by Anneset, Weston-super-Mare in 11/12 Plantin
Designed and produced by
PETER WHATLEY (Trowbridge)
for the publishers, Echoes of Service, Bath, Avon

Printed and bound in Great Britain by
Redwood Burn Limited, Trowbridge, Wiltshire

Contents

Acknowledgments

It goes without saying that the books in this series could not possibly be the work of one person. A certain amount of personal research has naturally been necessary, but the bulk of the information has been supplied by missionaries and very sincere thanks are due to them for their willingness to sacrifice time and effort in order to assist in this project. Without the details they have so readily furnished, the task could never have been accomplished.

A special debt is also due to Mr. S. F. Warren, whose energy and resourcefulness have been invaluable. The contribution he has made, particularly in securing information, is incalculable, and his patience in reading and re-reading drafts (often in the most illegible calligraphy) and in suggesting improvements and amendments deserves respect. We are also grateful to Mr. A. Pulleng, who with his wealth of knowledge of the mission field has so carefully examined every detail and whose encouragement in the project has been unwavering.

So many of the staff at *Echoes* office have been involved in one way or another in research, in planning and in typing that it would be invidious to mention anyone by name.

Mrs. M. V. Stockdale deserves special mention for her willingness to convert illegible manuscripts into legible typescripts, and David Restall of Shipham has given immense help in preparing the many photographs for publication.

If permission has not been obtained for some of the quotations included in the books, we tender apologies and trust that the sin of omission will be forgiven.

To ensure a measure of consistency the population figures quoted have been taken from the 1982/83 *Statesmen's Year Book* and the spelling of place names from the sixth edition (1980) of *The Times Atlas*. Where appropriate, earlier spellings are shown in parentheses. The information is, as far as possible, up to date as at March 1983.

List of Illustrations

List of Maps

Preface

On the occasion of the centenary of the magazine, *Echoes of Service*, it was decided to produce a history of the work of assembly missionaries in the foreign field up to that time, and a fully illustrated volume, *Turning the World Upside Down*, accordingly made its appearance in 1972. The first edition in cloth boards rapidly sold out, and a paperback edition is still selling and is obtainable from Echoes Publications, 1 Widcombe Crescent, Bath, Avon, BA2 6AQ.

Limitations of space made it impossible for the full story of the world wide missionary effort to be told: even with the curtailment of detailed accounts and the restriction to missionaries commended from the U.K., the book reached 671 pages.

As a further ten years has elapsed, it seems desirable to supplement the book with a series of others, dealing with the different fields of service and including a fuller reference to missionaries from the U.S.A., Canada, Australia and New Zealand.

In addition to those from U.K., our colleagues in the Missionary Service Groups in those countries have co-operated fully in this new project. It is obviously not practicable to trace the complete story of missionary endeavour and, of necessity, the account has been restricted to workers from brethren assemblies. (An explanation of the term 'Brethren', is given in Appendix I).

When *Turning the World Upside Down* was compiled, it was prepared for the press and seen through to the stage of final production by Dr. Fredk. A. Tatford. When the new project was contemplated, therefore, we naturally turned to Dr. Tatford, who has always been interested in missionaries and their work and has visited many of them overseas. He willingly agreed to undertake the task of writing the books.

The complete series envisaged, under the general title of 'THAT THE WORLD MAY KNOW...', is as follows:

1   The Restless Middle East
2   Dawn over Latin America
3   The Challenge of India
4   The Muslim World
5   The Mysterious Far East
6   Light Over the Dark Continent
7   Asian Giants Awake
8   West European Evangel
9   Red Glow Over Eastern Europe
10 The Islands of the Sea

The research entailed examining the source material covering many decades has been a rewarding exercise in which two earlier convictions have been confirmed and deepened. Firstly, that the work developed from small beginnings. Not infrequently it has involved the spirit of a pioneer constrained by love for Him and those He came to save. Secondly, that New Testament principles of evangelism and church planting are timeless in their relevance and universal in their scope. From continent to continent and country to country the gospel has been preached. Men and women have been converted and assemblies planted.

It is our hope and expectation that readers will find this account of practical help as a book of reference informing their minds about missionary personnel and the place, duration and nature of their service. If, additionally, the record increases devotion to the Lord Jesus and commitment to Him in the worldwide spread of the gospel, it will have well served its intended purpose.

A. PULLENG
S. F. WARREN

Mountains of Nepal   (Tear Fund and Air India)

1

The Land of Spices

The Book of Esther states that the dominion of Ahasuerus, or Xerxes I, extended from India to Ethiopia (Esther 1:1; 8:9), and it has also been claimed that Solomon, king of Israel, traded with India in the tenth century B.C., importing ivory, spices and precious gems from that country. It is certainly clear that he built a navy on the Red Sea and manned it with Phoenicians, who sailed to Ophir to obtain gold (1 Kings 9:26-28). Merrill Unger and others maintain that Ophir was located in Yemen, but some have argued that it was in India, near the delta of the Indus. In *Cargoes*, John Masefield portrays the great oared merchant ships sailing home from somewhere more distant than Yemen:

'Quinquireme of Nineveh from distant Ophir,
Rowing home to haven in sunny Palestine,
With a cargo of ivory, and apes, and peacocks,
Sandalwood, cedarwood, and sweet white wine.'

The region referred to in Esther (and possibly implied in 1 Kings) was probably the area of the Indus valley and plains to the east of the Afghan mountains, i.e. what later became known as the Punjab. Darius I definitely incorporated that area into the Persian empire and, according to Herodotus, made it his eastern boundary. In his masterly work, *Old Persian*, R. G. Kent confirms that Xerxes I included India in the list of countries over which he ruled. It has been established that, even before this, trade between Mesopotamia and India existed as early as 2100 B.C. – and possibly much earlier. 'India was the source of the war elephants used by Alexander and his Seleucid successors in Syria, and in the Graeco-Roman period many exotic products came from India, usually through the south of Arabia, either up the Red Sea or overland up the western side of India.' W. W. Tarn, in *The Greeks in Bactria and India,* also refers to Greek principalities maintaining themselves for some time in parts of north-west India.

It has been said, with some justification, that it would be more appropriate to refer to India as a sub-continent rather than as a country. It is virtually a union of a number of countries and races. Indeed, Queen Victoria converted it into an empire – primarily to acquire the title of empress for herself, of course.

According to a widely accepted theory, India's geological placement is possibly due to the drifting of continental masses over the surface of the earth after the breaking up of an ancient continent, usually referred to as Gondwanaland. The mass of peninsular India is thought to have collided with the south of the Asian land mass, the impact causing the forcing up of the Himalaya mountains. Subsequently, the erosive action of the rivers flowing down from the Himalayas resulted in enormous quantities of alluvium being deposited to form the immense Indo-Gangetic plain. That plain is, in fact, the greatest alluvial area of the world and, in consequence of its richness, it has also become the most densely populated region of this planet.

The Himalayas are the highest mountain system known to man and its snowy crests rise, majestic and serene, to amazing heights, Everest, for example, being 29,025 feet. Its ranges extend into Nepal and Tibet, but the earth's crust in Central Asia is still buckling and the mountains are imperceptibly continuing to rise and gradually to edge their way southwards. Great ice-fields spread out to a total area of 15,500 square miles; immense glaciers threaten to sweep down the valleys in destructive force; waterfalls tumble over precipices in sparkling beauty; and the whole scene is one of unparalleled wonder. The name 'Himalaya' means 'abode of snow', and there could be no more appropriate name, for the snow is always there.

It is a region of extraordinary contrasts. Says Jean Fairley in *The Lion River,* p. 24, 'The clouds of the monsoon break against the southern flanks of the Himalayas and they are clothed high

In the Region of Everest   (Indian High Commission)

up in lush vegetation, but in the Indian gutter to the north there is practically no precipitation, less than three inches a year. The mountains are barren, the few open spaces are mostly deserts. The air is parched and dusty and even the infrequent snow is not soft and feathery but granular, almost gritty. The surface rock is broken and fissured; mostly the skin of the earth is a pale powdery sand or a loose conglomerate in which rocks and stones are stuck in the clay like raisins in a cake. The Indus and its tributaries have left a series of terraces along their crumbling or rocky walls to show the higher levels at which they once ran and their beds are a jumble of water-rounded boulders and stones that might have been deposited by ancient glaciers or rolled downstream in last summer's spate.'

The Himalayas are India's northern boundary. To her north and north-west lie Tibet, Nepal, Bhutan, Sikkim, Sinkiang and Pakistan. On the east she has a frontier with Burma. (Bangladesh is an enclave in India on the east). In the south the shores of the peninsula are lapped by the waters of the Bay of Bengal on the east and by those of the Arabian Sea on the west.

Towards the Himalayas   (Indian High Commission)

Sri Lanka, of course, lies to the south, separated from the mainland by the Palk Strait and the Gulf of Manar. The Andaman and Nicobar Islands in the Bay of Bengal, as well as the Laccadive Islands and Minicoy in the Arabian Sea, are part of India's territory. The Maldives belong to Sri Lanka.

The total area of India is practically 1,222,713 square miles and there are three broad regions. The first is naturally the vast mountain area of the north, the Himalayas and associated mountains, extending across the country from west to east in a great irregular crescent. The second is the Indo-Gangetic plain formed by the basins of the Indus, Ganges and Brahmaputra; this immense alluvial plain is 1,500 miles long and up to 200 miles wide. The Vindhya and Satpura ranges, the Eastern and Western Ghats, the Nilgiri Hills, and the Aravalli chain, a mass of mountains and hills, up to 4,000 feet high, separate the plain from the third region of the Deccan plateau, which forms the rest of the peninsula.

For centuries the Himalayas effectively cut off India from the ancient civilization of China and later from the developing Islāmic world of the seventh century onwards, and threw the country back upon its own resources and philosophic thought.

The result was what has been described as a third stream of Asian history, originating in the civilization of Mohenjo Daro about 2500 B.C. Artefacts found at that site suggest, moreover, that it was out of the religion of the India of that period that modern Hinduism developed. So that, not only economically, socially and culturally – and, later, industrially, scientifically and politically – but also religiously and philosophically, India was thrown upon herself. It is an interesting theory, which can scarcely be disputed and one which may possibly explain some of the attitudes and reactions evidenced at the present day.

It is a country (and a people) of contrast and contradiction. Indeed, as one writer aptly remarks, 'Contrast and contradiction have penetrated deep into the Indian spirit, the Indian mind and soul, whether Hindu or Muslim, Sikh or Christian.' Although Hinduism has become a religion, 'Hindu' and 'Indian' are the same word and simply mean a man from the Indus. 'Every Hindu is divided against himself,' says Nirad Chandhuri in *The Continent of Circe*. 'The human personality is indeed contradictory everywhere, but normally one set of traits can push their opposites into the background and become dominant. But with Hindus the opposites almost neutralize one another, and the indecisive tug-of-war stultifies all their actions.' The result is what Arthur Koestler pertinently described as the Indian 'indifference to contradiction – the peaceful co-existence of logical opposites in the emotional sphere.'

India is a land of rivers. Apart from those of the Deccan plateau, the inland drainage basin and the coastal rivers, the three principal ones are the Indus, the Ganges and the Brahmaputra. The Karnati (sometimes distinguished from the others) is, in fact, a major tributary of the Ganges. It is claimed by Tibetans that all of India's northern rivers take their rise in the turquoise blue waters of the holy lake, Manasarowar, and run out of it to the four points of the compass, through the mouths of sacred animals, the Indus flowing north through the lion's mouth, the Karnati south to the Ganges through the peacock's mouth, the Brahmaputra east through the horse's mouth, and the Sutlej (a tributary of the Indus) west through the elephant's mouth. In the same valley there is a devil's lake as well as the holy lake, but none of the rivers owe anything to its waters. The valley is over 15,000 feet above sea level, in an amphitheatre formed by the Kailas range to the north and the

Great Himalayan range to the south. Heinrich Harrer describes it in *Seven Years in Tibet*, p. 45, as 'certainly one of the loveliest spots on earth'. Although the sources of all the four rivers are in the area of the lakes and of the Kailas range, the claim of the holy lake to be their source is today discounted.

According to the ancient animistic religion of the Tibetans, Mount Kailas is peopled with thousands of gods and spirits. The Hindus believe it to be the earthly paradise of Śiva, the Destroyer and Saviour. Buddhists claim that Buddha and 500 of his redeemer-saints dwell on the mountain-top. It is a sacred site and cairns, surmounted by poles carrying prayer-flags, are to be found on every approach road.

Taking its rise in the Vindhya mountains and flowing between them and the Satpura range, the river Narbada is an additional barrier to southern India. The Tapti flows past the Satpuras to empty its waters into the sea near Surat, while the Godavari leaves the Western Ghats to flow across the country into the Bay of Bengal. Each of these rivers is over 800 miles in length: those of the north are each, of course, over 1,500 miles long.

Hindus at worship in the Ganges   (R. Duff)

Practically all India's lakes are salt. The great Ran of Cutch is 190 miles long and between two and 90 miles wide and becomes a sandy waste in the dry season. Large quantities of salt are produced from the lakes.

The forest areas of India provide a variety of wood for export as well as for home use. Teak, bamboo, ebony, pine, sandal, rosewood, walnut and ironwood are the most common. Coffee, tea, rubber, ginger, pepper, coconuts, rice and a variety of other crops (of all of which there are two harvests every year) are produced, very largely for export. Bird and animal life is of the greatest variety, and almost every kind of wild and of domestic animal is found in the country. The jungles abound with elephants, bears, tigers, buffaloes, leopards, panthers and hyenas. The lion is found in the wilds of Rajasthan and Gujarat, the rhinoceros in the Ganges swamps, and the camel in the north-west. Wolves and jackals prowl in the ravines in search of deer and other prey.

In many parts of India, oxen are used to draw vehicles and to carry merchandise and, although regarded as sacred animals, they are often worked until, half-starved, they drop dead. As one writer declares, it is impossible to watch the bullock-cart passing in a city 'without discovering a dozen animals whose tails are not a zigzag string of breaks. It is easier for the driver to walk with the animal's tail in his hand, twisting its joints from time to time, than it is to beat the creature with his stick. If you ride in the bullock-cart, with the driver riding before you, you will discover that, from this position, he has another way of speeding the gait. With his stick or his long hard toenails he periodically prods his animals' genitals'. Domesticated buffaloes are employed in ploughing the fields but, despite their usefulness, they often have insufficient to eat. Goats provide the material from which Indian shawls and other garments are made – many of them homespun. If, with the inadequate nourishment they receive, they produce a little milk as well, it is almost a miracle.

India is rich in minerals. In the past she was renowned for her diamonds, rubies and other gems, and she still produces opals, amethysts, garnets, jaspers and cornelians. Gold is found in many of the streams and, as already mentioned, was possibly exported to Israel in Solomon's day and doubtless to other countries as well. Silver, lead, tin, antimony, iron and copper are

Oxen at work   (Tear Fund)

mined in various areas. It is known that there are petroleum
deposits, but these have not yet been exploited, primarily
because of doubts regarding the profitability of the enterprise.
Excellent marble is quarried from the Aravalli hills, and there
are thick seams of coal in the Damodar valley, as well as in other
localities.

The country is still awaiting full development and industrialization, although much has already been done. The
resources are available to make it rich. In the millions of her
population, India also possesses the reserves of labour required.
But it is a country of 547,000 villages and, for centuries, most of
the people have lived in the villages: the process of urbanization
is proving a lengthy and painful one. Indeed, with a country so
vast, with such a variety of races and with such a tremendous
population, the transformation into an industrial nation is a
herculean task, which might well daunt the most dedicated and
determined.

'At the centre of India's tricolour flag', writes William
Walker, 'is a small but very important Buddhist emblem – the
famous Ashoka Chakwra. This *chakwra*, a wheel, points back to
a glorious epoch in India's history, 273-232 B.C., the reign of

West Bengal—improved farming methods   (Indian High Commission)

Emperor Ashoka. The characteristic of that age was national unity, economic prosperity, discernment and peaceful co-existence. During Ashoka's reign, Buddhism became a mis-sionary-faith and spread rapidly south to Ceylon, then east to Burma, China and Japan. The Ashoka Chakwra represents the law as taught by Buddha. It has also come to mean life, movement, revolution and peaceful change. By these means India hopes to regain her place amongst the nations and relive the glories of her ancient past. D. Vable points out that India has witnessed three great revolutions in the past hundred years. 'First a social and religious revolution led by Swāmi Dayanānda Saraswati. Next a political and national revolution led by Mahatma Gandhi. Then an economic and industrial revolution led by Pandit Jawahartal Nehru.' It is obvious that Mrs. Gandhi has realized all the implications and is pursuing a path based upon the plans and concepts particularly of Nehru.

After independence had been achieved, Mahatma Gandhi 'strongly advocated village uplift at the level where five out of every six Indians lived. Agrarian reform and revived cottage-industries were the path upwards to a better life. The climb might be slow, but it would be sure; moreover, in the process the

West Bengal—the Durgapur steel plant   (Indian High Commission)

masses would escape the demoralizing effects of the machine age'. It sounded logical, but concepts of that kind were out of date in the twentieth century. Nehru, who saw much farther, was adamantly opposed to such a scheme, and maintained that the emphasis must be placed on heavy industry from the start. Only thus could the problems of India's starving millions be solved within a reasonable time.

Gandhi's assassination in 1948 averted any violent open disagreement. It took two years to integrate the 562 princely states which had been ruled personally by rajahs, maharajahs and nawabs. Then, in 1951, Nehru initiated his first Five Year Plan, in an ambitious programme of dam-building at Bhakra, Tungabhadra, Hirakud and Damodar. Hydro-electric power was successfully harnessed for irrigation and for industrial purposes. Food production was increased by 25 per cent. The second Five Year Plan of 1956–61 laid emphasis upon industry. Three big steel plants were constructed at Bhilai, Durgapur and Rourkela. The third Five Year Plan of 1961–66 was aimed at securing self-sufficiency in food and raw materials. Despite the achievements, problems still remain before India attains the position her leaders have set before themselves as an objective.

One of the biggest problems is the burgeoning population. With a population of 684 million, India adds over a million a month to that figure. She is second in size of population only to China. Because of the extreme poverty in some districts and also the difficulty of feeding everyone adequately, strenuous efforts have been made to secure some form of family planning, but most of these have been completely unsuccessful. One writer says, 'All forms of control have been advocated from time to time, so that a commuter with a civic concern has been able to drop in for a vasectomy at a clinic on Bombay railway station en route to the office, while a pair of newly-weds in Kerala have been liable to receive the nation's gift parcel of 144 condoms neatly packed among all their other presents.' Posters were everywhere to be seen proclaiming, 'First child a necessity, second child a luxury, third child a sin'. The campaigns and propaganda have been ineffective, however. In the rural areas, children are needed to help with the agricultural work and to provide for their aged parents and grandparents in years to come. In the urban districts there is little else than sex to relieve the monotonous tension of life, and for the vast majority there is no thought of contraception. The exploding population is one of India's greatest problems: not merely are accommodation, employment and health care at stake, but also the fundamental matter of actual existence.

2

The Story of the Centuries

The origin of the earliest Indians is lost in the mists of antiquity. A large percentage of the present population can probably claim descent from the Aryan invaders who, long before Hellas defied the Persian, were pushing back the earlier races of Hindustan with their animistic beliefs into the hills and forests where their descendants are now to be found. The history of that period has been preserved in the sacred Sanskrit writings or religious hymns, the Vedas, which portray the life of pre-historic India, the gods who were worshipped, the rites practised by the Aryan conquerors, the social life and culture, and so on. The date of the events recorded in the oldest Hindu epic, the Rāmāyaṇa, is estimated by Sir W. Jones as the twenty-first century B.C. The date of the Rig-Veda, the oldest of the four Vedas, is put by Max Müller at 1200 to 1500 B.C., and it is usually considered that the early Indus civilization could be dated as lasting from 3000 to 1500 B.C., and the Aryan civilization which succeeded it as running from 1500 to 500 B.C. The word 'Veda' simply means 'What is known', but the Vedas are practical in character and are not primarily records of historical happenings.

L. J. Trotter in his *History of India*, p. 8, says that the Vedas 'are full of the lifelike symbolism in which imaginative minds love to embody their impressions of the outer world. They sing the praises of the "Deva", the bright divinities of sun and dawn, of fire, storm, earth and sky. In them all nature is divine'. Sūrya the sun-god, Uṣas the dawn, Agni the god of fire, Indra the god of storms and rain, Vāyu the rushing wind, and a myriad others were worshipped, but in this Vedic pantheon no one deity was supreme. Later, the old imagery of the Vedic poets was absorbed into the metaphysical subtleties of the Upaniṣads and later still into the puerile grossness of the Purāṇas.

From some central point in Asia, waves of Aryan peoples moved westward and southward. A list of their old kiṇgs, given by Arrian the Greek historian, traces their history back to 3000 B.C. The people whom they displaced in India belonged to a less civilized race and spoke a different language. These Dasyas (as Aryan song termed them) apparently covered the whole of ancient India, and their descendants, to quote Trotter again, *op. cit.*, p. 23, 'make up the various tribes of Bhils, Gonds, Santhals, Kols, Mairs, Minas, Mangs, Kukis, and so forth, which still cleave to their ancestral hills and forests, or roam in quest of a livelihood from place to place. Dark-skinned, short, ugly-featured, with high cheekbones and scanty beards, these rude, scattered remnants of some aboriginal race differ "widely in appearance, language and habits" from the tall, light-skinned, full-bearded, comely-featured, subtle-brained Hindus of pure Aryan descent'.

These Aryan invaders apparently entered the north between 2000 and 1500 B.C. and swept south across the Vindhyan range into the Deccan. The story of the great war between the Pāṇḍus and the Kurus is recorded in the Mahābhārata, but how much of the record is true is not certain. It is, however, clear that the conquerors divided their new possessions into several kingdoms, such as the Punjab, Gujarat, Kananj, Tirhut, Magadha, and Bengal. Their régime lasted for at least a thousand years.

Invaders still poured into India; Scythians into Kashmir, Tartars into the areas watered by the Ganges and the Brahmaputra, and Yavons into Sindh. There is even a fantastic (and doubtless apocryphal) story of the Assyrian queen Semiramis leading myriads of horse and foot soldiers over the Indus, with thousands of camels disguised as elephants!

Soon there came other invaders from the west. Stories of the riches of the Indian kingdoms caught the imagination of Darius Hystaspes, and the Persian troops were flung across the Indus to the great desert between Sindh and Rajputana. Two centuries later, Alexander the Great of Macedon thrust his way through Afghanistan and the Khyber gorges to rout the forces of Porus on the banks of the Ganges before his warworn troops forced

Rajah of Mysore's temple

At a festival   (P. Marsh)

him to return home. Seleucus I, one of Alexander's four generals who divided his empire between them, determined on a further attack upon India, but compromised with Chandragupta, who had annexed the kingdom of Magadha. The Indian ruler paid him an annual tribute and was allowed to retain the kingdom he had seized.

Demetrius and his successor Eucratides reconquered the Punjab and Menander extended his dominions to Sindh. But, by the first century B.C., the Greek rule in Bactria and the adjacent provinces had given way to a succession of dynasties, Scythian, Parthian, Turkish and Hindu. Each change of dynasty was marked by a change of language, Greek gave way to Sanskrit and that to forms of Aryan, Turanian or Semitic.

About the third century A.D., the Gupta kings had begun to wield a leadership over the greater part of India. At that time, the strongest of the Indian rulers would win for himself the title of Lord Paramount of the Old Empire. This title was held by six of the Gupta princes, whose sway then extended as far as Ceylon or Sri Lanka, although there were, of course, many separate principalities which acknowledged his suzerainty.

From 200 B.C. to A.D. 400 invasions came from the Mauryans from the east, and then from the west by Bactrian Greeks, Śakas, Parthians, Kushans and Sāsānians. But in the fifth century A.D. the Huns poured into the Kabul valley, crossed the Indus and spread right across northern India. They ruled by terror and atrocity. But after a century of suffering, the Sāsānians, with the help of local tribes, rallied to drive the Huns out of the Indus valley. Unfortunately this was followed by constant inter-tribal warfare, until the forces of Islām swept in. The Arab followers of Muḥammad had overrun Persia, conquered Egypt, Syria and Mesopotamia, and they then not unnaturally turned their attention to India. In A.D. 664 one army marched into Sindh, and another set out for Kabul. The conquest of Bactria took only 50 years, but Aryan India proved a more difficult task and, despite minor victories, the Arabs were thrown back beyond the Indus in A.D. 812 and for more than a century and a half there was relative peace. Seventeen stormy raids were made upon the country by Mahmūd, the son of the King of Ghaznī, who had ridden with his father's forces through the high mountain passes down to the plains of Hindustan before he was fifteen. When he became king at an early age, his sovereignty was confirmed by the Caliph of Baghdād with his investment with the titles 'Right hand of government' and 'Guardian of the faith'. Young Mahmūd took the titles seriously and from A.D. 1000 commenced his mission to destroy the idols of India. By the end of his life, a large part of the Punjab had acknowledged Muslim control and his successors extended the area rapidly, but another Ghaznī ruler, Muhammad of Ghur, from 1186 onwards, achieved the Muslim conquest of India.

In the fifteenth century came the first real indication of Western interest in India. Vasco da Gama of Portugal rounded the Cape of Good Hope and in 1498 cast anchor near the city of Calicut on the Malabar coast. In 1500 a fleet of thirteen ships and a force of 1200 men under Pedro Cabral landed at Calicut and established a factory, which the Muslims indignantly destroyed. The consequence was inevitable: after a number of assaults, the Portuguese seized Goa and, in fact, conquered the area from Ormuz in the Persian Gulf to Malacca in the Malay Peninsula. The whole seaboard of western India was soon dotted with Portuguese factories.

Other powers became interested. In 1604 the Dutch wrested Amboyna from the Portuguese and made an unsuccessful assault upon Malacca. In 1612 a small English fleet defeated a Portuguese squadron at Surat, and ten years later another English fleet drove the Portuguese from their flourishing settlement at Ormuz. From that time, the Portuguese power in India gradually declined and their trade monopoly passed into other hands.

Around the same time a new personality appeared on the Indian stage. In 1504 a young chieftain named Bābur, a descendant on the male line from Tamerlane and on the female from Ghengis Khan, had seized Kabul and had made it the capital of his kingdom. Three times in the five years from 1519 to 1524 he made raids upon the Punjab, and in 1526, following an appeal from some dissatisfied Afghan nobles, he determined to make one more decisive attempt to gain the empire of Hindustan. With only 12,000 Mogul horsemen and a body of footmen, he set himself in the plain of Panipat against a Pathan army over 100,000 strong and completely routed them. That day marked the beginning of the Mogul empire in Hindustan.

Within a few months nearly all the Muslim provinces in the

Agra—shrines   (M. Browne)

Gondoliers   (Air India)

Villagers
(C. Gilmore)

Lucknow   (P. Marsh)

valley of the Ganges had submitted to Bābur's rule. West of the
Yamuna a mighty force gathered under the powerful Rānā
Sāngā, the Rajput sovereign of Mewār, and marched towards
Delhi. Despite the odds, the young Mogul was once more
victorious. Other kingdoms fell under his sway, but his glory
was shortlived, for he died in 1530 at the age of 49.

His descendants, the Great Moguls, 'held most of the Indian
sub-continent and Afghanistan for some 300 years. Their courts
at Delhi were famous for their exotic richness and splendid
pomp. But Delhi is a long way from the Indus, and all the power

of the Mogul emperors could not keep the people on their western borders under control for long'. The history of the empire was, in fact, a chequered one and Shāh 'Ālam, its last emperor, died in 1806, blind and helpless. During the last years of his life, the British allowed him to retain the dignity of his position without its power. To quote Michael Edwardes, in *King of the World*, p. 267, 'Within the walls of his palace, the king was permitted to exercise ruling powers. The inhabitants, servants, retainers, tradesmen, were his direct subjects, and members of the imperial family had immunity from British law. The ceremonial of the Court was maintained. Officials still bore the high-sounding titles of their predecessors and the formal rituals of court etiquette were rigidly adhered to.' But it was an empty and meaningless charade. The great Mogul empire was dead.

The Moguls were the last of the Muslim invaders who had established themselves in northern India since the beginning of the eleventh century. They brought a great deal of India under their rule, but the majority of their subjects were Hindus, whereas the Moguls themselves were Muslims and foreigners. Over the years a number of Hindus were naturally converted to the Islāmic faith, but they and the rulers remained a minority, 'encapsulated by an alien faith and alien social institutions'. Because of their numerical weakness, the Moguls made no serious attempt at colonization and, even for their civil administration, they were inadequate in numbers and were necessarily dependent upon Hindu support and labour. This partnership of Muslim and Hindu in administration resulted in the production of a common language, Urdu, the basic grammar of which was Hindu, and the alphabet Persian. Very rapidly, Urdu became the *lingua franca* of the educated class.

By Hindu tradition all land was deemed in principle to be the property of the king and, under Hindu law, he was entitled to one-sixth of its produce. The Mogul emperor Akbar (1556–1605) increased this proportion to one-third, and his successors increased it still farther to one-half, thereby reducing the peasantry to bare subsistence level. When bad harvests occurred and famine broke out, many died of starvation. The inevitable results of harsh treatment and pressure of taxation were civil disorders, shifts of population and general disruption of the rural economy.

Agra—Akbar's tomb   (Indian High Commission)

A later Mogul ruler, Aurangzeb (1658–1707), foolishly determined to impose the Islāmic faith upon the people. He destroyed a number of shrines of great sanctity to the Hindu, and ordered the demolition of all Hindu temples and schools, prohibited the great religious fairs and simultaneously revived a poll tax on Hindus.

It was the ill-advised actions of the rulers that aroused the antagonism of the landowners and the bitter resistance of the Hindu princes, and ultimately contributed considerably to the downfall of the empire. The various 'layers' of authority previously existing had been eliminated by the Mogul rulers, who centralized all power in themselves. All these factors contributed to a general spirit of bitterness and an innate resentment of authority which have not entirely disappeared in our twentieth century – and of which the Christian worker must take account.

The Persian invasion and the complete destruction of Delhi in 1739 gave Nādir Shāh little more than the Kohinor diamond and the peacock throne of Shāh Jahān, but they left a permanent sear upon the memory of the Indians. Soon afterwards, in 1748–62, north-west India was repeatedly invaded by the Afghans and both central and northern India were laid waste by the Marāthās, who continued to exercise their authority over those areas until the early part of the nineteenth century. The Marāthā princes and their armies were little more than gangs of robbers and adventurers, squeezing all they could possibly get out of the country. Their administration had not even the qualities of the Mogul régime, since they endeavoured to rule without regard to practice or custom. Yet, as one writer

West Bengal—the panchayat   (R. Duff)

comments, there was 'one surviving judicial institution left undisturbed by the Marāthās' – 'the *panchayat,* a representative body regulating village affairs and pronouncing judgment on matters of real and personal property'. Apart from this, chaos would have been complete.

'In the Punjab', to quote Michael Edwardes in *British India,* p. 9, 'where a powerful Sikh ruler, Ranjit Singh, had imposed discipline at the end of the eighteenth century, a system of controlled expropriation operated until the crisis in 1839, when wars of succession returned the country to the same uncontrolled anarchy as had preceded his reign. Village communities began to collapse under the pressure of civil war, and the country was finally annexed by the British in 1849.'

Portuguese, Dutch and French had tried to secure footholds in India, but it was the British who finally established themselves as rulers. In the year 1600 a company was enrolled by royal charter for the purpose of trading in the East Indies and it was given the monopoly of British Eastern trade for fifteen years. By 1619 the first British outpost had been established at Surat on the north-west coast of India to purchase Indian calico. Later in the century permanent trading stations were opened at Madras, Bombay and Calcutta, each under the protection of native rulers. Bombay had been the gift of Catherine of Braganza to Charles II on their marriage and was transferred by the king to the East India Company in exchange for a substantial loan. Gradually the Company expanded its influence over the whole of India and, to protect its factories and possessions, it became necessary to fortify centres and to employ armies for defence. As Michael Edwardes says again in *British India,* pp. 18, 19, 'The English had come as traders; then they became armed traders; soon they needed soldiers to defend their settlements; and as the Mogul empire disintegrated, "spheres of influence" became necessary if the Company was to survive. Slowly the rhythm of empire-building had imposed itself on the simplification of trade'. The anomalous position was created, therefore, that India was ruled by a company, primarily for the benefit of its shareholders, and it was not until the second half of the nineteenth century that this situation was rectified.

Over the years, reforms and political changes introduced by the British rulers caused no little unrest and uneasiness, but spasmodic outbursts against the authorities were quashed. In

1857, however, a relatively small event gave rise to a serious and widespread mutiny. The substitution of new Enfield rifles for those then in use involved using greased cartridges. The sepoys believed that the grease was made from the fat of pigs and cows – the pig being regarded as unclean by the Muslim and the cow as sacred to the Hindu. The sepoys refused to use the cartridges and finally open mutiny broke out. Other dissidents rallied behind them. Disaffection rapidly spread to the province of Oudh and the cities of Cawnpore (now known as Kanpur), Lucknow, Delhi, Meerut, etc. and massacres followed before order was finally restored.

In 1858 power was assumed by the Crown and the Company's powers and prerogatives were transferred. A Council of India was set up in London to advise the Secretary of State, final authority being vested in him and parliament. One consequence was that the areas and boundaries of over 500 princely states, occupying nearly half of India, became settled beyond dispute, and any fears of expropriation were dispelled. There were no further annexations and the rulers of the Indian states accepted the authority of the British government. On their side, the British carefully refrained from continuing any policy of social or political reform which might lead to anything comparable to the Mutiny. A war on Burma in 1885 led to that country being annexed as a province of the Indian Empire.

In 1876 Disraeli conferred on Queen Victoria the title of 'Empress of India'. The title of Emperor of India continued, however, only until the time of her great-grandson. Increasing pressure had developed for the end of British Colonial rule and the British Empire was in process of dismemberment. In India Mahatma Gandhi had started in 1920 the transformation of the Indian National Congress into a mass movement and used it to mount a popular campaign against British rule. The Congress used both parliamentary and extra-parliamentary means (including non-violent resistance and non-cooperation) in order to achieve its ends.

Ultimately Lord Mountbatten was appointed as Viceroy, superseding the then occupant of the post, with instructions to find a basis of agreement between all parties on which independence could be granted. The story has often been told of his long and successful struggle to provide the solution to what seemed an insoluble problem. Independence was finally

Calcutta—Queen Victoria memorial

granted in 1947 and India became a member of the Commonwealth of Nations, with Jawahartal Nehru as Prime Minister. An answer to the longstanding friction between Muslims and Hindus was found in the formation of Pakistan as a republic within the Commonwealth. The 562 princely states, which had enjoyed special status under the British, were made part of the Indian Union soon after independence.

In 1950 India adopted a new constitution and declared itself a 'sovereign socialist secular democratic republic'. The country has 29 states, including the Andaman and Nicobar Islands, and has a federal form of government. Executive power is virtually vested in the Council of Ministers, led by the Prime Minister. The President appoints the Prime Minister, who is designated by the political party or coalition commanding a parliamentary majority. The parliament, like that of Westminster, is bicameral. Each state has a governor, appointed by the President.

India is the largest democracy in the world and, as one writer remarks, 'It is largely due to British influence that India owes its open society with its democratic institutions, a parliamentary government, a well-trained civil service, a free press, universal education, genuine elections, and a *lingua franca* – English.'

A more concise history of India is given by the *Statesman's*

Delhi—Parliament building   (R. Duff)

Year Book, 1982-83, p. 609, 'The Indus civilization was fully developed by c. 2500 B.C. and collapsed c. 1750 B.C. An Aryan civilization spread from the west as far as the Ganges valley by 500 B.C.; separate kingdoms were established and many of these were united under the Mauryan dynasty established by Chandragupta in c. 320 B.C. The Mauryan Empire was succeeded by numerous small kingdoms. The Gupta dynasty (A.D. 320–600) was followed by the first Arabic invasions of the south-west. Muslim, Hindu and Buddhist states developed together with frequent conflict until the establishment of the Mogul dynasty in 1526. The first settlements by the East India Company were made after 1600 and the company established a formal system of government for Bengal in 1700. During the decline of the Moguls, frequent wars between the Company, the French and the native princes led to the Company's being brought under British Government control in 1784; the first Governor-General of India was appointed in 1786. The powers of the Company were abolished by the India Act, 1858, and its functions and forces transferred to the British Crown. Representative government was introduced in 1909 and the first parliament in 1919. The separate dominions of India and Pakistan became independent within the Commonwealth in 1947 and India became a republic in 1950.'

3

The People

As already mentioned, with a population approaching 700 million, India is the second largest country in the world, China alone having a larger population. To a great extent, the people are naturally the product of the many invasions which have taken place. Every conqueror left his impress upon the country and the people, but large numbers of the invaders settled down in the country they had overrun, and intermingled and intermarried with those whom they found around them. The *Encyclopedia Britannica* details the principal ethnic streams as the Caucasoid, Mongoloid, Australoid and Negroid.

The aboriginal Indians, i.e. the Kolarians, preceded the Dravidians. They included the Santals, Khonds, Bhils, Khols, Karens, and others. Originally located in the north-east, they were driven into the jungles and mountains of the Central Provinces, by the Mandians, who were apparently the first invaders of the country. The Kolarians were a fierce, primitive race, brave and ruthless warriors, prepared to fight mercilessly but never willing to compromise. Their descendants still remain and still possess the same characteristics, until reached with the gospel in comparatively recent days.

The Dravidians are usually described as the oldest inhabitants of the sub-continent, but this is obviously not correct. Their descendants are found largely in the south and include Telugus, Tamils, Kanarese, etc. They are normally short in stature and of a somewhat dark complexion, and are not of such

700 million to reach   (R. Duff)

a warlike temperament as the Kolarian tribes who preceded them.

The Aryans poured into India through the Khyber Pass in the sixteenth century, forcing the Dravidians southwards. While the latter were culturally superior, they were very definitely inferior in military strength and ability. The Indo-Aryans settled primarily in the north and their descendants are now to be found in Kashmir, Punjab and Rajasthan. They are obviously a distinct race from the short, dark Dravidians and are, in fact, generally tall and fair, with dark eyes and fine features.

The Hindustanis, who are to be found mainly in the Ganges valley, are the descendants of the intermarriage of Indo-Aryans with Dravidians. It would be difficult to find characteristics common to the race generally, but many Hindustanis, quite unjustifiably, would claim to be representative of the true type of Indian.

The Scythian invaders who settled in India also contributed to the medley of races. Intermingling and intermarrying with the Dravidians, whose land they had taken, produced the present Scytho-Dravidian strain found chiefly in Gujarat and the western part of Bombay. Numerically they are represented mainly today by the Marathis.

The Mongols, who originated in China and Tibet, had brought the whole of Central Asia from Korea to the Caspian under their control by the end of the twelfth century and, in the following century, they commenced their raids across the Indus – raids repeated over the centuries. They were possibly the most savage of all India's invaders. Cities were razed to the ground, the inhabitants brutally massacred, and thousands enslaved. They also left Mongoloid descendants in India, and they are still to be found in Assam and the eastern Himalayan region.

The intermarriage of Mongols and Dravidians resulted in a recognizable strain, of which the Bengali is a typical representative.

Quite apart from social and economic conditions and religious differences, there are cultural distinctions in the various races of India, which must obviously be recognized if acceptance is to be found. For an excellent example of the wrong attitude, one might quote from *The Land of the Lingam,* by A. Miles, in which he says, 'India can never be a nation until

Hinduism, with its superstitions and beastly rites, is wiped out. Not one step forward can be made in India while Hinduism, like a great snake, is allowed to crawl over the country, soiling every decent ideal and poisoning with its venom the bodies and souls of millions of people. The degenerate Brahmins will eat beef behind closed doors during some disgusting orgy if secrecy can be assured, and will drink themselves into a fine state of insensibility. Give an Indian a little power, and he becomes intoxicated with his own importance.' Hardly calculated to establish a *rapport!* To add that 'India is a land which has no history,' and then to wonder 'why Indian art is so crude', would scarcely endear the writer to an Indian.

Perhaps one could forgive the Indian student (whether or not his conclusions were justified), who declared that 'Your western philosophers like Plato, Aristotle, Kant, are rather shallow in comparison with our Indian philosophers. Our philosophy is very deep'.

Of course, there are defects in Indians as in people of every other race, but it is imperative to understand their background, culture, relationships, way of thinking, and so on. The Oriental is different in so many respects from the Occidental and would be horrified at some of the things that are tolerated in the west. One major problem confronts the foreign worker immediately he lands in India – the age-long one of caste. What is the solution? What attitude does he take? What action should be his?

Stephen Neill expresses it so admirably in *Salvation Tomorrow*, p. 84, that we venture to quote *in extenso*. He says, 'In India, missionaries found themselves faced by the challenge of the scheduled communities (Untouchables). Desperately poor, illiterate, sunk in habits which make it almost impossible for them to lift themselves up out of misery, these people did not seem to be exactly the material out of which flourishing churches could be built up. There were, in fact, two views as to the way in which they could be approached. One group held that social reform must precede evangelism; first improve social conditions and then the preaching of the gospel can follow. Others held that from the start the gospel of salvation must be preached. How can humanization be effected except by the direct and loving approach of a human being, in whom the oppressed can see the likeness of the Man, Jesus Christ, the One

After the cyclone   (Tear Fund)

in whom the true nature of human life is seen? How can a man become conscious of his own true being except through acquaintance with the living Christ, the true liberator from everything that mars and distorts the existence of God's children?

'The working out of the two views is interesting. Those who started out with the idea of social reform were singularly ineffective in bringing it about, and never got on to the preaching of the gospel. Those who started with a gospel of conversion, perhaps without intending it, brought about a social revolution, as believers became liberated from harmful habits and became aware with new self-respect that, even under the yoke of oppression, many things in their situation could be changed. It is a simple fact that two members of these oppressed communities are now bishops of the Christian Church.'

Another major fact to be appreciated is the prevalent poverty. It cannot be ignored, for example, that over a million people in

Calcutta live in a *bustee,* with open drains running down the narrow streets. The density of population is over 400,000 to a square mile. A dozen years ago 70,000 people slept in the streets of the city at night. Geoffrey Moorhouse writes in *Calcutta,* p. 81, 'They are to be found late at night and every morning throughout the centre of the city, lying under the arcades of Chowringhee and beside the standpipes of Bentinck Street. There are squadrons of them around the approaches to Howrah Station across the river, in addition to the platoons who sleep inside the station itself. You can find them at intervals along the great curving length of Lower Circular Road'.

Even in the day many still 'lie in the shade from the blistering sun, almost and sometimes totally naked, their hair matted, their sinews clearly visible, their skins bone dry and very dusty. They die like that eventually, and the kites, which forever swing lazily in the skies of Calcutta, congregate in a swirling circle high above the corpse, waiting for it to be alone'.

Calcutta is not unique for poverty. A tourist describes a scene in Bombay, for example, walking 'past the thin, dark shoeshine men squatting on the footpath, rubbing polish with their finger-tips into their customers' shoes; past the clamorous street-stall salesmen and the cunning-eyed, whispering, fingering money-changers; past a beggar couple who were old. The rags they wore and their own ragged skins were grey-brown, perfect camouflage against the grey-brown pavement they lay on'. Can the foreign worker enter into the thoughts and feelings and understand the circumstances of such?

Go to the Victoria Terminus railway station at Bombay and look at the vast crowded third-class waiting hall, full of sleepers for the night. Frances Letters in *People of Shiva,* pp. 252–3, describes the 'regulars' – 'a group of off-duty policemen, a couple of tattered old ladies, one thin dreamy man with the most alarming set of lower dentures. Numerous solitary young men also slept in one corner of the station, each one alone and silent in his huddled little world. Every night they came in one by one, hung their clean, dripping shirts on a seat to dry, and folded their trousers carefully with the creases just so. In this way not only did they have pillows for the night, but their trousers emerged neat and ironed next morning. Then wrapped in their *dhotis,* their sandals and plastic combs and mirrors and little scraps of soap hidden beneath their heads, they would lie down

Poverty and plenty   (S. F. Warren and R. Duff)

and sleep. In the mornings most of them rose early and went off to work, their hair plastered down, their clothes carefully smoothed'.

Some problems of the past have disappeared. No longer is the practice of female infanticide (confined largely in Rajasthan but practised in most parts of India) to be found, although there often still exists a comparative indifference to the welfare of female babies. As one official said bluntly some years ago, 'I very much doubt whether there is any active dislike of girl babies, but there is unquestionably passive neglect. The parents look after the son, and God looks after the daughter. She is less warmly clad, she receives less attention when ill, and less and worse food when well. This is not due to cruelty, or even to indifference; it is due simply to the fact that the son is preferred to the daughter, and all the care, attention and dainties are lavished on him, whilst the daughter must be content with the remnants of all three. The result is that the female death rate between 1 and 3 is almost invariably higher than the male death rate.' An example of this was experienced first-hand when triplets were born to one mother in a desert hospital in south India. There were two girls and one boy and it was evident that unless careful observation was kept the boy would have had an extra share of mother's milk so vital to survival. It cannot be said that, even in Britain, daughters always received the same consideration as sons, particularly so far as education and business opportunities were concerned. One ought to be thankful for the change in attitude in this matter.

Satī, the practice of high-caste Hindu widows perishing in the funeral pyres of their deceased husbands, was abolished in 1829 by Lord William Bentinck, but not before large numbers of women had lost their lives in this way. In 1780, for instance, the deceased Rajah of Maravar was joined in death by his 64 wives. Since a Hindu widow could not normally remarry, her lot was that of a menial in her late husband's house. In *Between the Twilights*, pp. 144–6, Cornelia Sorabji says that 'nothing can minimize the evils of her lot. For some sin committed in a previous birth, the gods have deprived her of a husband. What is left to her now but to work out his "salvation" and by her prayers and penances to win him a better place in his next genesis? ... For the mother-in-law what is left but the obligation to curse? ... But for this luckless one, her son might still be in the land of the living.... There is no determined animosity in the attitude. The person cursing is as much an instrument of Fate as the person cursed'.

Thuggu, i.e. robbery and murder, carried out by Hindus as a religious duty in the name of Kālī, has also long been stamped

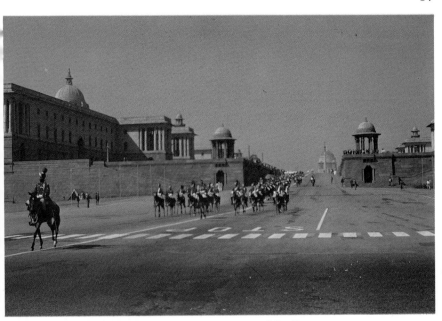

Delhi—presidential procession to the opening of Parliament   (R. Duff)

Delhi—beating the retreat, Republic Day   (R. Duff)

Delhi—Connaught Circus (R. Duff)

Delhi—Hindu temple (R. Duff)

out. To work in this country, however, it is necessary to realize
the thought pattern of the people and to understand how actions
of this type can logically be associated with religious devotion. A
Hindu may not take the life of an animal: that would be sin. But
he may allow a young calf such a small quantity of food that it
will die of starvation.

Until the Act of 1925, fixing a woman's age of consent at 13
within marriage and 14 outside marriage, it was normal for girls
of quite tender age to be married – some as early as seven years of
age. An official statement reported, for example, 'It can be
assumed, for all practical purposes, that every woman is in the
married state at or immediately after puberty and that
cohabitation, therefore, begins in every case with puberty.'
Gandhi described child marriage as a curse and wrote, 'It is
sapping the vitality of thousands of our promising boys and
girls, on whom the future of our society entirely rests. It is
bringing into existence every year thousands of weaklings – both
boys and girls – who are born of immature parenthood. It is a
very fruitful source of appalling child mortality and still-births
that now prevail in our society. It is a very important cause of the
gradual and steady decline of Hindu society in point of
numbers, physical strength and courage, and morality.' Not a
few child-wives became mentally deranged as a result of their
experiences. Fortunately, that curse has gone to a great extent,
but the mind of the child is corrupted from its earliest days by
the sight of the phallic symbols of Siva in the house, the temple
and the wayside shrine. And the sculptures and paintings on
temple walls, in street wall frescoes and in every conceivable
'religious' spot, can only defile the mind.

A particularly lovely child may be delivered to the temple
women for training in dancing and singing, to serve before the
shrine in the daily temple worship and, as Kathleen Mayo says
in *Mother India*, p. 52, 'in the houses around the temple she is
held always ready, at a price, for the use of men pilgrims during
their devotional sojourns in the temple precincts.' An attractive
young boy may become a male prostitute in the temple, used or
abused by the priests and other men.

One of the greatest curses of India is still the caste system.
Whilst its effect is tending to diminish slightly, it is still
prevalent and R. H. Glover's words in *The Progress of
Worldwide Missions* are still pertinent; he said that it 'permeates

Tomorrow's people   (R. Duff)

every phase of daily life with its vitiating poison. It promotes physical degeneracy by restricting the circle in which marriage is permitted, engenders bitter class hatred and obstructs intellectual progress.'

Language does not present an insuperable difficulty for the missionary today. The 1950 constitution made Hindi the official language for the whole of the country, with English as a second official language. In central and southern India Hindi is despised by many and there is a strong feeling against learning it. In 1967 it was laid down that either language could be used. In fact, India has 15 major languages and 700 dialects. In his *Linguistic Survey of India*, Sir George Grierson detailed the national languages recognized by the government as Assamese, Bengali, Gujarati, Hindi, Kannada, Kashmiri, Malayalam, Marathi, Oruja, Punjabi, Sanskrit, Sindhi, Tamil, Telugu and Urdu.

Whilst so many millions live in the cities, the great majority of people live in the country areas and it is there that the great variety of languages and dialects are freely spoken. Villagers may be prepared to listen to Hindi or English, but will often pay little regard to anything in another language from that commonly used in the area. It is, therefore, essential to have some knowledge of local languages if contact is to be established, and not to rely upon the major languages of the country.

4

Religions of India

It has well been said that, 'in spite of the fact that the new India has declared itself to be a secular state, in no other country does religion play such an important role.' The constitution guarantees religious freedom and for some years this provision was respected by the authorities. In the last twenty years or so, however, there has been a reaction against 'foreign' religions and all foreign-sponsored organizations. The official attitude is that there should be a complete 'Indianization' of all such bodies and that, as far as possible, the 'foreigner' should be eliminated. If Indian doctors and nurses are available, for example, those of American or English origin on hospital staffs should be replaced by the Indians. The posts of school teachers, clerks, dentists, lecturers, etc. should be filled by Indian personnel wherever practicable. Mission workers of other nationalities, particularly American, consequently often find admittance to the country refused or the grant of visas interminably delayed.

Mysticism has always been a characteristic of India, but it seems to be personified in the *gurus,* who are now to be found also in the west. J. Weldon says, 'The guru was supposed to be the living evidence that God was manifest in flesh in modern times; to follow his teachings was to make possible the acquisition of the spiritual ideals of deity. If one wanted to enter into the supreme knowledge of the gods, then one must follow the teachings of the guru, for the guru was the one who could lead to God. The guru would prescribe his *Sādhana,* or spiritual exercises.' Self, with its failures, worries and frustrations, must

New Delhi—at devotion   (R. Duff)

be handed over to the guru; through him one found peace, joy and fulfilment in the attainment of a divine life.

Despite all the efforts of other religions, Hinduism still retains an adherence of 83.5 per cent of the population; eleven per cent are Muslims; 2.4 per cent are classified as Christian, half of these being Roman Catholic; 1.7 per cent are followers of Sikhism, 0.7 per cent of Buddhism, 0.4 per cent of Jainism, and 0.3 per cent of Zoroastrianism and other religions. Most of the hill people are still basically animists. Religion permeates the whole of life in India and is the explanation of attitudes and conduct which seem totally incomprehensible to the western mind. A man is not merely a clerk or a salesman: he is also (and more importantly) a Hindu or a Buddhist.

In the west assaults and even murders can take place in crowded streets and the victims will be left without help by the passer-by. The ordinary person does not want to be involved, possibly for fear of being hurt, but more basically because he regards it as not his concern. In India it is equally true that normally no one would interfere to prevent theft, assault or rape, but the motive is more basic and more closely linked with religion. To quote once more, 'Hinduism through the ages has become rigid and static, a slave to form. It has grown away from its roots which, like those of Christianity, are grounded in love and humanity. The rules have become all-important. An Indian is not a member of society at large: he is a member of a caste. If he is to reach God, he must live every second of his life according to the rules, the duties, the *dharma*, of his caste. It is the *dharma* of a Kshatriya, a man of the warrior caste, to be soldierly and brave. The *dharma* of a holy man is to pray, to wear saffron robes, to meditate and to accept offerings from the faithful; nowhere is it stated that he must intervene in other people's quarrels. The *dharma* of a cobbler or a moneylender is to cobble or lend money; there is no specific mention of defending a stranger against his attackers.' To help someone in trouble may, in some cases, be regarded, not as a good or benevolent action, but as an immoral one. It is an attitude which the westerner finds difficult to understand.

The earliest inhabitants of India were evidently polytheistic and worshipped thousands of gods and goddesses. Their descendants, particularly the Santals, Bhils and Gondas, are still devotees of animism. The hill people see spirits in trees, rivers and streams, in hills and mountains, in storm, lightning and thunder and all the other elements of nature. All these must be appeased. The favour of the good spirits must be solicited, while the evil ones must be propitiated. They believe that the human spirit or soul continues after physical death has occurred and remains active in its disembodied state in the area where the person spent his natural life. In consequence, a form of ancestor worship is observed. A belief exists in a Creator, although it is ill-defined. W. T. Stunt says, 'The basis of animism is fear, constant terror night and day, of the spirits a man believes to surround him. These spirits are responsible for everything that happens to a man; there are no natural causes. All life, in its minutest details (birth, initiation, marriage, house building, seed-time, harvest, hunting, cooking, death), is bound up with the spirits, which must all the time be honoured and placated.' Some animists are adherents of Hinduism or other religions, whilst still continuing the customs and observances of past centuries.

Between 2000 and 1500 B.C. the light-skinned Aryans from Central Asia, pouring into India through the Khyber Pass, brought with them the worship of natural things such as the

Reading Hindu scriptures (R. Duff)

heavenly bodies, fire, water, winds and storm, and a large number of their own deities. They practised animal sacrifice, not because of a sense of sin or of a need for atonement, but rather to appease the gods who might otherwise be displeased with them for some reason. The dark-skinned Dravidians whom they conquered were mainly animists and did not practise sacrifice. During the ensuing millennium the Aryan beliefs suffered some amendment as the religions of conquerors and conquered gradually merged. The conquerors remained the sacrificing people (the priests), the warriors, merchants and the higher 'castes', while the conquered almost automatically became the lower castes. The Vedas, or holy books, took a more definitive shape and their contents were completed and finalized; it is clear that they are not entirely Aryan but contain elements of Dravidian origin, dating back to pre-Aryan days.

The Hinduism which has developed has become the traditional religion of India. One of its major features is the caste system, which, over the centuries, has permeated other religions and philosophies in India, and has become a completely divisive force throughout the country. The caste system has become an essential part of the Indian social life, which nothing can alter. As its full implications are realized, it presents the greatest possible shock to the foreigner on his introduction to the country.

Caste is not merely religious: it is socio-occupational. Grace W. Adams writes, 'Caste affects the wells and drinking water; a high caste person would not drink water from a low caste well; a low caste person is not allowed to draw water from a high caste well. Caste prohibits intermarriage, and touching by a lower caste person is defiling. Many high caste persons will not take tracts directly from our hands. . . . The gospel has been preached in the Godavari districts to all castes for over a hundred years, and many outcastes have accepted Christ. This has meant that the caste people look on Christianity as the outcastes' religion and comparatively few of these higher castes have become Christians. Caste feeling dies hard and its continuance among professing Christians constitutes a grave problem. Although different castes may partake of the Lord's Supper together, many will not eat food prepared by a fellow-Christian of a lower caste, not even at a wedding feast.'

In *A Global View of Christian Missions*, J. H. Kane gives an admirable summary of the system. 'At the top were the *Brahmins,* the traditional priests and intellectual leaders; next the *Kshatriyas,* the warriors and rulers; then the *Valayas,* the traders and merchants; and finally the *Sūdras,* the servants and labourers, who performed all the menial tasks for the other three groups. Below this structure were the *Pariahs,* or untouchables, more recently referred to as the "scheduled classes." Constitutionally, "untouchability" has been outlawed in the new India, but in practice, an outcaste must still live outside the village. In the urban centres the problem is rapidly disappearing; in the rural areas, caste remains one of the biggest obstacles to social and economic progress. So strong and pervasive is the influence of caste that even the churches in south India have been unable to eradicate it completely.'

Although the oldest of the religions of India, Hinduism is not a distinct, clear-cut religion. It has been described as an utterly diverse conglomerate of doctrines, cults and ways of life. Some of the Vedic literature is as old as parts of the Old Testament and contain reflections of Jewish laws and practices, e.g. the Nazarite vow (Numbers 6). Yet, as Dr. R. E. Harlow says in *Faces of Asia*, p. 27, 'Hinduism is extremely polytheistic – every village has its own temple and special gods and goddesses. A common saying is that there are more gods in India than grains of sand on her shores.'

It is the most extraordinary and illogical combination of concepts and beliefs. To quote another, 'Primitive magic and fetishism, animal worship, belief in demons, occur beside, and

Hindu goddess and priest   (R. Duff)

often combined with, the worship of more or less personal gods, or the mysticism, asceticism or esoteric doctrines.' All forms of belief, worship and practice find a home in Hinduism. It is accepted that there must be some good in all religions and they cannot, therefore, be discarded. There is no need to be specific and selective: so that a Hindu may embrace another religion, either partially or wholly, without ceasing to be a Hindu.

The Hindu believes in the doctrine of Brahman, i.e. an all-embracing principle compassing being and non-being, which is eternal, infinite and uncreated. Brahman alone is reality and is the ultimate cause of all existence. The universe emanates from Brahman, and Brahman is itself the universe. Brahman is discoverable in all things and is the Self, or *Ātman* of all living things. It has, however, no qualities or attributes, but is entirely impersonal. Yet, contradictorily, Brahman is to be identified with the all-pervading and sublime Supreme God, adored as Vishnu or Shiva. Since all souls originate in Brahman, the real object of life is to find the way back into that supreme essence. To this end, the individual experiences continual reincarnations and, after long years of discipline, penance, and expiation, he finally loses his individuality entirely and is absorbed into the divine essence.

There is a sacred Hindu Trinity or *Trimūrti* (i.e. the One in Three Forms), sometimes shown as having one body with three heads. Vishnu is the protective and preservative aspect of the sublime Being. Shiva is the destructive aspect. In the background is the mighty demiurge, Brahma; the priest who led devotions was called the Brahmin. In ancient Sanskrit the word Brahma meant 'prayer' or 'devotion', so that, not unnaturally, lest it should be deduced that this is a reflection of the Triune God of the Bible, or that it is a trinity of divine beings inseparably united in one, it should be appreciated that the *Trimūrti* are impersonal, although all-pervading.

Brahma, the Creator, is regarded as all-pervading and unchanging. Vishnu, the preserver, has had nine avatars, or incarnations and a tenth and final one will take place after 425,000 years. On previous occasions, he has come as a fish, as Rāma (a moral god), Krishna (whose life was immoral), Buddha (who was holy), etc. Śiva, the destroyer, is both loved and feared, since he is both the giver and destroyer of life, and represents the elemental powers of the universe. He is frequently shown with four arms, dancing and shaking the world. But he is also represented as an ascetic, with his body smeared with ash, a snake around his neck and a trident by his side. Animals accompany him and his elephant-headed son, Ganeśa, is often at his side. As the fertility god, Śiva's worship reflects something of the ancient fertility rites and is attended by considerable sexual immorality.

Śiva has a consort in Kālī, the mother-goddess and the fertility deity, to whom women pray for health and for children. Yet she is portrayed as the merciless goddess of destruction, with long black hair and almost completely naked, and holding swords and human hair. At her temple at Calcutta (i.e. Kālī-ghat), blood sacrifices take place every day. She has thousands of temples in India: the one at Calcutta is the private property of a family of Brahmins, and the shrine is always crowded by pilgrims from far and near, bringing their offerings to Kālī. In *Mother India*, p. 15, Kathleen Mayo describes the 'deep, semi-enclosed shrine in which, dimly half-visible, looms the figure of the goddess. Black of face she is, with a monstrous lolling tongue, dripping blood. Of her four hands, one grasps a bleeding human head, one a knife, the third, outstretched, cradles blood, the fourth, raised in menace, is empty. In the shadows close about her feet stand the priests ministrant.' Every day between 150 and 200 goats are slain to her, and women and dogs will join in lapping up the blood. Just below the temple runs a muddy brook, the most ancient remaining outlet of the Ganges, filled with worshippers who, when they have finished their ablutions, drink of the filthy water in which they have just bathed.

In addition to the principal deities and to innumerable local gods of the animists, there are 330 million lesser gods and goddesses in the Indian pantheon.

The body of ancient religious literature in Sanskrit, known as the Vedas, is regarded as possessed of absolute and final authority. This Vedic literature is composed of (1) books called the four Vedas, (2) the Brāhmaṇas, subsequent writings that explain, illustrate and direct the ritualistic use of the old texts or hymns of the Vedas, (3) the Upaniṣads, appended to the Brāhmaṇas and intended to elicit and apply more fully and systematically the references in the earlier writings to the great problems of the universe. The four Vedas are a collection of

Tamil Nadu—idol shrines   (S. F. Warren)

hymns, commentaries, poems and formulae, said to have existed
for three and a half millennia. The oldest Vedic literature
consists of 1,028 hymns, celebrating particularly a trio of gods:
Indra, the deity supposed to yield dew and rain; Agni, the god of
fire; and Sūrya, the sun-god.

The Vedic literature is said to be the revelation of
fundamental and unassailable truth. Its traditions and teachings
can be discerned only in the sanctity and pious lives of the
Brahmins. These are a special class, allegedly possessing a
spiritual superiority acquired by birth, and portraying in their
lives the ideal norm of ritual purity and social prestige.

Respect for life is inculcated because the bond of life unites all
living things. The protection of the cow is compulsory. The
Hindu believes in the transmigration of souls and he may be
reborn in any form. His life and actions will, according to this
doctrine, determine his future. His position at rebirth will be
determined by the merit or demerit of his present life. A man's
life consists of actions, ritually good and bad, each bearing fruit,
so that when he dies, there is an accumulation of *Karma*, merit
and demerit, to be worked off. This determines his status in his
next life – he may become a god, an outcaste, a woman, a dog, a
plant, for example. A man is not really responsible for what he

does – it is the result of a former life. Everything is attributed to Karma.

There is a cycle of life, so that there is a ceaseless return from death to life. There is virtually no beginning or ending and it is not surprising that a spirit of fatalism develops. Emancipation can come only along the path of duty, of knowledge and of devotion. For the ordinary Hindu, the aim of life is conformity to social and ritual duties and to the traditional rules of conduct for his caste, family and profession. These constitute his *dharma*. The Indian philosophers have constantly sought a way of release from the endless process of birth and re-birth, and look for it in Nirvāṇa, when by the knowledge of the Supreme Truth of the Brahma-ātman, the soul is released from its ceaseless pilgrimage by absorption into the nothingness of the heart of the universe. Ātman (soul or self) is one with the Ātman everywhere, i.e. the Brahma, the soul of the universe.

There are six forms taken by Hinduism, viz. Vedism, Brahmanism, Vaiṣṇavism, Śalvism, Trantrism and Śāktism. It is a religion devoid of any real hope.

It should not be ignored, moreover, that there is a definite sexual undercurrent. Krishna, for example, is alleged to have seduced over 3,000 million women and to have changed himself into millions of forms to enjoy the attractions of so many women. Śiva, says Kathleen Mayo, *op. cit.*, p. 31, 'is represented on highroad shrines, in the temples, on the little altar of the home, or in personal amulets, by the image of the male generative organ, in which shape he receives the daily sacrifices of the devout. The followers of Vishnu, multitudinous in the south, from their childhood wear painted upon their foreheads the sign of the function of generation. And although it is accepted that the ancient inventors of these and kindred emblems intended them as aids to the climbing of spiritual heights, practice and extremely detailed narratives of the intimacies of the gods, preserved in the hymns of the fireside, give them literal meaning and suggestive power, as well as religious sanction in the common mind.... And, even though the sex symbols themselves were not present, there are the sculptures and paintings on temple walls and temple chariots, on palace doors and street-wall frescoes, realistically demonstrating every conceivable aspect and humour of sex contact.'

Khanapur—idol
prostitutes
(S. F. Warren)

Tenkasi—temple
cart
(S. F. Warren)

For centuries young girls were used as temple prostitutes and even had their own caste, the *devadāsīs*, or 'prostitutes of the gods.' Amy Wilson Carmichael's *Lotus Buds* and other books tell the story of the horrors and consequences of this religious prostitution. The effect is evident at every level of life. To quote Kathleen Mayo again, *ibid*, p. 33, 'the mother, high caste or low caste, will practise upon her children – the girl "to make her sleep well", the boy "to make him manly", an abuse which the boy, at least, is apt to continue daily for the rest of his life.'

One of the religious pictures of India, which a visitor never forgets, is that of the typical *sādhu*, who gives himself completely to the Hindu faith. To quote Letters' description of these 'holy men', *op. cit.*, pp. 192–3, 'Gaunt, bearded, and wild-haired, their naked or near naked bodies smeared with ash, they haunted the ghats and the roadways, sitting cross-legged in meditation or standing alone with eyes fixed on some unseen faraway vision. Their cloaks and loin-cloths were stained ochre, their uncut hair was wildly bedraggled or matted into long solid lumps like grey wadding; and from their necks drooped strings of nutbeads and flowers. *Sādhus* own nothing, and live on whatever comes to hand, wild fruit and berries or the offerings of the pious. Their paths to release are many and varied. Some spend their lives wandering from place to place, some become hermits, living alone in caves and on mountain-sides. Each *sādhu* sect practises a different form of worship and seeks the inner consciousness by its own particular austerities; by vows of silence, long arduous fasts and meditations, going naked in the Himalayan winter, abstaining from sleep, or sitting on beds of nails. Years of yoga studies have made them able to spurn their bodies, and have freed them from the laws of nature that tie other men to the physical, materialistic world.'

While the majority of the people are Hindus, some are adherents of Jainism, which broke off from Hinduism in the sixth century B.C. It has two million followers, mostly in Gujarat and Rajasthan in western India. Its basic principles of asceticism and non-violence inspired Mahatma Gandhi and he adopted them in his 'resistance' to British rule.

Jainism has been described as both a philosophy and a religion, but it is more the former than the latter. The name was derived from Jina (victor) and was applied to 24 great religious persons, the example of whose lives is the focus of the religion.

Jainism was founded by Vandhamāna Mahāvīra in protest against certain of the teachings of the orthodox Vedic cult. It teaches the 'three jewels' of right faith, right understanding and right morals. The principal characteristic of the religion is the doctrine that no injury should be done to any other living creature, since all life is connected.

Jainism is dualistic. It divides the universe into two independent eternal categories of life (*jīva*) and non-life (*ajīva*), but does not recognize an initial creator. The ideal is to be attained through the perfection of man's nature, and this is achieved primarily through monasticism and asceticism. Jainism rests on *māyā* (point of view) and teaches that there are many sides to reality, so that it is impossible to make an absolute and positive assertion on any subject. It has two sects – Śvetāmbaras and Digambaras – and has many wealthy and influential adherents.

Sikhism, which is also virtually an offshoot from Hinduism, rejects caste, idolatry and the supremacy of Brahma, and its followers rely upon *gurus* (after Guru Nānak), or divine guides. J. Lloyd Bone says that Sikhism was founded in the sixteenth century by a Hindu, named Guru Nānak Dev, in an attempt to abolish idolatry and unite the Hindus and the Muslims. 'The cause was carried on by nine successive gurus, who tended to turn Sikhism into a military democracy. Gorrind Singh, the last of these gurus, consolidated the religion by giving its adherents the following external peculiarities, which distinguished them from people of other faiths: (1) They must never cut their hair (keṣa) or shave their faces, a symbol of saintliness and strength. The hair is done up in a kind of bun and covered by a bright coloured turban, which is worn at all times in public. (2) A comb (kanghā) must always be worn in the hair, keeping it in place and being available at all times when needed. (3) An iron bracelet (karā) must always be worn on the right arm, a sign of sternness and constraint. (4) A knicker (kacch) was to be worn to ensure briskness of movement in time of action and an easy underwear for times of rest. (5) A sword (kirnān) kept always by his side was a weapon of offence and defence, also a symbol of power and dignity. To bind them still further together, every follower had to assume the name "Singh," which means "lion," the symbol of strength.' It is interesting to note that, during ten years' service in Punjab, Mr. Bone did not see a single Sikh confess Christ.

Near Srikakulam—rural markets

(C. Gilmore)

56

Delhi—street market

(Air India)

India's tomorrow

(C. Gilmore)

Inside a Sikh temple   (R. Duff)

The Hare Krishna movement, or the International Society of Krishna Consciousness (ISKCON), is a variation of Hinduism which has invaded Britain and America. It is said to have originated from the teachings of Krishna in India about 3000 B.C. Krishna is alleged to have had a number of incarnations, the last being in A.D. 1486. The most recent guru, Swami Prabhupada, was initiated in 1933. He died in 1977, but the movement still flourishes. It teaches that 'to attain salvation, one must abstain from the four primary sins, chant a minimum of 1,728 times daily, and obey 64 different rules and duties.'

The Divine Light Mission, led by another guru, Maharaj Ji, at first claimed that he was divine. It is also an offshoot from Hinduism, which has found ready acceptance in the west. Most of the gurus 'bring with them teachings highly destructive of morality, commonsense, spirituality, and Christian values. Their open advocacy of various forms of occultism and psychicism (e.g. yoga), spiritism, and sexual immorality (e.g. tantra) have ruined thousands of lives.' It is not generally accepted in India, although it has found many followers in the west.

Transcendental Meditation began in 1957, when Maharishi Mahesh Yogi was allegedly commanded by his spiritual master, Guru Dev, to develop a simple technique that would allow the common masses of people to attain the state of Hindu God-realization. An offshoot from Hinduism, it has spread extremely rapidly in the U.S.A. and has now over a million adherents. It has an international controlling organization, the World Plan Executive Council, and its branches include the Spiritual Regeneration Movement, the Students International Meditation Society, etc. It has centres in 90 countries. It claims to be the 'Science of Creative Intelligence,' and presents itself as a natural method moving forward to a greater field of happiness.

John Weldon says that 'one becomes a meditator by attending three public lectures and undergoing the initiatory rite, or *pūjā* (a Hindu word meaning "worship"). During this time one receives his own mantra... there are only sixteen principal mantras dispensed by age categories (*eng, em, enga, ema, ling, lem, unga, iema, shirim, shiring, kirim, kiring, hirim, hiring, sham, shama).* ' 'The true nature of TM is Vedantic Hinduism in the non-dualist *(advaita)* tradition of Shamkara. Maharishi's four principal texts are replete with thinly veiled Hinduism, particularly his *Commentary on the Bhagavad Gītā* and *Meditations of Maharishi Mahesh Yogi.* ' The mantras are related to Hindu deities. The pledge signed by every TM teacher states that he recognizes his duty 'to serve the Holy Tradition and spread the Light of God to all those who need it.'

The ceremony of initiation includes the following: 'Guru in the glory of Brahman; Guru in the glory of Vishnu; Guru in the glory of the personified transcendental fulness of Brahman, to Him, to Shri, Guru Dev adorned with glory, I bow down.' Although it is sometimes claimed that TM is purely secular, there is no question that it is religious and of Hindu origin. To quote Weldon again, 'Through meditation we progress to a recognition of the Absolute. We perceive our self (body and personality, etc.) as unreal and recognize our true Self as Divine. Reality lies beyond all duality – good versus evil, man versus God, etc. Everything is One, and if we obtain this knowledge (proved to us by our experience in meditation), then – and only then – can we progress spiritually and have no need of reincarnating into another life.' The meditator accepts that *ātman,* the true self, is Brahman, the final, impersonal god of

Khajraho—Kandariya Mahadeo temple   (Indian High Commission)

Hinduism. TM claims that men are not separate from God; they *are* God.

Parseeism, or Zoroastrianism, derives from the teaching of the Persian sage, Zoroaster and the sacred writings of the Zend-Avesta. Zoroaster (or, more properly Zarathustra) lived for many years at the court of Darius Hystaspes, and attempted to reform and systematize the Indo-Iranian polytheism and to establish it on an ethical basis. He was said to have been also the master of the Greek philosopher and mathematician, Pythagoras. He introduced a class system which bears resemblance to the caste system later adopted in India. In Parseeism, worship is of the sun, moon, stars, earth, air and water, although the enlightened regard these merely as

representations of God. Ahura-Mazdā is worshipped as a great
and good god but his power is limited and he is always opposed
by Angra Mainzu, who created evil. Life is regarded as a
continual conflict between good and evil. Those who overcome
pass into eternal happiness, but the wicked are eternally lost.
The world is soon to be destroyed in a tremendous
conflagration. Zoroastrianism apparently entered India initially
through Afghanistan and then through Persian refugees fleeing
from Muslim persecution. It has not a large number of followers
in the country today.

Buddhism originated at roughly the same time as Jainism and
is named after its founder, Gautama Buddha, an Indian prince
who was born in 563 B.C., about 130 miles north of the city of
Banaras. At the age of 29, he voluntarily assumed a state of
mendicancy to devote himself to philosophical meditation.
After six years of this simple life, combined with intense mental
activity, he claimed to have achieved 'enlightenment', and
recruited sixty disciples to propagate his teaching. Buddhism
knows nothing of a Supreme Being. It teaches that suffering is
universal, that desire is the cause of suffering, and that suffering
ceases when desire ceases. The origin and the end of all things is
a state of nothingness, in which thought, emotion, desire,
affection and feeling cease, and in which there is neither
personality nor change nor emotion. The highest state for a
human being is Nirvāṇa, or absolute extinction, and it may take
thousands of rebirths to obtain complete detachment or
enlightenment. In the Tripiṭaka, or three sacred books, the four
sublime virtues are stated to be: '(1) the utter and hopeless
misery of all conscious existence; (2) the transmigration of souls;
(3) the attainment of Nirvāṇa; (4) right belief, right speech, right
means of livelihood, right memory, right aspiration, right
conduct, right endeavour, and right meditation.' (Collett). This
is the 'path' which leads to the cessation of suffering.

Although a Supreme God is not recognized, statues of
Buddha are to be found on every side, and Buddhist temples are
full of images of deities and also of demons and legendary
animals. Buddhism gained widespread allegiance under the first
great Indian empire, the Mauryan, which eventually spread to
most of the sub-continent. The number of adherents today,
however, has declined considerably.

There are two main schools of Buddhist thought. Hīnayāna is

the more conservative and conforms more closely to Buddha's original teaching. It is found in Ceylon rather than in India. Mahāyāna tolerates other ideas and incorporates much local animism. It acknowledges a supreme reality, and believes in the deification of Gautama Buddha. The way of salvation is through faith in him and a vast number of Wisdom Beings (Bodhisattivas) who abstained from Nirvāṇa to help deliver their erring fellows. The idea of attaining enlightenment has given way to compassion for humanity. Mahāyāna is found in Nepal rather than in India.

Zen, which claims to be the true Buddhism, originated in India in the sixth century A.D. and is one of the divisions of Mahāyān Buddhism. It spread to China, Japan and Korea and in the present century, to the west, but is not very prevalent nowadays in India. It has two main schools – Sōtō and Revizai. The goal of Zen is 'enlightenment' *(satori)*. This, as C. Wilson says, 'may literally take nine years of staring at a blank wall, as it did with Bodhidharma, the founder of Zen'. It has no basis of belief, D. T. Suzuki says quite frankly in *The Gospel According to Zen,* pp. 228, 229, 'Zen has nothing to teach us in the way of intellectual analysis, nor has it any set of doctrines which are imposed on its followers for acceptance. If I am asked what Zen teaches, I would answer Zen teaches nothing. Whatever teachings there are in Zen, they come out of one's own mind.' There is no need to believe in anything in order to experience the 'enlightenment' Zen offers.

J. Weldon and C. Wilson put it clearly in *Occult Shock,* p. 62, 'Prior to enlightenment, we perceive the world in ignorance and distortion, . . . as having good and evil, subject and object, life and death, as duality. However, when we experience *satori,* we see reality as it truly is – one entity. . . . In Zen, enlightenment is achieved through meditation *(Zayen)* on paradoxical questions or statements *(Kohns).* The purpose of the *kohn* is to open the mind to truth, to help it to achieve *satori.* ' Freedom is experienced when we cease to look at the world logically, morally, reasonably, or scientifically. All is one, and knowledge of our true self is a knowledge of all nature. And this intangible nonsense is spreading like wildfire in the west.

Judaism was brought to India by Jewish traders and merchants, who established settlements in a number of towns, one of the principal centres being Cochin. It did not make a

Gaya—Buddhist (Bodh Gaya) temple   (R. Duff)

great impact upon the sub-continent and little is heard today of the Jewish faith.

From the seventh century onwards Aryan and other traders brought the teachings of Islām to India, and the new faith became firmly established during the Mogul empire from the sixteenth century onwards. Muḥammad's teachings were evidently derived from a mixture of Judaism, Christianity and paganism, and his 'inspired' utterances of the 'revelations' given to him were recorded by his followers and, on the instructions of the Caliph Omar, brought together in the Koran. The faith is known as Islām, i.e. 'submission'. Islām is monotheistic and claims that God has had four principal prophets – Noah, Moses, Jesus and Muḥammad. It rejects the Divine Sonship of the Lord Jesus Christ and substitutes Ishmael for Isaac as the chosen seed. The 'five pillars' of Islām are detailed as (1) recitation aloud of the Kalima, (2) prayer five times a day, facing Mecca, (3) almsgiving, (4) fasting during the month of Ramaḍān, and (5) pilgrimage to Mecca at least once in a lifetime. Sir M. Monier-Williams succinctly summarizes the teachings of Islām: 'Cease from your idolatries; worship the one God; pay strict attention to your religious duties – prayers five times a day, fastings for the whole of one month, almsgiving, pilgrimages – and then trust to God's mercy, be resigned to His decrees, and look for a Paradise hereafter, a material condition of bliss – beautiful gardens, cloudless skies, running streams, and the companionship of lovely women'.

When independence came in 1947, the areas in which Islām was the major faith were split off to form West Pakistan and East Pakistan (now Bangladesh), but a minority in other parts of the country retained their loyalty to Islām.

These are the faiths with which Christian missionaries have had to contend. S. Eddy says in *India Awakening* that India is 'the home of religions, a vast religious area where the world's great faiths are on trial and where finally only the fittest can survive.' These many religions are more clearly defined today than when the apostle Thomas first brought the gospel to India, and this may be one of the reasons why Christianity has not taken root to a greater extent in this vast country. The growing spirit of nationalism has unquestionably been an important contributory factor, and the ever-present poverty is doubtless another. Nevertheless there is cause for thanksgiving that some impression has been made, even if the need seems greater than ever.

There is obviously no room for complacency, and the problems of the future are probably far greater than is commonly realized. The situation was very clearly described in a review written by William Walker in *Echoes of Service* nearly 20 years ago and we make no apology for quoting *in extenso*.

He says, 'The breakup of the Moghul Empire in the eighteenth century was the end to seven hundred years of Muslim dominance in India which had greatly weakened the vital forces of Hinduism. By the nineteenth century, further decline was noticeable in the popular faith of the masses. Child-marriage, female infanticide and suttee (the immolation of widows on their husbands' funeral pyres) were widely practised and caused strong revulsion of feeling amongst the educated classes. Many cultured Hindus believed that they should break with a religion so degrading and, for a time, it seemed that they might turn to faith in Christ. That they did not do so, was probably due to two important developments which followed, viz. the rise of nationalism, and the introduction of certain reforms within the Hindu fold.'

The first reformation movement of note was the Brahmo

Muslims at prayer   (R. Duff)

Samāj. This was a religious society which attempted to work out a synthesis of all that was best in Hinduism and Christianity. Christ was given a prominent place in the system, but His teaching was put on the same level as the ancient Hindu traditions. Ram Mohun Roy (1770–1834) and Keshub Chundu Sen (1838–1884) were its first leaders. These men frequently spoke of Christ in terms of devotion. In a speech in 1879, for example, K. C. Sen said, 'You cannot deny that your hearts have been touched, conquered and subjugated by a higher power. That power, need I tell you, is Christ. It is Christ who rules British India, not the British Government. None but Jesus shall have it.' *(Moving Millions,* ed. by J. E. Speer.) Such fervent protestations of faith were very misleading, however, for Christ's divine claims were never seriously considered. The Brahmo Samāj made little progress outside of Calcutta. The movement was confined mainly to the rising middle class families of the Bengali intelligentsia. Lacking originality and dynamic stimulus, the Samāj did not long survive the cultural impulse which gave it birth.

The second movement was the Ārya Samāj founded by Swāmi Dayanānda Saraswati (1824–1883). This movement differed greatly from the Brahmo Samāj. There was no secret admiration of Christianity, but open hostility to the cause of Christ. The Swāmi publicly attacked Christianity (as well as other non-Hindu religions) and sought to re-convert Christians to Hinduism. His criticism of Christianity was twofold. First, the belief that God became man violates the basic doctrine of monotheism. Second, Christianity is a foreign religion brought into India by foreign missionaries and supported by foreign funds. The Samāj has steadily increased its influence in North India. It has been estimated that there are between 40,000 and 50,000 members meeting in more than 100 centres of the metropolitan area of Delhi. An official spokesman of the Ārya Samāj stated deliberately, 'Christianity is a fraud; it is anti-national, a foreign movement. Hinduism is the religion of India and fully adequate for our people.' *(The Church in Delhi,* by J. P. Alter and H. J. Singh, p. 72).

The third movement is more difficult to trace and define, but it may be said to have started with Rāmakrishna Paramahamsa (1834–1886). Rāmakrishna professed to have experienced mystical union with the founders of various faiths (including

Students of Muslim theology   (R. Duff)

Christ), and taught that all religions are true and lead to the goal of self-realization. His experiences were believed to be remarkable confirmations of the Hindu text which says, 'All men reach you, the Supreme, even as all rivers, however zigzag their courses, reach the sea.' (Mahimnastava). At Ramakrishna's death, his views were brilliantly expounded by his disciple, Swāmi Vivekānanda. From the moment that he made his historic appearance at the Parliament of Religions in Chicago in 1893, the success of the Rāmakrishna Mission was assured.

Vivekānanda was a powerful orator in English and Bengali, and made a deep impression on those who heard him. He was widely acclaimed and made an extensive tour of the U.S.A., preaching the Hindu philosophy of the Vedanta. When he returned to India, he had successfully transplanted Hinduism to many parts of the western world. The financial support he received in America enabled him to arrange for the wide extension of the Mission's work in his own land. The activities of the Rāmakrishna Mission now cover libraries, reading rooms, lectures, symposia on cultural subjects, worship meetings, free dispensaries, and clinics for the treatment of tuberculosis. The ideas which Rāmakrishna taught and which Vivekānanda popularized in the west, were later dramatized in politics by Gandhi, and given intellectual content by Dr. S. Radhakrishnan, the greatest interpreter of Indian thought.

The reaction of the east against the west then has followed a distinct pattern: first a period of anxious withdrawal, next a period of bold return, and third a period of quiet advance. The mood has changed from timidity to a sense of equality and now to superiority. The apologetic tone has gone. The confident accent is clear. There can be no doubt that we are in the last phase. It is constantly being said that what India needs is not conversion, but reform through gradual development. In learned circles the hint is dropped that, 'if a Christian approached a Hindu teacher for spiritual guidance, the latter would not ask his Christian pupil to discard his allegiance to Christ, but would tell him that his idea of Christ was inadequate, and would then lead him to a knowledge of the real Christ, the incorporate Supreme.' *(The Hindu View of Life,* by S. Radhakrishnan, p. 24). Hinduism is, by implication, not only superior to all other faiths, but has universal significance.

Bruce Nicholls says in *Missionary Strategy,* pp. 9, 10, 'Non-Christian religions are no longer on the defensive, but are each confident that they have the answer for the salvation of man and the renewal of society. The Church now faces a twofold attack: annihilation by the sword and assimilation by doctrinal absorption. Communism threatens the young churches with annihilation. Islām once successfully wiped out the church of North Africa; will this be repeated elsewhere? Assimilation or, to use the more technical word, syncretism, is the major threat from Hinduism and Buddhism. This is the coming encounter.'

The role of the traditional missionary has, in any case, completely altered. The political changes of the last few decades have made it imperative that Indian Christians should take the initiative in evangelizing their own people. As far as Hinduism is concerned, the great need is for Indian believers themselves to prove that Christianity is not a foreign religion brought into India by foreign missionaries and supported by foreign funds, but the very life of Christ Himself revealed in those who love Him.

5

The Coming of Christianity

There has for centuries been a tradition that the gospel was brought to India by the apostle Thomas about A.D. 52 and that he spent twenty years preaching in the country. According to the story, the first half of that period was spent in evangelistic work in the north of the country around Lahore, where he enjoyed the protection of the king Thanavalla. When the king was murdered in A.D. 63, he was advised to move south and actually settled in the area of Madras, where he again started to preach the gospel. According to P. Thornton-Flett, in *South East Asia Journal of Theology*, vol. 6, no. 3, pp. 43–51, 'the area from Madras to Cochin is studded with reminders of his work.' Thousands are said to have been converted through his ministry. When the new king's wife was converted in A.D. 72, however, Thomas was seized and martyred at Mylapore in Madras. When, in the year 180, Pantaenus of Alexandria was sent to India to preach to the Brahmins, Jerome declares that he found Christians who were using a Hebrew version of the Gospel of Matthew, said to have been left by Bartholomew (see Eusebius' *Ecclesiastical History*, 5:10). Later commissaries were apparently sent by the Bishop of Alexandria in 193, but little is known of their labours or the results therefrom.

Doubt has sometimes been cast on the story of Thomas' ministry in India, but the Mar Thomas (or Syrian) Christians of South India claim that their churches owe their existence to the apostle and his preaching. It is, in any case, remarkable that the faith should have been maintained so long and in the face of strong opposition, unless a strong foundation had been laid for it by some pioneer possessed of considerable authority. With no contact with fellow-believers in the west and surrounded, as they were, by the floods of Hinduism, they retained their loyalty to the apostolic faith and principles for centuries. It was not until the coming in the seventh century of the Nestorian Christians, fleeing from persecution in Persia, that they received any support.

The Nestorians were well established in Madras and in other parts of India when John of Monte Corvino visited the country in the thirteenth century. When the Portuguese invaded the country in 1498 they found 1,400 Nestorian churches with about 200,000 members spread across India, and at Chinsaprise there were a hundred villages composed entirely of Nestorian Christians. A Nestorian tablet dating back to the seventh century, found near Madras in 1549, bore a dove and also Scriptural quotations in Syriac and Pahlavi. Nestorian Christianity had put down its roots firmly.

As in Brazil, the Portuguese invaders prepared the way for the conversion of the people to Roman Catholicism. Franciscan missionaries accompanied Cabral when he landed in India in 1500. Three years later they were followed by Dominicans with the same object in view. Goa, on the west coast, was captured by the Portuguese in 1510 and became an important colony. In 1533 it also became the centre of an enormous Roman Catholic diocese stretching from the Cape of Good Hope to Japan. Rome intended to make India her own. It was at Goa also that Francis Xavier laboured among the Portuguese colony. According to L. A. Marsh in *In His Name*, p. 147, 'One of the early Jesuit missionaries to India was the Italian Roberto de Nobili, who arrived in 1605 and, adopting the attitude of "an Indian to the Indians", worked around Madurai in South India, learning Tamil, Telugu and Sanskrit, and living in the mode of a Brahmin, he drew many thousands into the Roman Catholic Church.'

It was not until the following century that Protestant missionaries entered the country. When Denmark established its first trading colony at Tranquebar on the east coast, Protestant chaplains also took up residence to care for the spiritual needs of the colonists. They were followed a hundred years later by missionaries to labour among the Indian people

Ootacamund, 1934—W. Stunt and C. F. Hogg outside Montauban Rest Home

themselves. The first were Germans who were graduates of Halle University in Denmark and had been influenced by August H. Franke and Count Nikolaus L. Zinzendorf. They mastered Tamil fairly quickly and the first, Bartholomäus Ziegenbalg, who sailed for Tranquebar in 1706, translated the New Testament and part of the Old Testament into Tamil within three years and later produced a Tamil grammar and dictionary. This was the first translation of the Scriptures into any Indian language. He was accompanied by Heinrich Plütschau and, within a short time, they were followed by Philip

Frabricius and Christian F. Schwartz. The last-named mastered not only Tamil, but Persian, Hindustani, English and Portuguese. He remained in India until his death in 1798, spending his life in Trichinopoly and Tanjores in central and South India and becoming one of the great figures in missionary history in India, well respected and loved by rulers and common people alike. Through the Danish-Halle Mission a great deal was accomplished and it is said that by 1719 there were 355 converts and that a school, a seminary, a paper mill, a type foundry and a printing press had been established. The mission continued until the end of the eighteenth century and, during that time, 50,000 converts had been won, most of whom came from the Śūdras and Pariahs.

At the end of the eighteenth century, Protestantism was represented in India primarily by the traders and troops of the East India Company, but the chaplains of the Company – particularly David Brown, Henry Martyn and others of this same character, several of whom had been greatly influenced by Charles Simeon of Cambridge – laid the foundation for future missionary work. Their association with the Company was perhaps not the most acceptable recommendation to the Indian people, and the work may have suffered somewhat in consequence of this. It certainly did from the attitude shown by the officials of the Company in later years.

The first British missionary was William Carey, who went under the auspices of the newly-formed Baptist Missionary Union. Carey (1761–1834) was apprenticed to a shoemaker at the age of fourteen. Originally an Anglican, he left to join a dissenting body, following his conversion at the age of eighteen. He commenced preaching wherever he had the opportunity and was finally persuaded to join the Baptist denomination and to become ordained in 1787. He still continued his secular employment, but also taught school on weekdays and preached on Sundays. He devoured every book within reach and taught himself Latin, Greek, Hebrew, French and Dutch.

Through reading *The Last Voyage of Captain Cook*, his interest was aroused in missionary work and he commenced reading every book he could obtain regarding the countries of the world. He made his own map of the world and noted on it every item of information he could discover. The result was perhaps inevitable. In 1792 he published a small book of 87

Dussehra festival   (Indian High Commission)

pages, entitled, *An Enquiry into the Obligations of Christians for the Conversion of the Heathen,* and then commenced striving for the formation of a society to send missionaries to needy countries. He found little enthusiasm among the Calvinistic Baptists with whom he was associated. At one ministerial meeting, when he proposed a discussion of the Great Commission, he was sternly rebuked by Dr. John C. Ryland, when he retorted, 'Young man, sit down. When God pleases to convert the heathen, He will do it without your help or mine.'

But nothing daunted William Carey. Soon afterwards, at the Baptist Ministers' Association at Nottingham, he preached on Isaiah 54:2, 3 and urged, 'Expect great things from God; attempt great things for God.' It still took further effort but eventually he secured the formation of The Particular Baptist Society for Propagating the Gospel among the Heathen. Difficulties abounded, but on the 18th June, 1793, Carey and his family and two others set out for India – a land to which he gave 40 years of unbroken service. His letters and labours aroused missionary interest in Europe and America and the extent of his influence cannot be exaggerated. He was truly 'the father of modern missions.'

Because of the unsympathetic attitude of the East India Company, he was unable to work in British India and he

Reading Telugu
scriptures
(M. G. G. Harvey)

accordingly settled in the Danish colony at Serampore, fifteen miles up the Hoogley River from Calcutta. He and his co-workers gave themselves to the missionary cause unreservedly. Funds received were used primarily for the work and they lived as frugally as possible. Three times a year they met to read a compact they had made, 'Finally, let us give ourselves irrevocably to this glorious crusade. Let us never think that our time, our gifts, our strength, our families, or even the clothes we wear, are our own. Let us sanctify them all to God and His cause.' They did!

Carey's capacity was amazing. He compiled and published grammars in Sanskrit, Bengali, Marathi, Telugu, and Sikh, and dictionaries in Bengali and Marathi, as well as translating the

Scriptures and publishing other works. He and his colleagues founded 26 churches and 126 schools with a total enrolment of 10,000. In addition, he produced the first vernacular newspaper in Bengali. He also translated the New Testament into Bengali. In 1799 he was joined by William Ward and Joshua Marshman, a printer and a weaver, and the three were forced by the continued restrictions of the East India Company to concentrate the work in the Danish settlement of Serampore, some fifteen miles from Calcutta. On Carey's death in 1834, he and his colleagues had been responsible for the translation or publication of the Scriptures into 40 languages or dialects. The entire Bible had been issued in six languages, the New Testament in 23 more and portions of the Scriptures in nearly a dozen other languages.

From 1792 to 1813 the East India Company had been opposed to missionary work in India and had inhibited all religious and educational activities in their dominions. Strong pressure was brought upon the British Parliament to override the Company's decision and it was mainly through the advocacy of William Wilberforce that the battle was won. Referring to his speech on the motion, he said later, 'It was late when I got up, but I thank God that I was enabled to speak for two hours, and

Hearing the "Good News" (R. Duff)

with great acceptance, and we carried it, about 89 to 36. I heard afterwards that many great men had been praying for us all night.' The new charter granted to the Company provided that missions should be tolerated. In fact, however, the Company continued to hinder everywhere and to encourage heathenism. Large sums of money were spent in replacing temples, providing new idols and supporting a pagan priesthood. But despite the Company's insincerity, the provision was in the charter.

Not only the Baptist Missionary Society but other societies took early advantage of the opportunity. The London Missionary Society started on a large scale in the Ganges country and also in the south, as well as in Madras, Belgaum, Calcutta and Banaras. The Society for the Propagation of the Gospel took over a work in the Tirunelveli (Tinnevelli) district. Alexander Duff of the Free Church of Scotland commenced a great educational work in 1830. The greatest spiritual success was met with in the extreme south of India. As early as 1822 it was estimated that 5,000 had embraced Christianity at Travancore.

In spite of all these efforts, heathenism still held sway with all its cruelty completely uncurbed. Still thousands of widows every year were compelled to burn to death on the funeral pyres of their husbands. Still, year by year, devotees were crushed to death beneath the car of Juggernaut in its annual procession. Converts faced trial and persecution, not only among the higher castes, where a profession of Christianity often meant death, but even among the lower castes. 'The Brahmins had almost absolute power,' writes Prof. A. Rendle Short in *A Modern Experiment in Apostolic Missions*, p. 30. 'This was dangerously shown in the "upper class" riots of 1827 and 1858. The low caste women of the Travancore district were forbidden by custom to wear any clothing above the waist, to show their inferiority. Under the refining influence of Christianity they began to feel the indignity of this restriction, and the lady missionaries made them a loose jacket, to which some of them added a scarf. Bitter persecution followed. The women were beaten and their clothes torn off; the Christian men seized and imprisoned; the chapels burned down. In 1829 the government issued a decree forbidding the "upper cloth," and as a compensation allowed the low caste Christian women exemption from Sunday labour and from employment in idolatrous service. In 1858, the Christian women having gradually resumed the obnoxious garment, more riots broke out, and for weeks there was nothing but a reign of terror in the Nagercoil district. At last the Madras government conceded the right that a *coarse* upper-cloth might be worn, thus giving the higher caste women an opportunity to emphasize their superiority by the fineness of their attire.'

The first assembly missionary to India was Anthony Norris Groves. As a young man he had felt the call of God to India but, for a variety of reasons, had been diverted to Baghdad. His real burden had always been for the millions of India and when Colonel (later General Sir) Arthur Cotton presented the needs of India to him, there was no doubt regarding his reaction. In 1833 he paid a visit to that country, travelling extensively and working among missionaries of various denominations and societies. He was in his element. Although he left his sons and others at Baghdad, that chapter was closed for him and the greater part of the next twenty years of his life was devoted to India.

It cannot be said that he laid the foundation of the present-day missionary work in India, but his ministry was richly

The god-car entering a village

blessed to the missionaries with whom he had fellowship. His experiences in Baghdād and his personal study of the Bible had led to the formulation in his mind of certain principles for missionary work. The conditions he discovered in India only served to confirm his views and he did not hesitate to propound them to those of other 'persuasions'. He was not diffident in discounting the value of ordination or in questioning the authority of missionary societies, the difference in status and conditions between foreign and national workers, the principle of fixed salaries and regular payments, or in emphasizing the oneness of all Christians.

He repeatedly exhorted missionaries to live simply and to trust God to supply their needs, although his words did not have wide effect among denominational workers; in fact, at times they aroused considerable (though friendly) opposition. For him the Christian life was one of faith and he confidently looked to God to sustain him. But he found few who were prepared to commit themselves to this way of life. One young convert, John Christian Aroolappen (brought to the Lord by C. T. E. Rhenius), who acted as Groves' translator for some time, did adopt his mentor's principles and became a full-time worker living by faith. Through Aroolappen's ministry, a revival broke out in Tirunelveli in South India and many assemblies were formed. Groves visited this area initially to help in a dispute regarding the ordination of Indian catechists, and was later described as the greatest enemy the Church of England had in India.

After a year's furlough in England, he returned to India with a small party of missionaries in 1836 and commenced work in the Godavari Delta. Groves continued preaching and teaching in India until ill-health made it imperative for him to return home in 1852. Years of trials and privations exacted their penalty and his condition slowly deteriorated until he slipped away to be with his Master in May 1853 – two months before the first issue appeared of *The Missionary Reporter* (a predecessor of *The Missionary Echo,* later *Echoes of Service,* of which his older son, Henry, later became an editor). A prince and a great man fell that day and his memory will live as long as foreign missions continue.

Anthony Norris Groves was unique. The value of his contribution to the missionary enterprise cannot be over-emphasized, although it springs rather from the inspiration his activities provided than from the measurable results of his ministry. His life of utter devotion to Christ and of complete dependence upon Him for his every need established a pattern which thousands since have sought to emulate.

Since Groves has aptly been described as 'the father of faith missions' and since his principles still represent those adopted by assembly workers today, it may be justifiable to spare a little space to mention his views.

The need of India had, of course, exercised the hearts of Christians long before the assembly outreach commenced and missionary work was being carried on in various countries by denominational organizations. Policies and principles governing the operation of their missions were naturally determined by the bodies concerned. Anthony Norris Groves, however, was completely unfettered by tradition or precedent and regarded the principles and practices of the missionary societies as having no validity or relevance to himself. It was to the Word of God, therefore, that he turned for his guide-lines.

He had already shown a readiness to accept new concepts revealed in the Scriptures, and it was through him that the group of ministers and others at Dublin had commenced breaking bread after the New Testament pattern. He was evidently also the first to affirm that ordination of any kind to preach the gospel was not required by the Scriptures – a view which was later to be adopted on the mission field (particularly in India) and to create problems for the Anglican Church there.

Groves had long determined his attitude to money. In the light of Biblical teaching, he regarded possession of money as a stewardship, and considered the deliberate accumulation of wealth as a hindrance to personal piety. Indeed, he felt it a duty to use all material possessions in the service of God and repeatedly maintained that such use induced love and communion with God, since it necessarily made the believer utterly dependent upon Him. When his professional income rose to £1,500 a year (a substantial amount 150 years ago), he and his family lived on a bare minimum and gave the balance to the Lord.

His life on the mission field was essentially one of complete dependence upon God, and the principle he enunciated of living by faith is a characteristic of assembly missionaries to this day.

Beggars
(R. Duff and S. F. Warren)

Rather paradoxically, he attempted to provide support for John C. Aroolappen, but the latter declined on the ground that he would be accused of preaching for payment. An attempt Groves made to introduce a means of support for the work ended in a loss and he said that, 'This first departure from the way of faith was ... followed by most bitter consequences.' When, at Sarepta, he found Moravians supporting their work by secular projects (and the missionary work declining in consequence), he had learnt his lesson and said, 'I see here the greatest evil of having anything mercantile connected with missionaries'.

How many missionaries have since gone forth from assemblies to follow the same course, with no guarantee of support, but in simple faith and trust in a Father God to supply all their needs! And how many, tried and tested as he was, have also testified to the faithfulness of the One in whom they placed their trust.

Sources in England, from which Groves anticipated financial support, dried up and there was no evident alternative source of supply. He was thus compelled to leave his case in the hands of God, confident that He would supply all his needs. He acknowledged that, in the midst of famine, pestilence and war and in the absence of financial support from anyone in England for over a year, the Lord had not suffered him to want or to be in debt. Even though the necessities of life at one time had increased by 2,000 per cent, every need had been met. He repeatedly praised the Lord for His providential care. Even when reduced to a food supply that would last only five or six days, he cried, 'Blessed be His Holy Name'. Appropriately, the Lord's servant said, 'My soul is led to abhor more and more that love of independence which still clings to it, when I see how it would shut me out from these manifestations of my Father's loving care'. He was satisfied that, if sources failed, the Lord would provide for the support of His servant.

An important extension of the principle was added by Groves' argument that the life of faith was applicable to national converts as well as to missionaries. Indeed, he implied that the establishing of an indigenous church was dependent upon the implementation of this principle. He pointed out pertinently that, where a native worker was deprived of other help, he was thrown upon God and that this was calculated to develop character: the European missionary was naturally inclined to

Godavari—in the rice fields   (P. A. Pritchard)

take the place of responsibility, but this was undesirable. Those who had been taught in practice to depend upon God would not be shaken in times of political and other change.

The weakness of the 'rice Christian' has been clearly evidenced since that day. It is also plain today that the interposition of any prop, either material or human, which deprives the national believer of his sense of dependence upon God will detrimentally affect faith and communion. Groves was farsighted enough to see what many a missionary has had to learn by long experience.

The principles by which he guided himself must, in some cases, have seemed revolutionary to other missionaries with whom he worked. They readily accepted his dictum that what missionaries most needed was first love and then patience and that they should live the gospel as well as preach it. But they were not so ready to accept his criticism of their disinclination to translate into the vernacular instead of in the language of the scholar. The masses did not understand this, he contended, and the preaching was unintelligible. The use of colloquial language was essential, he declared.

Again, he argued that missionaries should not remain stationary, but should itinerate and preach the gospel from place

Godavari—gardening   (P. A. Pritchard)

to place. When they founded a church, they should place someone in charge and continue evangelizing. The same principles, of course, have been repeatedly re-enunciated since.

The attitude which Groves had shown to social distinctions in his earlier days re-appeared in his condemnation of the caste system in India. He went farther, however, in maintaining, as a principle, that the missionaries should live among the Indians and not in better conditions and should not assume a higher status. He declared that no lasting impression could be made until the missionaries mixed with those among whom they were working in a way which had not been attempted. His argument, of course, was completely sound and we may still need the reminder occasionally.

A refreshing feature of this outstanding man was that he was never concerned about results – or the lack of them. He claimed that his task was to preach Christ. He never doubted that the work in which he was engaged was the Lord's work, to which he had been directed, and that the ultimate benefit to the church would be greater than if he had remained at home. Some friends pressed him to give up and return home, in view of the lack of results when he was earlier in Baghdād. This kind of argument was completely ineffective with one of his character and he bluntly replied that the fluctuations of judgment thus displayed arose from a too restricted view: a broader view of God's plan and purpose was essential for a true judgment.

One of the fundamental principles of his life was the recognition of the unity of all believers. He constantly endeavoured to demonstrate his fellowship with all who belonged to Christ and paid no regard to denominationalism. He stated clearly that one of his purposes in going to India, when invited by Arthur Cotton, was 'to become united more truly in heart with all the missionary band there and to show that, notwithstanding all differences, we are one in Christ'.

When, very much earlier, after his baptism, a friend had assumed that he would now join the Baptist Church, he had trenchantly answered that he would not join one party and thereby cut himself off from others. He was not concerned with sects and parties: he recognized individual believers as members of the body of Christ and sought to have the fullest possible fellowship with them. He never considered himself restricted from visiting a denominational meeting to receive the benefit of another's ministry or to afford them the benefit of his own.

General Sir Arthur Cotton

He rejected entirely the sectarian attitudes and practices which were being introduced by some of his earlier associates in the homeland and regarded them as a denial of the Biblical principles on which brethren first gathered. 'The theory of unity by separation... is false', he wrote, 'the unity of God is found in the union of all who possess the common life from Jesus'. His undeviating objective was to show himself one in heart with all God's children, irrespective of their denominational affiliation, and he had no sympathy with any spirit of sectarianism. 'I do not object to anyone's enjoying the forms he holds to be more Scriptural', he said, 'but I do absolutely object to his imposing his yoke on the back of his fellows'. Such an attitude inevitably attracted criticism, but such were his transparent honesty and sincerity as well as his saintliness, that criticism melted away.

He found catholic spirits in the sects, who were ready and willing to help and succour those who belonged to other bodies. Yet, he declared, in circles, where there was a plain absence of systematic sectarianism he detected in practice a most sectarian spirit, which would have nothing to do with others who were separated from them – an attitude which he rightly described as a holiness in form, but alienation of heart in reality (Isaiah 48). One cannot help wondering what his comments would have been on the developments which have occurred since his day.

He consistently maintained fellowship with all the family of God, without exclusive attachment to any section of it. This was, of course, the position originally taken by brethren.

Groves' views on the church were clear and definite. He condemned the union of church and state as unscriptural but, on the other hand, had no sympathy with a spiritual democracy, such as is often seen today. 'I would join no church permanently', he wrote, 'that had not some constituted rule. I have seen enough of that plan, of everyone doing what is right in his own eyes and then calling it the Spirit's order, to feel it to be a delusion' and 'far more dishonouring to God'. He equally rejected J. N. Darby's thesis of a 'church in ruins' as absurd.

He pertinently commented after two years on the mission field, 'Jesus meant His church to be a body. The miserable substitute of men's arrangements for the Holy Ghost's, has destroyed the true unison and order of the church of Christ by substituting that which is artificial for that which is of God; by

Christian bookstall   (R. Duff)

appointing men to be the artificers of a work God alone can accomplish. Now the church presents a disunited aspect; the unity being marred, among other things, by the unscriptural distinction of clergy and laity, which confines ministry to a few, leaving the many without one office or service; this is not of the Spirit'.

Although he held strongly (as assemblies still do) the priesthood of all believers, he insisted that recognized pastors and teachers were essential to the good order of all assemblies and that this was required and commanded of God. A stated ministry was vital to the well-being of the assembly.

He condemned preaching and teaching without previous preparation – what he described somewhat contemptuously as 'impulsive ministry'. He maintained that, in the whole of the New Testament there was not an allusion to waiting for an impulse from without in connection with ministry. Those whom God had called to be ministers should prepare thoroughly and should supply spiritual food which they had discerned to be needed by the flock.

It is perhaps in his personal devotion to Christ that Anthony Norris Groves had most affected lives. He desired that nothing should stand between him and his God and his conscience was always sensitive to the possibility. When, having lost his beloved wife, he was also bereaved of his baby daughter, he deemed it to

Chagallu—heathen festival   (P. A. Pritchard)

be the Lord's mercy, in removing every object of affection so that his heart might be devoted to Him. He rejoiced in friendship, but was jealous that any attachment to himself might not spring from love to Christ.

The humility shown in his life is still an example. He declared that he never felt fit for God's service, but rejoiced in His mercy to him. Always willing to take the lowest place, he was prepared to be stripped of everything that Christ might be supreme.

If space has been devoted to this servant of God, it is not merely because he was the first assembly missionary in India, but rather because he set the pattern for missionary work, not only in India, but wherever the Lord's servants have laboured since. These are still the principles which govern the work of missionaries commended by assemblies today.

The following pages record something of the labours of these missionaries over the years. The Republic of India has 22 states, viz. Andhra Pradesh, Assam, Bihar, Gujarat, Haryana, Himachal Pradesh, Jammu and Kashmir, Karnataka, Kerala, Madhya Pradesh, Maharashtra, Manipur, Meghalaya, Nagaland, Orissa, Punjab, Rajasthan, Sikkim, Tamil Nadu, Tripura, Uttar Pradesh, and West Bengal, and also nine union territories, viz. Andaman and Nicobar Islands; Arunachel Pradesh; Chandigarh; Dadra and Nagar Haveli; Delhi; Goa, Daman and Diu; Lakshadweep; Mizoram; and Pondicherry. To avoid confusion, the following chapters follow that order. There is no other significance in this somewhat arbitrary arrangement. Sri Lanka, Nepal and Bhutan have also been included as a matter of convenience.

Ritual bathing in the Godavari · (S. F. Warren)

Holland Wharf Hostel · (P. A. Pritchard)

Nidadavolu, Hebron Hostel
on Christmas Day
(C. Gilmore)

6

The Godavari Delta

When Anthony Norris Groves first visited India in 1833 at
Colonel Arthur Cotton's suggestion, he travelled extensively,
visiting different mission fields and missionaries. It soon
became apparent to him that, if the gospel was to spread in such
a vast country, it was essential for there to be many more
missionaries. When he returned to Britain for a brief furlough,
therefore, he presented the spiritual needs of India at every
possible opportunity. Consequently, on his return to India in
1836, he was accompanied by two young men aged 23 – George
Beer, an intelligent young shoemaker from Barnstaple who had
been temporarily assisting a local farmer, and William Bowden,
a tall young stonemason of powerful build, also of Barnstaple –
together with their wives.

Groves now had his own helpmeet once more for he had
married the daughter of General Baynes of Sidmouth. There
were others in the party. Mr. Brice of North Devon, a young
schoolteacher, and Mr. Kalberer of Würtemberg, a tailor, who
were both going out to join Mr. Stark in Patna; Mlle. Marie
Monnard, a teacher whose service was soon ended by ill-health,
and Mlle. Julie Dubois, a farmer's daughter (later Mrs.
Gundert), both from French-speaking Switzerland; Dr.
Hermann Gundert, also of Würtemberg, an outstanding
linguist, who later enriched Malayalam literature by his
monumental dictionary of that language, and who became a
leading member of the Basle Mission. In addition to the
missionary party, there was Miss Emma Groves, a cousin of

The Godavari river   (P. A. Pritchard)

Anthony who became the wife of Mr. Lehner (one of the founders with Greiner and Hebich) of the Basle Mission; her brother John, whose debts Anthony had paid and who was accompanying him to help in any practical way possible, and his wife (a believer praying earnestly for John's conversion); Mrs. Groves' brother, George Baynes, a gay young fellow going out to join the army, whose debts Anthony had also paid, who later became a Christian and an earnest worker with his brother-in-law.

The captain of their ship had served with Admiral Horatio Nelson at Trafalgar and was apparently not very sympathetic to religious activities. At first he gave Groves permission to hold a public service on deck for the whole of the ship's company, but then he withdrew it when some of the crew and the passengers expressed hostility. In *They Were Men Sent From God*, p. 18, Eustace B. Bromley describes the commotion when the missionary party's luggage was brought aboard. 'As they had to provide their own commissariat, a brother had kindly gone to Scotland and there bought the necessary livestock and brought them to the ship – 40 rams, 20 pigs, cows, goats, geese, etc. – to the great astonishment of the novices of the party when they went on board and were shown the pens. It was promptly dubbed "Noah's Ark"'.

The party settled first in Madras, where Groves contributed to the support of the others by working as a dentist, while one of the Swiss ladies helped by teaching French. The Beers and Bowdens went to Masulipatam in order to learn Telugu and from thence moved to Narasapur (Narsapur) (then known as Madapollam, which gave its name to a type of hand-woven cloth exported from this town). This town in the state of Andhra Pradesh had formerly been a very important port, but its industry had been paralysed and there were no European residents there. On the bank of the river Godavari, the missionaries found a large unoccupied Dutch house, with walls and roof intact, and there they settled and commenced a work which still continues to the present day.

In the meantime, Groves' sons from Baghdād joined him, as also, for a short time, did Dr. Cronin and John Parnell (later Lord Congleton). Subsequently, George Baynes, Groves' brother-in-law, who had been converted since leaving England, resigned his commission in the army and joined him as a full-

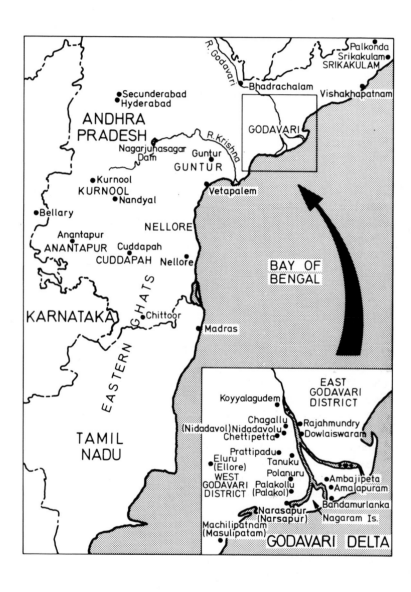

time missionary. The hostility of other Christians in Madras led to Groves, Baynes, Gundert and the Swiss ladies moving to Chittoor, near Arcot. Not long afterwards, Dr. Gundert left (with Julie Dubois as his wife) to work elsewhere and joined the Basle Mission but, to Groves' delight, two ex-army officers, named MacCarthy and MacFarlane, joined them in his place.

The Beers and Bowdens spent their first eighteen months in the Godavari District without a single letter from home – a serious trial to faith as well as to natural feelings. A strong reaction against missionary work had very surprisingly set in at home and this naturally affected the financial support given to the missionaries. As Bromley says, *op. cit.*, p. 41, 'Their would-be regular supporter had come to accept the strange view now gaining wide currency amongst brethren that it was not the responsibility of the church now to promote missions to the heathen, that being the task assigned to another dispensation! The logical conclusion of this conscientious brother was that he must withdraw his offer of a yearly donation'. This intimation was their first letter from home! Their circumstances entailed clear privation, but their confidence was in God and not in man.

Groves' diary indicates that his young co-workers were being tested quite severely at times – something he had also known from personal experience. He writes concerning them, for example, 'Each family lives on 30 rupees a month. They tell me they have received from Mr. Thomas some bread and cakes, from Mr. Jelicoe bread and wine, and from some unknown person 30 rupees; they still have enough for the present and, I doubt not, will not have finished the old store before the new comes in'. Again, his diary records, 'We heard from dear Rhenius last night; he is reduced to a fortnight's provision of bread, but has in hand a good stock of faith and trust'.

Since the apostle Paul had been prepared to support himself by tentmaking, Groves decided 'to start an industrial mission', writes Rendle Short, *op. cit.*, p. 32. 'He rented some land, planted mulberry trees, and commenced to cultivate silk. At first, the expenses were heavy and the profits small; also, at this stage, conversions were not recorded in his diary, probably because there were none visible. Someone offered to lend 30,000 rupees to develop the mission. It seemed like a godsend. The money enabled the missionaries to undertake irrigation works, and employment was offered to many Indians under Christian auspices. But the industry did not prosper. The silkworms died off from disease. Mr. Baynes had to return to England. In 1845, after three years' trial, the silk experiment had to be given up, and the borrowed money had to be repaid with heavy interest, which more than used up all the little personal property of the family. Then sugar cultivation was tried, but once more financial misfortune followed. These troubles, the relative ill-success – as far as the human eye could see – of the evangelistic work, both in schools and in preaching services, and the death of Mr. MacCarthy, cast a heavy shadow over Groves' heart'.

George Beer and William Bowden reached out to neighbouring towns and villages, going into the bazaars with tracts and engaging the Indians in conversation. When the Beers subsequently moved to Masulipatam, the Bowdens moved to Palakol, then the largest town in the Godavari delta area and a busy trading district with a large weekly market. William Bowden preached regularly on the streets. The Saturday market, attended by hundreds from the surrounding countryside, afforded unrivalled opportunities for evangelism. It was six years, however, before the first convert was gained. The lack of conversions greatly exercised the missionaries and William prayed specifically, 'If it is Thy will I continue in Palakol, let me see some souls come to Jesus. If not, show me another place'. The first convert was Achoma, an outcaste, the former concubine of a European. She opened her house to women and many were won for the Lord. Among the caste Hindus also, many believed and were baptised. When Peter, the first such, was baptised publicly in the river, he consigned his gold *lingakaya* (a charm worn by worshippers of Śiva) to the waters. His descendants have provided preachers and teachers to the assemblies. Many others were baptised in 1842, the beginning of a church in Palakol.

Dispensaries were opened and the sick came from far and near to receive treatment and medicines and, at the same time, heard the message of the gospel. Bowden became a skilled homeopathic practitioner and, *inter alia*, he produced the well-known ointment, *Bowden's Indian Balm*. The workers began to go farther afield, evangelizing in the hill and jungle tracts to the north-west of the delta, frequently witnessing horrifying rituals at the festivals they visited. By the middle of the nineteenth century an assembly had been established at Narasapur, which

Palakol—temple
(P. A. Pritchard)

Baptism in the
Godavari
(C. J. Tilsley)

grew rapidly. A cholera epidemic at this time took toll of many lives, but William Bowden, showing little concern for his own health, moved about ministering to the sick and dying.

A great opportunity arose in 1847 when a huge project was initiated at Dowlaiswaram to irrigate the surrounding area with water taken from the Godavari river. In the initial work over 10,000 were employed and even in 1848 to 1850 the average number was no less than 6,500. The whole project was under the charge of Colonel Arthur Cotton, who naturally could not remain indifferent to the spiritual needs of these labourers. He sought God's guidance that some capable worker should be found to undertake their evangelization. Almost by 'accident' he came into contact with Bowden and invited him to undertake the work and put a dwelling-place at his disposal. Without hesitation the Bowdens moved to Dowlaiswaram, and every day went from camp to camp, preaching the gospel, and on Sundays, there were the Europeans to be ministered to.

In 1849 they returned to Palakol. In those early days the influence of the caste system was extremely strong. Whilst most of the early converts were from the outcastes, there were divisions even among these, each division being completely shut off from the others in all ordinary forms of social intercourse, particularly as regards eating and marrying. A convert, who survived all the pressures brought to bear upon him as soon as he showed any interest in Christianity, ceased to be a Hindu if he was baptised. He was usually cast out and his possessions confiscated. He lost his employment and the missionaries were faced with the problem of how a livelihood could be provided for those who were compelled to leave their villages and settle at the mission station.

Because of the prevalence of illiteracy, the missionaries deemed it necessary to open simple primary schools where, at first, the Telugu New Testament, Pentateuch and Psalms were the main textbooks. (It was not until 1860 that the complete Bible in Telugu was printed). At that stage the plentiful palmyra leaves were used for paper and the letters were scratched on them with stylos. Since then, schools have proved a fruitful means of winning many for Christ.

When the Beer family returned to Narasapur, a primary school was established there on very modest lines. It was not until 1850 that an assembly was commenced in this town, but

George Beer did not confine his activities to the immediate area. He had boundless energy and itinerated constantly over a wide field, visiting the many festivals, distributing tracts and the Scriptures. It was during one of his many visits to the unhealthy Reddisema hill country that he suffered congestion of the brain, consequent upon exposure to the sun, and passed away in 1853 at the early age of 41.

At the time of his death there was a total of 40 baptised believers at Tirugudemetta, Narasapur and Palakol, and there were also over 100 children being instructed in Bible truths. Schools could have been multiplied if there had been sufficient means and if teachers had been available. Mrs. Beer threw herself into the school work and she also opened a school for caste girls, which soon had an attendance of 32. She served the Lord faithfully in this sphere for many years and eventually laid down her life in India.

William Bowden had to divide his time and ministry between the three centres where converts were gathered, but he continued in the all-important work of preaching in the villages. The rains of 1854, however, brought the worst possible epidemic of cholera and it raged around Palakol and Narasapur for weeks. During that time, Bowden was constantly moving around, ministering to the sick and dying. The promising school work was broken up and losses in the Christian community were severe.

Martha Bowden's grave   (S. F. Warren)

It was just at that time that help came. Thomas Heelis, a young officer in the merchant navy, the son of an Anglican rector, had been converted through the life and conscientious work of a Lascar seaman. When attending an assembly meeting in London, he heard William Yapp praying that the Lord would fill the gap in the Godavari mission left through the homecall of George Beer. He responded immediately, resigning his appointment and sailing to India in 1855, to give 55 years unremitting service, with only one furlough. He became a specialist in Telugu and a very able gospel preacher. He married twice, his second wife, Helena Cowling, becoming the acknowledged 'Mother' of the Godavari Christians on Mrs. Bowden's death. At the same time, the ranks of keen Indian workers were augmented by the conversion of a Muslim, named Ali Sahib, who became one of the finest evangelists in the Godavari Delta, and soon after, of another Muslim, Sooban Sahib. About the same time a high-caste Hindu of the Haju (kingly) caste was converted and commenced witnessing for the Lord in spite of bitter persecution.

Joined by Ali Sahib and a very gifted preacher from the outcaste Madiga community named Francis, the missionaries continued to penetrate into the jungle country with the gospel as far as the Godavari river gorge, their objective being to preach to the huge crowds at the Bhadrachalam festival. Having encountered fierce opposition from the temple Brahmins there, who were enraged at the evangelists' invasion of their religious domain with the gospel message, they were returning, when Tom Heelis strayed into the jungle. Suddenly a very large tiger sprang out close to him, uttering tremendous roars. Fortunately he did not lose his nerve, but faced the tiger with his gun – and the beast slunk off without making an attack.

The revival experienced by John C. Aroolappen in the Tirunelveli district in the Tamil area spread to the Godavari district in 1861. Just then the visit and the powerful preaching in Palakol and Narasapur of the Brahmin convert and gifted hymn-writer, Chowdhuri Purushottam, impressed many Brahmin young men, who came to study the Bible with Tom Heelis and at least one of these accepted Christ. Brahmins and other caste Hindus were reached and saved through the witness of the Narasapur school, raised to high school status by John William Beer, whose Scripture expositions attracted not only

Bowden-Beer memorial   (J. S. McNaught)

his students but also many high caste Hindus. This resulted in a rapid expansion in the numbers and spiritual strength of the assemblies. He also started and edited the Telugu monthly magazine, the *Rayabari,* which is still published today.

Both of George Beer's sons gave themselves to the work, the younger, Charles Henry Beer continuing from 1866 until his death in 1921. William Bowden continued until 1876, active to the last. His death proved a call to his son, Edwin S. Bowden and his wife, to fill the gap. They later moved to Chettipetta, which lies at the junction of several canals, and he used his houseboat to travel extensively on the canals, extending the work, evangelizing the villages and exhorting the believers in the assemblies.

The principal methods of work were visiting villages and preaching and also holding day schools for children. There were not the thrilling scenes and great ingatherings as at Christianpettah, Tamil Nadu, but instead there was a long, consistent record of conversions in ones, twos and little groups. By 1865 there were 50 Indian believers in fellowship at Narasapur and some of the converts were men of spiritual power. At one time the assembly had 400 members. There were also Indian evangelists giving their whole time to teaching or preaching. An Indian doctor, named Allasahib, preached Christ everywhere to the sick as he visited them. On one occasion he was in a house in which there had been a heathen altar for generations, the owner, Brammaja being the priest, and his mother the oracle. When the gospel was preached, Brammaja accepted the word spoken, and immediately broke down the altar; his mother gave up her sorceries, and he began preaching on every possible occasion.

Financial support was not plentiful, although the missionaries' needs were always met. On one occasion they had reconstructed the boys' school-room to provide a meeting-room, but it was destitute of furniture and they looked to the Lord to supply the need. On another occasion, they had to decide not to employ an additional teacher because it would cost *£1 a month* to support him! They did not come home on lengthy furloughs to stir up interest. There was no committee behind them. George Müller was able to help them to some extent financially, but they were unknown to many Christians in the homeland. Yet they proved the faithfulness of God in every circumstance and in every hour of need.

Many another has trodden the same path and has proved experientially that God is still the same. It is not by chance that a remittance arrives on the day the rent is due, or that food is mysteriously left at the door when there is none in the larder, or that a new pair of shoes arrives when the old ones can no longer be worn. There is a Father in heaven who cares for His children.

A valuable addition came in Mr. and Mrs. James Norman Macrae from Scotland in 1876, who went first to Narasapur for language study, and who later negotiated with the C.M.S. to take over the work and properties of the Church mission in Amalapuram. Before the end of the nineteenth century, many had been won for the Lord and baptised and a number of assemblies started on that side of the River Godavari. In 1890 Miss Ruth Lynn (commended from U.K. in 1888) joined them in Amalapuram, but later went to Bandamurlanka on the Bay of Bengal. There she was joined in 1901 by Misses Margaret Robertson and M. J. Marshall from Scotland, who laboured there tirelessly for over a quarter of a century.

Miss Lynn later served the Lord for some years in Nagaram Island and later in Tanuleu, until her homecall in 1945. Mrs. Macrae opened a girls' boarding school and a caste girls' school

Early Godavari missionaries. From left to right (*back row*): E. Charles and Ethel Adams; Anna and Eustace B. Bromley; Amelia C. Bromley, Edith and John M. Boyd; Alice and Matthew Brown; Agnes M. Clarke; (*front row*): Mrs. Bromley (senior); Henrietta Bowden; Martha Bowden; James N. and Mrs. Macrae; Henrietta Bowden (senior); Ada J. Brealey; Elizabeth A. Collins.

and taught the Indian women and girls to produce the crochet lace which was to provide them with a livelihood for many years. Mr. and Mrs. Edwin Bowden also opened a girls' boarding school at Chettipetta, of which Miss Lily Bowden was in charge until she left India to marry Mr. Thomas Tilsley of Müller's Orphanage at Bristol. She was succeeded by Miss Henrietta Bowden (commended from U.K. in 1893) until the latter's homecall in 1956.

The Godavari was proving a fruitful field and the early part of the twentieth century saw a number of additions to the band of workers. Mr. and Mrs. Robert J. Bryant, using a houseboat, extensively evangelized the villages among the canals, as well as visiting and ministering to many of the assemblies in the area. Archie Naismith often spent school holidays touring with the Bryants and preaching the gospel. Several converts were won from the Goldsmith and Raju castes. Mr. and Mrs. Bryant had been commended from the U.K. in 1901, and Miss Elsie H. Bryant joined her parents in 1934 and continued in the work there for 18 years. Mr. Bryant had a carpet loom erected in his compound at Prattipadu and for some years supervised the manufacture of Indian rugs and carpets, with a crippled Christian lad in charge of the workshop.

When the Bryants retired, A. George and Edith Phair (commended from U.K. in 1936 and 1930 respectively) continued the assembly work there, expanding south beyond Ellore, the capital of the District, George was a truly missionary statesman who was much used of God. They were succeeded for a number of years by Mr. and Mrs. David Drown. During that time, Miss Patricia M. J. Heads used the bungalow and premises there as a dispensary and a centre for leprosy treatment. She had been commended from New Zealand in 1951 and had joined Misses Beach and Margaret E. Hampton (from U.K. 1924) at the Leprosy Hospital at Narasapur. Having learnt Telugu, she visited villages for leprosy clinics with Miss Hampton, until she moved to Tanuku in 1955, where, in addition to the clinics, she was busily engaged in women's meetings.

In 1963 she had a new centre at Koyyalagudem, where she continued holding clinics. The mobile leprosy clinics, in which she worked for so many years, were highly organized. In two old Landrovers, specially equipped for the work, they used to start out early in the morning and, arriving at a village, would begin treatments, while the evangelists preached the gospel and distributed literature. In 1970 Patricia moved to Prattipadu, where some old buildings were cleaned and renovated, and the gospel was preached. Miss Sybil R. Taylor (N.Z. 1924) also helped in this work and in 1971 an assembly was commenced in the jungle area and many were saved and added to the church.

After service first at Amalapuram and then at Chettipetta, and before they went on to the Fiji Islands, Mr. and Mrs. Robert W. Rawson (U.K. 1897 and 1892 respectively) served the Lord in Dowlaiswaram for a considerable time from the end of the nineteenth century. They were joined by Mr. and Mrs. E. Charles Adams in 1901 and 1903 respectively (from U.K.), who later opened a new centre at Chagallu. With his excellent knowledge of the language, Charles Adams established a printing press there, edited the *Rayabari* magazine, printed a Telugu hymnbook and wrote many tracts in Telugu. Miss Grace W. Adams (U.K. 1931) joined her parents and, for some years, with Miss Ivy E. Barnard (U.K. 1947), carried on a busy

Miss Ada J. Brealey

dispensary and a work among women. After the Adams's left Dowlaiswaram, Miss Ada J. Brealey (U.K. 1906) and Miss Grace E. Morice (U.K. 1924) transformed the school buildings into a dwelling, from which they reached out with the gospel to the women in the surrounding area.

Mr. and Mrs. Eustace B. Bromley (U.K. 1903 and 1905 respectively) concentrated their energies on training the youth of the Delta in their large boys' boarding school at Narasapur, then a higher elementary institution, and short-term Bible schools for teachers and preachers in village assemblies. Having supervision of the many primary schools throughout the Delta, he arranged a curriculum for Bible instruction and a faithful evangelist, M. Anaraam, ensured that they were carried out.

In the early thirties the Bromleys went to live in the hill country among the Koyyas and Reddis, evangelizing and planting assemblies there. After Mr. Bromley's homecall in 1946, Mrs. Bromley, blind from glaucoma until her death, retired to England. Kevin H. Osborne, commended from New

Zealand in 1942, continued the work and also supervised the printing press and literary work in Chagallu for some years. The ship on which he was travelling to India in 1942 was sunk by an enemy raider and he was interned in Japan until the end of hostilities. Repatriated to New Zealand in 1945, he went to India in 1946. After language study at Narasapur, he moved to Dowlaiswaram in 1948 and was active in school teaching and in visiting villages. In 1949 he married Miss Jean Fitzgerald, who had been commended from New Zealand that year, and they made their home at Chagallu, taking Mr. Adams' place, while still retaining his interest in gospel activities in Kovoor and other places. In 1951 they moved to Koyyalagudem, where there were twenty assemblies, but still supervised the printing press at Chagallu. There was a tremendous demand for literature and a new press was obtained in 1954 and a million tracts in Telugu produced each year. He was a great help in Bible schools and was concerned with the Telugu Bible school in Madras. The Osbornes eventually retired in 1965.

Another devoted worker, Miss Elise Revington (U.K. 1928), having made her language studies at Koyyalagudem, spent her time evangelizing in the jungle with tracts as far as the foot of the Eastern Ghats, but she contracted malaria and died in the Mission Hospital at Narasapur in 1936.

A great deal of work was done by houseboat on the canals of the Godavari Delta. Among the many who worked in this way were Miss Rhoda Bridger and Miss Katie Hindman, both commended from Australia in 1909. In their boat, *The Harbinger,* they contacted large numbers of women along the waterways. Katie laid down her life in the work, dying of cholera in 1921. Rhoda then moved to Chagallu to work among women until ill-health compelled her to return home in 1928.

Mr. and Mrs. Matthew Brown, commended from Scotland in 1904, joined Mr. and Mrs. Norman Macrae in Amalapuram and, after some years there, moved to Ambajipeta, a beautiful island in the Delta, about 30 miles from the sea. It is thickly populated and is surrounded by coconut, banana, sugar and rice plantations. There was a healthy assembly there and while Mrs. Brown carried on dispensary work among the women, he laboured in neighbouring assemblies and villages until his death in 1937.

Dr. Irene Leeser started another hospital on the island and in

Ambajipetta—antenatal clinic
(C. Gilmore)

Palkonda—tribeswomen
(C. Gilmore)

Ambajipetta—theatre block
(S. F. Warren)

Prattipadu—Patricia M. J. Heads
at leprosy clinic
(S. F. Warren)

Ambajipeta—
assembly hall
(Dr. I. Leeser)

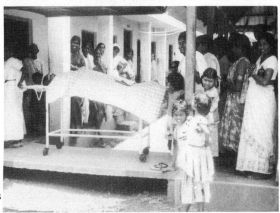

A patient arrives
(Dr. I. Leeser)

Labour ward
(Dr. I. Leeser)

1969 was joined by Miss A. Sylvia Wright, commended from New Zealand in 1957, who had first been at Koyyalagudem with Kevin and Jean Osborne and then temporarily at Narasapur. She later joined Grace Adams and Ivy Barnard at Chagallu for six years, taking over the printing press, but gladly handing it over to David Drown (N.Z. 1959), who transferred it to Narasapur. Pauline Hodgkinson (Australia 1965) joined the hospital in 1971 but had to return home to care for her mother in 1978. Colin Tilsley and Tony Grove had a 'workshop' for outreach on the island in 1978.

In the early days of the work one of the major tasks was obviously to improve the standard and extent of literacy and this was effectively done by the many schools which were established in town and village. This only resulted, however, in a need for literature. A monthly magazine for believers, entitled *Ambassador,* was published from 1877 (and is now edited by K. Wilson of Narasapur), but it was evident that a printing press of a reasonable size was required for the production of tracts, leaflets and magazines. This became a matter of prayer, but the answer came rather unexpectedly. Returning from furlough, E.

Chagallu—
E. Joyce Harding
and K. Wilson
outside the press
(P. A. Pritchard)

Grace W. Adams
(P. A. Pritchard)

Charles Adams found – to his surprise – that a large part of the living room of his bungalow was taken up by a treadle printing press which had suddenly arrived from nowhere! He had no alternative but to construct a building, make cases, purchase equipment and operate the press. He managed the Chagallu Mission Press for twenty years, pouring out a steady stream of literature for the avid new readers and for the work of evangelization. He was succeeded by Kevin Osborne and then by Sylvia Wright. Before Ivy Barnard retired, the old home of the printing press was converted into a very busy dispensary which operated for some years.

On the east side of the Godavari is Nagaram Island, where Percy C. Whitehouse (brother of Mrs. E. Charles Adams), laboured for 56 years. Commended from Birmingham in 1909, he had been courting a young lady, who was prepared to accept him but not to go to India. So he sacrificed the dictates of his heart for the Lord's work. Fifteen years later, on his second furlough, he again sought the lady's hand, only to receive the same reply. He went back to the Godavari and, save for a short period in 1928-29, did not return home again in all the succeeding 41 years of missionary service. He made his centre at Razole and, assisted by capable Indian brethren, developed a very successful work. The island proved singularly fruitful and had some of the largest assemblies in the Delta, some numbering up to 500. When he first went to Nagaram there were scarcely a dozen baptised believers on the island; at his death there were thousands he had led to Christ. His loved Indian friends referred to him as Thatha, or grandfather. He travelled everywhere by bicycle. On one occasion, caught in a heavy rainstorm which made the road a quagmire, he simply dropped the cycle into a canal and walked home, returning next day to retrieve the machine. He refused to rest and eventually passed on in 1965 in his 85th year.

David B. Burt had been interested in the mission field from his earliest days and in 1934, when he was teaching in New Zealand, he was invited by Alfred Redwood to become temporary principal of Clarence High School, Bangalore, to relieve Wilfred Wilcox. He accepted and after visiting other missionaries, saw the great need for helpers. Commended from New Zealand in 1936, he took up teaching at Narasapur and for some years shared in the work with Archie Naismith and helping in some 30 assemblies in the area. With George Phair he also visited scores of jungle villages near Koyyalagudem among the Kois.

In 1943 he was invited by Eddie Bury to relieve him at Breeks School, Ootacamund. At Montauban he met Catharine Garrett a missionary from Tasmania who had been commended in 1929 to work with the Irvines in Belgaum and in the villages around Sulge and Hindalge among the leprosy patients. David married her and she had to move from the west to the east coast, learn another language and undertake a totally different type of work. Bible school work was started to equip Indian brethren to preach amongst the 250 assemblies in the Godavari District. They were also responsible for administering 30 elementary schools, a large secondary school and a hostel. At the time Mrs. Burt gave help to Dr. Edward Short at the leprosy hospital. When Percy Whitehouse died they moved into his bungalow at Razole and the Bible School was started on Nagaram Island. The Burts retired in 1972 and a committee of Indian brethren took over the Bible School.

Miss Edith M. Morgan, commended from South Wales, in

David Burt crossing the Godavari   (P. A. Pritchard)

1914, laboured for many years in and around Narasapur until her homecall at the age of 84. She had great acceptance with the caste Hindu women, who invited her to their homes and, for years, assisted by a Bible woman and a Brahmin woman convert, she conducted a Sunday school for caste children.

After the first World War there was a great accession of missionaries to the Godavari, and in the decades that followed the number of baptised believers grew tremendously. In 1920, Crawford J. Tilsley from U.K. joined his grandparent, Mr. Edwin Bowden, in Chettipetta to evangelize and care for the 60 assemblies in that part, reaping the harvest of the seed sown by earlier workers. Mr. Tilsley was fluent in Telugu and addressed large conventions of Christians, often numbering 2,000 to 3,000. He married Marjorie King in 1922. Their daughter, B. Joy C. Tilsley (U.K. 1954) and Olive Rogers gave help there.

In 1921 Jesse Webb and Wilfred Hitchcock came to Narasapur. For two years the assemblies in many parts of the region were edified by the former's powerful ministry of the Word. In 1922, Miss Helen M. Munro, (U.K. 1922) went to Narasapur for language study before going on to join Misses M. J. Marshall and Margaret Robertson at Bandamurlanka. For some years, in cooperation with Miss Emily Starck, she taught in the caste girls' school in Amalapuram, before giving her remaining years to Bandamurlanka and the surrounding villages. Emily Starck had been commended from New Zealand in 1904 and, with Cora R. Newport, had joined Mr. and Mrs. Charles H. Beer in the work pioneered by Mr. Beer's parents in 1836. Charles served the Lord there for 55 years. She met the tragedy of India almost immediately – the body of a 12 year old girl was recovered from the river; her husband had died and her head had been shorn and, ashamed to live, she ended her life in the murky water. In 1909 Emily Starck joined Mr. and Mrs. Tom Heelis, who had been in the Godavari since 1855, and helped in selling Scriptures, teaching girls' classes, and helping evangelize jungle villages by houseboat. By 1920 there were 1,500 in fellowship at 25 centres. In 1918 Miss Jane A. Rhodes (U.K. 1899), who had started the girls' school at Amalapuram, died and Emily took over the responsibility, and until her death in 1952 continued to visit villages by houseboat with Helen Munro.

Miss Margaret E. Hampton came to the area to establish

leprosy clinics in various places, assisted for some time by Miss Edith Black. Margaret spent 50 years serving the Lord among leprosy patients. In 1926 Miss Afra A. Dyason spent some time in Narasapur learning Telugu, before joining Edith Morgan on a houseboat in East Godavari, and later moving to Amalapuram to link up with Helen Munro for twenty years in village evangelism by houseboat. They visited over 100 villages a year, and eventually concentrated on Bandamurlanka, where there were three large canals and hundreds of villages accessible from each. Afra returned in 1946 to New Zealand to care for her aged mother, and in 1950 married Frank E. Cooper. After two years' work in Fiji, they returned to India in 1952 for a year at Coonoor Rest Home. After his death in 1956, Mrs. Cooper returned in 1959 to visit some of the 100,000 people whom she and Miss Munro had visited years before. In 1963 she moved to Ambajipeta and made it a centre for village evangelism and Bible school work. In 1966 she participated in Dr. Irene Leeser's hospital project. From a temporary dispensary, a full-scale hospital developed, so that when she retired in 1970, they were treating 600 outpatients a day, many of whom were saved in consequence of being contacted for Christ there.

William A. Morrison, commended from Scotland, went to the Godavari District in 1925. Miss Anne Good, also

Meal time at Holland Wharf   (P. A. Pritchard)

Chagallu Clinic—Ivy E. Barnard   (S. F. Warren)

commended from Scotland, followed in 1926 and was received
by Miss Emily Starck and Miss Helen Munro. William and
Anne were married in 1928 and began their married life in a
small house made of mud and wattle, which Mr. and Mrs.
Eustace Bromley had used when they began the evangelization
of the hill tribes in the Koyyalagudem area. The Morrisons'
medical training equipped them in opening a dispensary in
Koyyalagudem, which opened many doors for the Gospel.
There was a cholera epidemic when they arrived and both
became so ill that Jesse Webb took them to Amalapuram and
they worked with Mr. and Mrs. Webb here and then later at
Rajahmundry. Mr. and Mrs. Matthew Brown, who followed
Mr. and Mrs. Norman Macrae had done a good work in this area
and a number of assemblies had been established, which needed
teachers. Mrs. Webb, Mrs. Morrison, Mrs. Cooper and Miss
Munro worked hard among the women and some caste women
were saved.

Mr. and Mrs. Albert Lilley, commended from Australia,
remained in India after working in a Gospel Literature
Outreach team in Madras. They found a home in Narasapur,
engaged in village work and Bible teaching and conducted an
Emmaus correspondence school.

One of the most significant features of the work at Narasapur is the hospital, opened in 1915 by Dr. Charlotte E. Pring (commended from U.K. in 1909) for women and children. Although crippled from birth, Dr. Pring personally examined and prescribed every day for large numbers of outpatients, as well as inpatients, with the assistance for over 30 years of Miss Daisy Shrimpton, commended from Australia. Daisy's language teacher, a bigoted, orthodox Brahmin, was converted through her witness and joined an assembly of humble believers. Daisy was a great help to young missionaries in their early years in India and was greatly missed when she died in 1962 at the age of 86. For a shorter period Miss Margaret Hampton was a great help there. The gospel was (and still is) faithfully preached in the hospital grounds each morning, and a follow-up work is continued as ex-patients are visited in their homes, sometimes in distant villages.

Dr. Christine Vine (a daughter of Mr. W. E. Vine) joined Dr. Pring in 1930 and spent four years at the hospital, until her marriage in 1935 to Gordon Fountain, when they moved to Kerala.

Miss Sybil R. Taylor learned Urdu in order to reach the many Muslims in India, and went on to learn Tamil and Telugu. She joined the hospital in 1928, but three years later took up houseboat evangelism at Amalapuram and continued in it for nearly 40 years.

In 1950 she was joined by Miss Jessie F. Anderson. Commended from Scotland in 1936, Jessie was almost persuaded by her unconverted parents (who later became Christians) not to go. Eventually she procured their approval and set forth with intention to serve among the women of the various castes, who at that time were forbidden to attend meetings held by missionaries on pain of eviction from their homes and villages. During their visits Sybil and Jessie would contact these women while their husbands spent all day working in the fields. At first the results were disappointing, but with time they witnessed great blessing among the caste women. The houseboat was, however, completely destroyed by a cyclone in 1969, Sybil moved on to Nidadavolu (Nidadavol) to engage in leprosy work (as she had previously done) with Patricia Heads until she retired to New Zealand. Jessie Anderson continued to distribute literature, going to weekly markets, high schools, junior colleges and the Nidadavolu railway station, where there

Children at Joyce Harding's hostel   (P. A. Pritchard)

were opportunities to sing and speak the gospel to the many who would gather round and listen. She retired in 1978.

Miss E. Joyce Harding (U.K. 1949) is now located at Nidadavolu at the Hebron Hostel. Joyce Harding wrote fairly recently from Nidadavolu, telling of the tremendous convention being held at Chettipeta and of her responsibility for the children's meetings there. Ninety children came to each session. The little assembly at Nidadavolu is always overflowing and larger accommodation is necessary. In 1931 Miss Doris Yates joined the missionary nurses in the hospital and continued there until 1968, much of that time as matron, Miss Joan E. Holt (U.K. 1944) followed in 1952 and continues there, having done much to accredit the standard of the Nurses' Training School there, which was opened in 1967.

Crawford and Marjorie Tilsley lived very largely on a houseboat, visiting villages and staying a few days near villages whilst visiting and teaching. Peravali, Polamuru, Rajahmundry, Koyyalagudem, Nidadavolu, Narasapur, Palakol, Kotagiri and other places were visited. The Narasapur annual conference used to attract 12,000, but grew to such an extent that it became necessary to substitute four regional conferences, which are each attended by over 4,000. At least six of the assemblies in the area each have over 600 in membership.

In 1924, eight years after the opening of the Women's Hospital, the Bethesda Leprosy Hospital was opened in Narasapur, primarily through the efforts and personal sacrifice of John M. Boyd (U.K. 1911). He procured three acres of land, included in the site of the present Women's Hospital, and constructed nine huts for patients. Dr. Williams joined him in the work, but Mr. Boyd was struck down by typhoid fever within eight years. His death would have closed the hospital, but for the courage of Dr. Charlotte Pring. Although her hands were more than full already with the Women's Hospital, she saw the need at Bethesda as a call from God which she could not refuse, and, with Miss Margaret E. Hampton, she took over the responsibility.

Miss Winifred M. Osborne had felt the call to leprosy work at the age of sixteen and, after completing her nursing training, she applied to the Methodist Missionary Society, but was not accepted. Some time later she came into contact with an assembly at Birmingham and found happy fellowship there. After meeting Miss Edith Morgan and learning of the need in India, she was commended and booked her passage in 1949. Her parents' illness prevented her going, but in due course she joined Miss Morgan in 1950. Apart from a year in Chagallu, to

Crawford J. Tilsley's houseboat

relieve Ivy Barnard, she spent the whole of her time at Narasapur, helping Miss Morgan in her work among women and girls, and assisting Margaret Hampton in leprosy clinics. In 1953 she joined Dr. and Mrs. Edward S. Short at the Leprosy Hospital.

Dr. Edward Short (U.K. 1951) arrived just a month before Dr. Pring's homecall at the age of 72 after increasing disability and pain, and during his service there the number of patients grew tremendously and many came to know the Saviour. Mr. and Mrs. David B. Burt, Sheila M. Waite, A. Jennifer Whitehurst (now Mrs. Michael J. Steggles), Sandra M. Medland and others helped for varying periods. Dr. K. Vandanan, Dr. R. S. Murthi, Mr. V. Ramayya, and Mr. Thomas Patient have helped for longer or shorter periods and Miss Eileen Rogers helped for a year in physiotherapy and occupational therapy. When Dr. Edward Short had to return home in 1978 for the sake of his family the work was looked after by Dr. Ben Walkey seconded from B.M.M.F. until he finally retired in 1982. The work is now supervised by Indian doctors.

Dr. Pring was succeeded at the Women's Hospital in 1946 by Dr. Betty D. Holt, who had been commended from the U.K. two years earlier. With the help of Doris Yates and Mary Bardsley (U.K. 1946), she recommenced an antenatal clinic and found that practically every case was abnormal: 3,000 cases a year are treated now. Dr. Dorothy Munce, commended from U.S.A. and Dr. Irene Leeser joined in 1953 in view of the expansion of the work. At the same time many of the staff were running Sunday schools in a number of hamlets, as well as holding special meetings at which 150 or more Hindus came. Dr. Leeser remained there until she started the hospital at Ambajipeta in 1967.

Mary Bardsley moved to Tiruvalla in 1955, but Enid Wagland (U.K. 1962) and Helen P. Thomson (U.K. 1968) later joined the others at Narasapur. Dr. Prabhakar and his wife Miriam who had worked in the hospital and among the young people and children in the assembly, after spending several years in England and America, felt led to return to take over the hospital. Later, Indian staff nurses and doctors became available and Dr. Kalyani took charge of the maternity side.

New buildings were erected from time to time because of the rapid expansion of the work, and in 1965 funds were provided to

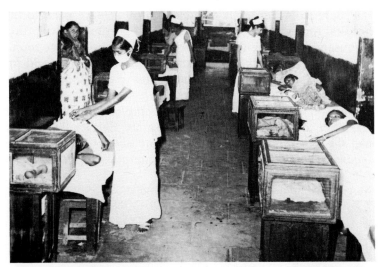

Narasapur—maternity ward   (B. D. Holt)

Narasapur—waiting patients   (B. D. Holt)

put in running water in the hospital. The nurses training school
was opened in 1967 and training commenced in Telugu, Miss
Assir Wadan being appointed as director and Misses Grace
Morice and Devas Das as instructors. When Miss Morgan died
in 1972, her bungalow was reconstructed to constitute an
operating theatre, etc. There are now ten full-time doctors at the
hospital and men as well as women are treated.

People from hundreds of villages around have been to the hospital for treatment and have received portions of Scripture. Thousands have heard the gospel. Two Bible women go round the hospital wards every day, and gospel services are held for outpatients every morning. Rallies for girls are held every Saturday.

The story of Godavari would be incomplete without a further reference to the school work at Narasapur. Eustace B. Bromley had the supervision of all the assembly mission schools in the Godavari Delta and, because of the interest of John M. Boyd,

Narasapur—Enid Wagland and Joan E. Holt   (B. D. Holt)

Archie Naismith of Scotland was invited to take charge of the largest of these, the Junior Secondary School in Narasapur. He married Miss Alice M. Cannon in 1922 and they sailed for India, where they spent 36 years of useful service. After five years Mrs. Naismith took over from Mrs. Boyd the responsibility for the boys' hostel, instructing the boys in the Scriptures for over 30 years and leading meetings of young women. The school was raised to the status of high school and has over 1,000 pupils. David Burt joined in 1936 and proved invaluable. Archie engaged in intensive ministry and in short-term Bible schools to equip the Indian brethren. This project had the whole-hearted cooperation of Eustace Bromley, Crawford Tilsley, Jesse Webb, William A. Morrison, David Burt and George Phair. Archie was also responsible for instigating the preparation of a Telugu Bible Concordance.

Antarvedi festival—
Mary Short selling
gospels
(E. Shapland)

Antarvedi festival—the pilgrims arrive   (A. N. Liddell)

Antarvedi festival—the temple   (A. N. Liddell)

In 1959 Indian brethren held an all-Godavari Crusade, in which the missionaries helped. Eight to twelve thousand attended and 1,870 people were counselled. The government eventually took over the High School and appointed Indian headmasters.

Irene W. Williamson (now Mrs. Roy German), Olive Rogers and E. Joyce Harding all went to India in 1949. With Miss Ada

Sybil R. Taylor's houseboat   (P. A. Pritchard)

Mary Short's Hindu girls rally   (P. A. Pritchard)

Narasapur leprosy hospital—patients (P. A. Pritchard

Brealey and Miss Grace Morice, Joyce Harding and Olive Rogers spent their first six years at Chettipetta, learning the language and helping Miss Henrietta Bowden in the school. E. W. Rogers (Olive's father) was one of the visiting preachers at the annual conference. In 1954 the school was moved to Nidadavolu, where Joyce Harding has a hostel for girls and engages in work amongst caste women and the local assembly. Hebron Hospital was destroyed by fire, but Berachah was acquired in its place. Olive Rogers moved to Narasapur to engage in further teaching and also became involved in the press work. She was responsible for many years for a Bible School at Narasapur for educated young women. Olive Rogers' knowledge in the Scriptures equipped her for work among students in Hyderabad and now at Secunderabad.

David J. Drown, commended from New Zealand in 1959, joined Kevin Osborne at Koyyalagudem after studying Telugu in Narasapur. In 1962 he married Miss Rose Trail (N.Z.) and they took over the large hostel in Narasapur and also helped in the Bible School. In 1963 they moved to Prattipadu to give more time to teaching the many assemblies in the area, as well as teaching in Bible schools and at conventions. David also took on responsibility for the Emmaus work with 1,500 students. They moved to East Godavari to relieve Mr. and Mrs. A. George Phair, where there were over 100 assemblies to help. They spent all available time in Bible school work and in encouraging Indian brethren, retiring to New Zealand in 1970 to take up secular work.

One of the greatest events in the Godavari Delta for many years was the annual festival at Antarvedi, a little fishing village, six miles up the river from Narasapur, which can only be reached by boat. Thousands of pilgrims came to the festival. The big day was the marriage of the Hindu gods and after that the ceremony of bathing in the sea. The god-car was drawn around the town by 100 men, while people threw fruit and flowers into it. Assembly workers used the opportunity to distribute literature and to preach the gospel to the crowds – not always receiving the most favourable reception, especially at the hands of the Brahmin priest. This is the India which many missionaries know only too well.

A guru being carried in procession by his disciples   (Indian Realities)

7

The Telugu Witness

(Map page 94)

Under the Muslim rule, Andhra Pradesh formed part of the Northern Circars, one of which had its capital at the ancient city of Rajahmundry, a fortress situated on the eastern bank of the Godavari, a few miles above its bifurcation. Another Circar had its capital at Ellore, famous for its carpets. The modern state is 106,272 square miles in size and its capital is Hyderabad. It has a population of over 53 million, 80 per cent of whom are Hindu and the remainder Muslims, Christians, Jains, Sikhs and Buddhists. It is the only state in which Telugu is the universal language. The Godavari Delta area is only a fifteenth of the area of the province, but a considerable amount of space has been devoted to it in the previous chapter because it was in that region that assembly work was virtually commenced and was most extensive and fruitful. A larger number of assembly missionaries went to the Delta than to any other part of the country. But the remainder of the province has not been without a witness for Christ. The largest town is Secunderabad and Mr. and Mrs. Robert W. Rawson worked there for a time in the early part of this century. Miss Olive Rogers is now located there, although continues responsibility for the Press at Narasapur.

The state is particularly interesting as having been the scene of the growth and development of indigenous autonomous local churches to a greater extent than elsewhere in the country. These assemblies have been formed and have become powerful witnesses for the Lord in many areas without the example and instruction in Scriptural principles of gathering by missionaries

Hyderabad—
Char Minar
(Air India)

such as the Godavari Delta enjoyed. Some 50 or 60 years ago, a movement commenced that was very similar to the brethren movement in Britain a century earlier.

In the past, many missions have occupied parts of this populous province and have established a fruitful Christian work, but the inroads of modernism and dead formalism, accompanied by a decrease in evangelistic effort weakened the spiritual witness of many of those mission churches. From several of such missions, truly regenerate Christians, seeking in vain spiritual food and revival in their denominational groups, began to meet together for prayer and Bible study in small companies in various places scattered over wide areas. In this way they learnt from the Scriptures the truths of the priesthood of all believers and the privilege of all such to meet to break bread as disciples of Christ, in obedience to His command, without the need of an ordained presiding minister or pastor. Following the apostolic practice, they set aside every Sunday for the remembrance of the Lord. Thus enlightened by the Holy Spirit and desirous of following and practising the principles enunciated in the New Testament, even if it involved separation from companies with which they had been associated, they began to meet together, disowning any Mission connection and taking only the name *Visvasulu*, which means 'believers'. In those early days, a gifted Canadian brother, Silas Fox, who had a roving commission for the Lord in India and who preached in the Telugu language with great acceptance and power, visited several of these indigenous groups and instructed them further from the Word of God. His ministry was fruitful in conversions and in the building up of these young assemblies.

So these churches continued steadfastly in the apostles' doctrine, in the fellowship, in the breaking of bread and in prayers. With true evangelistic fervour, they preached the gospel regularly in streets, bazaars and villages in the vicinity of their homes. With an ardent desire to learn the whole counsel of God, they invited missionaries and mature national Christian workers from assemblies to their large conventions to instruct them in the Scriptures. Brethren from other language areas also visited them and taught them in the ways of God, speaking in English, while good interpreters translated into Telugu.

This has undoubtedly been a movement of the Spirit of God, and the Lord is adding daily to these churches. Some time ago, Roy G. German reported that, according to reliable statistics given him by a gifted Indian evangelist, S. Prabhudas, who moves constantly among them, there are now over 150 such indigenous local assemblies in Andhra Pradesh in Anantapur, Cuddapah, Guntur, Kurnool, etc. – all outside the Godavari Delta. Over 30 brethren, commended from those assemblies, are engaged in full-time service for the Lord. Unfortunately, these companies seem devoid of literary talent and there is, therefore, a great need for writers of Telugu gospel tracts and expositions of the Scriptures – preferably written direct in the language rather than being translated from another language. The rapidly growing Jeethi Jotham Press at Narasapur is making a massive contribution to this need.

After an initial period of Telugu study, Roy German settled in Rajahmundry in 1951 and started a Christian Publishing

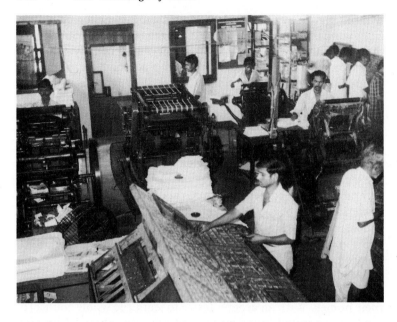

Narasapur—Jeethi Jotham Press and Bookshop

House there in 1952, producing mostly books. The most outstanding production has been a Telugu Bible Concordance. Roy moved to Bangalore in 1974. Not only is there an increasing demand for Christian literature, but it is particularly essential that more should be produced to combat the teachings of Marxism and of the many false cults.

It was really through Roy German that the Lord called Patricia A. Pritchard to India, commended from Folkestone in 1963. She learned Telugu at Chagallu then helped with secretarial work and also amongst women and girls. In 1966 whilst living at Rajahmundry she gave some help to Dr. Short before moving to Narasapur in 1967 to help at the Holland Wharf Hostel. After a course at the Missionary School of Medicine she returned in 1969 to Nidadavolu for a time, going on to Chagallu and Bangalore. She went wherever help was needed, finally returning to England in 1974.

A revival broke out in 1957 through the preaching of Silas Fox and K. P. Agrippa, which began in Anantapur and an assembly was started nearby at Hubli (Karnataka). It spread from there to Vetapalam, where another assembly was started, then to the Guntur District where 25 assemblies were commenced. Blessing was also seen at Bellary (Karnataka) and Nandyal. In the Vellore District the story was repeated and twelve more assemblies were founded, and in the Kurnool District another twelve assemblies started. They were days when the windows of heaven were opened in blessing. Some 200 assemblies came into being altogether.

Although the work in the rest of the province has not developed so completely as in the more thickly populated Godavari Delta, the area is free from some of the difficulties which are beginning to arise in the Delta. Of necessity, evangelism in the Godavari area was based largely upon institutions established by the missionaries – hospitals, clinics, schools, hostels, orphanages, etc. Many of these are now being taken over by the government and will gradually become secularized. As one writer pertinently comments, 'Institutions tended to centralize the work and the communities of Christians built up around them were isolated from the mainstream of Indian life. Many of these Christians became dependent upon the institution for their livelihood and inevitably upon the missionaries for spiritual leadership and initiative. It was very

Patricia A. Pritchard with the children

difficult for a truly indigenous church to develop in such circumstances, for the Indian believers were generally the employees of the institutions which were managed by the missionaries. A second major drawback of institutional work was that it forced many of the missionary workers to become static. Many who had been called of God to evangelism and church planting were localized by institutions'.

These problems do not arise so much in the rest of Andhra Pradesh, but unfortunately there have not been so many workers attracted to the towns and villages there. With the government's reluctance to admit new workers on a permanent basis, the work of evangelism is thrown back upon the small number of Indian believers, and much prayer is needed for their help and guidance.

A recent report by William F. Forward describes the indigenous Telugu assemblies in the area just south of the Godavari District and stretching across to Bellary (Karnataka). 'These assemblies are independent and they have elders who are recognized as God-given men. Meetings often go on for several hours. The believers sit on the ground, with the sisters on one side and the brethren on the other. There is an extended session of hymn-singing while the villagers straggle in. After this a time of praise and prayer follows as brother after brother leads the saints in worship. Then several brethren will open the Word with meditations and after this thanksgiving is offered for the emblems and the believers partake of the bread and wine. Generally there are many unbelievers in the gathering to observe what takes place.

'A baptism is a time of real witness. A meeting is held to instruct the candidates in their responsibilities and then all the believers march in a procession to the nearest water-hole or open well where the baptism will take place. The candidates are in the front of the procession and the entire assembly sing and witness as they go.

'Evangelism is largely entrusted to the full-time workers, who move in groups of four or five to the surrounding villages. Three to five day Bible classes are organized in a central area and 200 to 300 will gather from many miles around. The programme is a full-day one from 5 a.m. on. Brethren lead the congregational singing with traditional Indian musical instruments, such as little hand-pumped organs, cymbals, tambourines and tablas or drums. Each speaker speaks for at least an hour and the meetings go on until at least 10.30 p.m.

'When it is remembered that these assemblies are very poor and have had no missionary help apart from visiting to teach and encourage, it is amazing what they are able to do. Visitors are all provided with the first meal as a "love feast" by the host assembly, and after that are invited to purchase meal tickets which entitle them to the three meals provided daily. The cash received enables the local brethren to buy more rice and vegetables for the next day. The system can cater for 1,500 or more for the five days.

'We may confidently expect the work to increase and be more fruitful. The assemblies are growing in the Lord and in numbers and are reaching out to previously unreached areas. Greater emphasis than ever is being placed on the need to build up the believers in their faith.'

One can scarcely leave south Andhra without a little further reference to the work of Silas Fox, who left the Ceylon and India

"Breaking Bread"   (C. J. Tilsley)

Preparing the "love feast" (P. A. Pritchard)

General Mission and trusted the Lord to meet his needs. He made Anantapur his base for some 25 years and among those who were saved were some remarkable young men from caste Hindus like Paul V. Gupta and S. Prabhudas. K. Agrippa became a close associate of Silas Fox, earning for himself the sobriquet of the 'Black Fox'. Through the efforts of those who had caught the vision of Silas (the 'White Fox') over 150 virile assemblies came into being in the next two decades. The inspiring story of Silas Fox has been told in *The White Fox of Andhra,* by D. S. Fox.

In the whole of Andhra Pradesh there are over 400 assemblies, but the need is still very great. In a brief campaign at Vishakhapatnam, Don and Jill Stanton found attendances of over 3,000, and in four nights more than 250 people turned to the Lord for salvation.

8

The Home of Tea

(Map page 260)

Bounded on the north by Tibet and China, on the east by
Burma, and on the west by Bhutan and Bangladesh, Assam is
almost completely isolated from India. The 500 miles long
Assam Valley is occupied by the middle course of the River
Brahmaputra. The broad river divides and reunites several
times. Not far from its banks is flat alluvial land – almost a
marshy waste – given over to cotton-growing. Rice, tea and oilseeds are the principal crops, however. Two small oil-fields at
the eastern end of the valley augur well for the state's future
prosperity. There are refineries in Bihar as well as in Assam.

The main product is, of course, tea and Assam tea is world-
famed. The tea shrub is a hardy sub-tropical plant. In Assam,
there are sixteen pickings a year, as compared with three in
China. Until 1850 China supplied the entire tea needs of the
world, but the Assamese supplies gradually increased until
today Assam supplies half of the world's requirements. Assam
was, in fact, the original home of the tea plant and it was
discovered there growing wild. Tea plantations are situated on
the slopes of the hills on both sides of the Brahmaputra.

The state is 38,300 square miles in extent, its size having been
reduced by the carving out of another state from its territory. As
R. Wilson says in *Asia Awakes,* pp. 233–4, 'In 1968 the Indian
government announced plans to form the new autonomous hill
state of Meghalaya within Assam to cater for the special needs of
the Garo, Khasi and other tribal peoples. But the "balkaniza-
tion" of Assam is naturally resisted by the plains Assamese

Grading tea seeds   (Indian High Commission)

themselves, and since the whole area is so important for India's defence along two hostile borders (with Bangladesh and China) there is bound to be further difficulty ahead'. The capital of Assam, viz. Shillong, is also shared with Meghalaya.

The population is nearly twenty million and the people are of the Mongoloid type, originating in China and Tibet. For several months of the year, however, the country is flooded with Nepalis and Biharis, working temporarily on the tea plantations or wherever they can secure employment. The main languages spoken are Assamese and Bengali.

There is not much Christian activity in Assam. In fact, there is definite opposition to Christian workers. *The Hindu Weekly* (Madras) of the 21st August 1967, p. 11, for example, said that recent information confirmed 'that the current unrest in the sensitive hill areas of Assam is mainly, if not wholly, the result of the activities of these foreign missionaries'. The supporting evidence was not published, so that refutation was impossible. But in the same year, several missionary families, American, Canadian and Dutch, were expelled from Assam on charges that they 'helped rebel uprisings'. Some 80 other missionaries were informed that their residence permits would not be renewed when they expired. Fewer than one per cent of the population is even nominally Christian.

Health Visitor with villagers   (R. Duff)

The first missionaries to work in the state were Baptists in 1829. Assembly work was commenced in 1847 at Tezpur, when Captain James Gordon, then in charge of the Darrang District, felt constrained to establish a testimony, at the time the only one on the north bank of the Brahmaputra. Captain Gordon reported that the Assamese were an effeminate and indolent race, whose morals were exceedingly depraved. They were addicted to the use of opium. For a time he was helped by Mr. Merk, but after a short time both men fell sick and were compelled to leave the work. Captain Gordon survived only a few months after reaching England.

Their places, however, were taken by Messrs. Deubla and Hesselmeyer from Germany. The latter soon married a young lady who had been engaged as a missionary teacher in Dacca. Subsequently Mr. Deubla joined the Baptists, and the Hesselmeyers continued the work alone. They had ten orphan children under their care, and he also superintended a nearby school. During the difficult early months the Lord encouraged them through the conversion of their Assamese language instructor. When the cold season came between November and March, they would set out together, accompanied by the male orphan converts, and would engage in itinerant preaching throughout the villages of the Darrang District. Of these preaching journeys, Mr. Hesselmeyer wrote, 'There are some villages with a population of between 4,000 and 5,000 souls, chiefly weavers, who also cultivate land, amongst whom the Word of God seems to be taking root. I have received this impression from the way in which my preaching has been received; and I feel that the mass of my hearers are but waiting the signal, in the conversion of one of their village elders, to leave idolatry *en masse.*' Nowhere in the area had Hinduism become the religion of the people, even though social conformity obliged many to be Hindus. Evidently the labours of the Hesselmeyers and their national helpers were much used and blessed of the Lord at the time but a lasting work does not appear to have resulted.

M. Mathew, a national assembly worker, has served the Lord in Tezpur for the past eight years, but has not found a very encouraging response. There is a small assembly at Tezpur, but this is apparently the only one in Assam.

Hundreds of believers from assemblies in South India have come to Assam, seeking employment, but the great majority have become members of Pentecostal churches. Others have shown no further interest in spiritual matters.

143

Rajahmundry—near the station

(P. A. Pritchard)

Vetapalem—listening to the Word

(M. Browne)

Vetapalem—a baptism   (M. Browne)

9

Santal Refuge

Bihar, in the north-east of India and bordering on Nepal, is
67,184 square miles in extent. A prominent feature is the river
Son which flows through Shahabad Province and past the towns
of Arrah and Sasaram. It has a population of nearly 70 million.
The capital is at Patna and the language spoken is Hindi. The
population is 65 per cent Hindu, twenty per cent Santal and ten
per cent Muslim.

The Biharis are quite distinct from the other races of India in
many respects. They are said to be slow-thinking, but vigorous
and disciplined, a contrast to their Bengali neighbours, who are
quicker in thought but less vigorous in action. In *Asia*, p. 291,
Professor Dudley Stamp says, 'the Biharis live in their fields
rather than in villages like the people of the Upper Ganges Plain
and the Punjab. The population is dense and the pressure on the
land so severe that there is a large annual emigration. Many of
the Biharis go every year in the cold season to work in the mills
of Bengal or the docks of Calcutta, returning to their homes after
four or five months in time to cultivate their land during the
rains. Others go to the tea gardens of Assam.' There is no little
poverty in the state and, even during the last fifteen years, there
have been reports of starvation because of inadequate funds to
buy food.

It is the land of the Santals. These people, who number about
two million, derived from the aboriginal tribes of India and were
very little affected by the Aryan civilization. Their Parganas
(country) forms the southern part of the Bhagapur division of
Bihar. They are basically animistic and their principal god,

Ranchi—HIndi Braille   (M. G. G. Harvey)

Moran Buru, is revered as the chief of the spirits. The superstitious Santal feels himself surrounded by spirits and demons, who may easily become enraged. The death of a relative, the experience of sickness, the loss of crops, or the death of cattle, for example, are all deemed to be the effects of the displeasure of the spirits, who must consequently be appeased by sacrifices and religious ceremonies (often involving drink and immorality). They are gradually being influenced by Hinduism with its myriads of deities, but this does not diminish their fear of the spirits and their constant attempts to secure the favour of the spirits. A century ago, hundreds of Santals professed faith in Christ but, in recent years, there has been very little response to the preaching of the gospel. In fact, there seems a general antagonism to the message on the part not only of Santals, but of Hindus and Muslims as well.

The Santals, who are a fairly simple people, suffered long under Hindu oppression and were often fleeced by Hindu money-lenders. They found little justice in the law-courts because of their inability to speak the language and their ignorance of the proceedings. Eventually, in sheer frustration, in 1856–58, they rose in revolt. The rebellion was quelled by troops, but the government realized that there was legitimate ground for grievance, and accordingly special laws were enacted, which are applicable to the Santal country and are designed to protect them from their oppressors.

Writing 60 years ago, Paul Cansick said that the Santals lived happy and contented lives and were seen to the best advantage away from the railway and the crowded coal-mines, in their quiet, clean, white villages (so different from the usual dirt and ugliness of Indian villages) in the jungle. The cultivation of their few fields and the care of their cattle provided their chief occupation, and they had little ambition beyond the provision of food and clothing for themselves and their families. Their main pleasures were in hunting and in the keeping of religious festivals with all they entailed (the feasting and merriment). They could sometimes be seen, going off joyously into the jungle, armed with bows and arrows and sticks, intent on hunting. Their language is not of Sanskrit origin and has been described as 'belonging to the agglutinative class of languages, where every syllable is a word, and every word a sentence.'

Mr. Start (U.K. 1833) was to have been accompanied by Mr. Caldicott, but the latter was hindered by illness. In a lecture given at Bethesda Chapel, Bristol, in 1854, Mr. Start could not remember more than one instance of a national of Patna being converted, although the city had a population of over 200,000. Not infrequently those from the surrounding villages who were interested mysteriously disappeared. In those days tracts were

Near an agricultural community   (Tear Fund; R. Duff)

often torn up, the homes of believers burnt down, their possessions and crops plundered, and the believers themselves severely beaten.

Mr. Start also laboured at Gaya, which he described as one of the great seats of idolatry. Then it contained 1,300 Brahmin families, who depended for their livelihood on the offerings made by about 100,000 visitors to the shrines of their god. The opposition of the Brahmins was very bitter, and Mr. Start was frequently attacked. Little outward result was apparent. Mr. Start also visited Arrah, where Mr. and Mrs. A. Sternberg laboured for several years. There many made professions. Two of the members of Anthony Norris Groves' party in 1836 – Brice of Devon and Kalberer of Wurtemberg – went to India in order to join Mr. Start, who was then working in Patna.

From Germany in 1838–39 came Mr. and Mrs. L. Brandin, Mr. and Mrs. H. Ott, and Mr. and Mrs. A. Sternberg to Muzaffarpur. From the same country Dr. F. Ribbentrop, Mr. and Mrs. C. Baumann and Miss Schoris went to Chapra. The last mentioned died soon after arrival but the others extended their ministry to Motihari, Darbhanga, and Dhooli and distributed literature at the numerous fairs. In spite of considerable opposition, much fruit attended their efforts. Dr. F. Ribbentrop wrote: 'Our consolation and our joy are the school children, after visiting whom we nearly always return home pleased: we should like to cover the land with schools. If the old make sport of us, we receive a hearty welcome from the young; they answer our questions in a way that puts the sages to shame.' At that time the missionaries had no less than eight schools in and around Chapra. But there were setbacks too. At Karantia for instance, cholera carried off six brethren (also from Germany) who out of love took charge of cholera patients. The mission was abruptly ended although it began so successfully.

In the provinces of Chota Nagpore and Ramgath, other German brethren worked at Ranchi where Messrs. Behrens, Bohn, Herzog and Schatz resided, helped by Mr. and Mrs. F. Batsch and Mr. and Mrs. Brandt. There were other workers from Germany at Gobindpur Mr. Conrad; at Schardegga Mr. and Mrs. Gerndt; and at Hazaribagh Mr. H. Batsch and Mr. and Mrs. Sieek. In 1853 came Messrs. F. Dodt and H. Höpper to Buxar, where they joined Mr. and Mrs. E. Greiff, Mr. and Mrs. W. Ziemann, and Mr. Van Gerpen, also from Germany.

Greatly used of the Lord, all engaged in preaching the gospel as far as the borders of Nepal and particularly in the town of Hajipur. Their labours did much to break down the seemingly insurmountable prejudice and antagonism that Mr. Start had encountered earlier. Somewhat later, through hearing of the spiritual needs of Bihar from Capt. Johnston, a retired Indian Army officer, Mr. and Mrs. William S. Body (U.K.) felt constrained to give themselves to this work and in 1870 they settled in Jamtara and commenced a school. Within two years, however, William Body had died.

Travelling from Sweden to India, Edward Cornelius, a member of the ship's crew, was converted and immediately determined to give his life to God as a missionary. When the ship arrived at Calcutta, he accordingly applied to be released from the crew and permission was somewhat surprisingly granted. Packing his few belongings, he began to walk inland towards Bihar, without any clear idea of his ultimate destination. Although he met Swedish missionaries en route, he declined to throw in his lot with them, saying that he preferred to learn the language by living among the people. In his journeyings, he arrived at a place 25 miles from Jamtara, where he built a hut for himself. After a brief while, he heard the story of Mr. and Mrs. Body's apparently abortive effort at Jamtara and of Mr. Body's untimely death. Learning that Mrs. Body was in Calcutta on her way back to England, he at once sought her out and persuaded her to marry him and return to Jamtara, where they continued in service for their Master until she was called home in 1909 and he in 1916. During their period of service there, many were saved and an assembly was started at Jamtara.

They were joined from 1888 onwards by other workers, commended from the U.K., including Miss Hughes and Miss Emmeline Hollyer, Mr. and Mrs. Walter N. Hearn, who in 1888 started a work at Karmatam and were joined there by Mr. James E. Johnston in 1905, and by the latter's wife in 1911.

Wesley Crawford was burdened with the need of China, but J. E. Johnstone of Bihar presented such a picture of the condition of the villages of North India that he realized that this was to be his field of service. He qualified as a nurse and, after additional medical training, was commended from Ulster in 1944 and joined the Johnstones. The boat trip was with 24 other

Olive M. Bland

nurses – all ladies! After a period of language study, he was soon involved in dispensary work, village visiting, leper work, etc. There were six assemblies in the area.

Lilian H. Wright was saved at 21 after much spiritual turmoil and met Wesley at the Missionary School of Medicine. She was commended from the U.K. in 1946 and they were married in 1947. At the birth of their first child, the registrar had no birth certificates, so amended a death certificate for the purpose. In 1977 they returned home for the sake of the family, but took up work in Ireland.

Mr. and Mrs. Fred Rowat went to Mihijam in 1888 and received the support of Miss R. M. Sparks in 1923, of Miss Eileen E. Lindsay in 1936 later Mrs. E. Gordon Williamson. Olive M. Bland having qualified as a midwife went from U.K. to Banaras in 1951 to join Mr. and Mrs. Alex Smyth and for language study, moving to Mihijam in 1953 where she continued to serve the Lord until 1972 when for family reasons she was unable to return to India after furlough in the U.K. Mr. and Mrs. Kenneth J. Newton commenced at Katoria in 1903.

A small orphanage was opened at Jamtara to receive a number of orphans from Gujarat at the time of a terrible famine which swept that state. At Kadhar, a Hindi-speaking town, Mr. E.

Gordon Williamson in 1929 opened another small orphanage. Gordon also preached in a large number of villages in the area and saw some measure of blessing. He was able, in addition, to establish an assembly at Kadhar composed of Santals and Biharis. It seemed that interest had now been aroused in the needs of Bihar for, from 1899 to 1910, there was a further increase in the number of workers, and stations were opened at Sagjuria, Banka, and Katoria. By 1910 the number of workers in the state reached its peak of 23. After that date the numbers gradually declined, but a work for God was done during that time.

Throughout the years the emphasis has been on evangelism, the missionaries ceaselessly itinerating throughout the area. Festivals and markets, where crowds congregated were obvious opportunities for preaching the gospel and distributing evangelistic literature, and the missionaries took full advantage of the opportunities thus afforded. Roughly 130,000 tracts a year were distributed at that time and many a soul was won for Christ. William Walker, Wesley Crawford, Alex Smyth and others have been used of God in this state.

Dispensaries were opened at the different stations. Thousands came for treatment in the course of the year and, in consequence, a certain amount of prejudice was broken down and contacts were facilitated. The native quack doctors treated almost every form of illness with doses of crude calcined mercury; for rheumatism, fire was applied to the affected part of the body; for other ailments equally absurd remedies were prescribed. Yet many of the people seemed to have greater faith in the completely ineffective treatment of these quacks than in the healing ministry of the missionaries.

In fact, despite all the activities, Bihar proved a hard and relatively barren field. But this did not affect the devotion and self-sacrificing love and care of the servants of Christ. The pressure of Hinduism, the effect of the caste system, the cost of ostracism and rejection by the family, with the problem of practical support of the converts, all tended to limit the response. The work was almost entirely in the rural areas where, in the early days especially, practically all of the people were illiterate. This made it difficult for them to understand the gospel message and also for brethren to be raised up among the new believers who would be able to lead the assemblies.

Nevertheless, several assemblies were established and continued in spite of the absence of qualified workers. The schools which were started at that time have been handed over to the government and the orphanages have had to be given up. (In any case, the need for these is not so great as it was formerly).

Miss Amy Roper (N.Z. 1906) first served in Ceylon with Mr. and Mrs. Arthur F. Witty and then moved to Bengal with the Watsons before going on to Mihijam in Bihar. She married Henry Rees (U.K. 1903) in 1908 and they moved to Jamtara to help in the orphanage. At the same time he engaged in preaching in the markets and visiting the villages, while she helped in dispensaries and in women's meetings. They commenced a small Bible school to help local believers to teach their own people. In 1934 there was a devastating earthquake and 700 people were killed. They retired in 1948 and Henry died in 1962 and Amy in 1967.

Miss Grace George (U.K. 1944) heard the call to Bihar through an address by Mr. Rees and she joined Mr. and Mrs. Rees at Jamtara. At that time, Mr. and Mrs. Paul Cansick (U.K. 1906 and 1907 respectively) were at Mihijam, having been previously at Sagjuria, and Wesley Crawford (U.K. 1944) was at Karmatam with the Hearns and Johnstons. The orphanage at Jamtara had thirteen boys and girls and there was also a small home for leprosy patients. In view of the need, mobile leprosy

The Cansicks

Bihari children receive scriptures   (M. G. G. Harvey)

clinics were held regularly at different centres. The rapid
growth of the medical work made it essential to open a number
of dispensaries. A primary school with three Christian teachers
was also started.

Grace was joined by her sister, Bee George, in 1946 and by
Kenneth W. Smith in 1947. In the following year Ken and Bee
married and took charge of the small leprosy home, orphanage
and school. In 1953 they moved twelve miles east of Jamtara and
opened a dispensary. They also preached in a local refugee camp
and at a site where a large dam was being built. Grace added to
her responsibilities a Sunday school of a hundred and an adult
gospel meeting. The assembly, which had 25 members, had an
attendance of 50, but relied upon visiting speakers and for help
in the breaking of bread service. In 1962 Philip Singh, his wife
and family, moved to Jamtara: he was employed at Kulti 25
miles away, but was able to live at Jamtara and to help the
assembly.

Because of the extreme poverty of many of the patients, Miss
George had six wells dug and arranged for wheat and rice to be

grown, thus providing work for many who were unemployed – as well as the food so much needed.

E. Gidleigh Wheeler (U.K. 1920) came to assist at Kadhar in 1921. When Mr. and Mrs. John F. Smele left for Calcutta in 1927, Gidleigh took over the work. Two years later he married Miss Ivy Williamson (U.K. 1926) and together they laboured at Kadhar for eighteen years. They returned to England in 1947 and he died in 1964. Miss Rose M. Sparks (U.S.A. 1923) and Gordon (U.K. 1924) and Eileen Williamson (U.S.A. 1936) have served the Lord in this state. They were married in 1937.

Since 1957, with the discovery of rich coal deposits, large industrial concerns have been established in Bihar. Thousands of workers were brought from many parts of India, transforming hitherto completely rural areas. At the same time, however, full-time Indian commended workers have moved into the state. One lives at Patna, which has a population of a million. A number were converted and, although some have moved elsewhere, there is now a well-established assembly there. T. E. Easow, besides maintaining the usual assembly meetings, conducted a Bible correspondence course, mainly for local college students, and also a regular meeting for nurses in the government hospital. In addition, he had cottage meetings in various parts of the city.

A brother from Kerala, named Samuel Kurrin, is working in Dhanbad, the centre of the coal-mining area. He commenced there in 1964 and, despite determined opposition, has been able to form an assembly there. Another assembly was commenced at Bokaro by another brother from Kerala and there is reason for encouragement at the blessing apparent in many centres.

T. E. Easow of Kerala went to Patna in 1961 and the assembly activities still continue. K. G. Varghese of Kerala went to the industrial city of Ranchi in 1968; there has been an assembly there since 1962 and the gospel has been taken to all the surrounding villages. O. V. Poulose and others have been helping the assembly (founded in 1967) in this steel city, which has the biggest steel project of Asia. Samson Nayagam was able to establish an assembly at Nalanda, which was the centre of Buddhist education at the time of Ásoka. O. M. Skariah has moved to Deoghar to help the small assembly in this pilgrim city.

10

Bombay's Offspring

In the reconstruction of 1960 the former Bombay State was administratively divided into two new states on the basis of the language spoken in the area. The northern part, including Kutch, Kathiawar and Gujarat, in which the major language was Gujarati, became the state of Gujarat. The remainder, in which the major language was Marathi, became the state of Maharashtra, and this contains the city of Bombay, where, one writer cynically remarks, 'only one man in three is a local Maharashtran.'

Gujarat is 72,236 square miles in area and stretches from about 100 miles north of the city of Bombay to the border of Pakistan, and it has a long coastline on the Arabian Sea. Although it has numerous small hills, it is mainly a lowland area. In the north, where it embraces the former state of Saurashira, is desert; in the south there is a very wet region. The area known as Kutch is almost encircled by the vast marshy wastes of the Rann of Kutch. It is almost completely barren: there is not a sign of tree or bush for miles. Rocks frequently break through the surface of the ground and, in places, become ridges, on which nothing can be grown.

Kathiawar is a large peninsula, in the centre of which is the Gir Forest – a group of forest-covered hills – which is well-known as the haunt of the only lions to be found in India. Rocky ridges are divided from one another by barren sandy valleys where few people live.

The northern region of Gujarat itself is dry and flat with poor

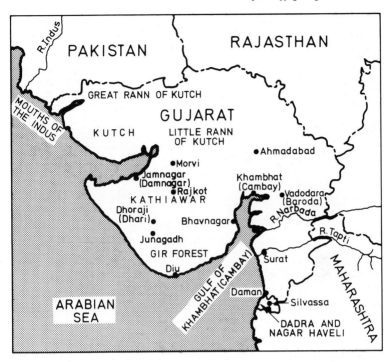

sandy soil. Its area includes the former rich and prosperous
native state of Baroda. Many of the people inhabiting this region
are the primitive Kolis, who earlier used to plunder their richer
neighbours. The central region is wetter, but rice grows freely in
the stretches of alluvium on the banks of the rivers, although
more attention is paid to the cultivation of millet and cotton.
The southern region is very wet, but is thickly populated. The
rich black soil in the broad strip of land near the coast produces
cotton, rice and sugar cane.

The principal towns include Daman, which was once a
Portuguese possession; Surat, a large and important town near
the mouth of the River Tapti, which was the principal town on
the west coast prior to the rise of Bombay, and which was the
location of the first factory of the East India Company; Cambay,
Bhavnagar and other smaller towns around the Gulf of Cambay,
none of which has any real claim to importance; Rajkot, Morvi,
and Junagadh in the Kathiawar peninsula; and Ahmadabad, the
capital of the state, which has large industrial works, a modern
textile mill and a busy railway junction.

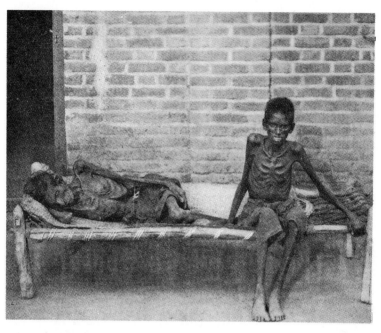

Victims of famine   (*Links,* Februrary 1912)

Gujarat has always been a relatively poor region, but in 1900 it suffered seriously from crop failure and an unparalleled famine struck the state. A large number of people died and hundreds – if not thousands – of children were left destitute. In answer to the appeals for help, H. Handley Bird and his sister, Miss Florence P. Bird, unhesitatingly went there and took over the responsibility for a hundred starving children who had been left orphans. On the journey back to Kollegal a dozen or more of the little sufferers died, and the emaciated bodies of those who remained alive taxed the patience and love of Miss Bird and her colleagues for a long time. The total number rescued by H. Handley Bird at that time is not known, but his charitable actions and unreserved willingness to help left an indelible impression. It was out of this tragedy that the orphanage at Mount Zion was established and continues under Indian leadership.

The population is approaching 34 million. Parts of the state are almost uninhabited, but the people are concentrated principally in the more fertile areas in and around Damnagar and the cotton-growing tracts near Dhari. Some live near the salt deposits at the coast and others in isolated wheat-growing sections where there is good irrigation.

T. I. Joseph and M. G. Mathai have been preaching the gospel with blessing and a number of believers have been baptised. At Baroda, G. K. Bhatnagar, K. M. George and F. G. French successively cared for the assembly, but T. S. Koshy moved here in 1977 and is now giving his full time to the work. Mr. and Mrs. Justus Samuel were able to help at Ahmadabad, where the assembly commenced in 1962. T. C. Chacko has been there since 1964 and has helped in the growth of the assembly. Bakht Singh has followers in Gujarat and some assemblies, it is gathered, have been formed. The assemblies he has founded in India now number hundreds and are patterned on those of the brethren.

Work in Gujarat is somewhat hampered by the poverty existing in many places and the consequent bitterness expressed of those in that condition. Some years ago V. G. Desai wrote critically in *Young India* of the Salvation Army being allowed the use of 560 acres of public grazing land in Gujarat for farm purpose. He said, 'In ancient times . . . cattle enjoyed the benefit of common pastures and had also the free run of the forests. The

K. George   (O. Rogers)

maintenance of the cattle cost their owners practically nothing. But the British Government cast a greedy eye upon this time-honoured property of the cattle, which could not speak for themselves and which had none else to speak on their behalf, and confiscated it, sometimes with an increase in the land revenue in view, and at other times in order to oblige their friends, such as the missionaries. . . . The result of this encroachment upon grazing areas has been that at the present day in India the proportion of grazing grounds to the total area is the smallest of all countries. . . . It is not, therefore, a matter for surprise that our cattle should have rapidly deteriorated.' The criticism may not be entirely justified, but it is the kind of thing which cannot be ignored by the foreign missionary.

Despite the poverty and the bitterness and the now almost complete absence of expatriate missionaries, assembly work in Gujarat continues and expands. The beginning in much privation, watered by prayer, is bringing forth fruit.

11

The Green Place

Over 30 years ago a not inconsiderable part of north-west India comprised the province of Punjab, but in 1947 it lost a third of its area when the country of Pakistan came into being. In 1966 it suffered a further loss, when it was divided to make two states. The northern one retained the old name of Punjab and comprised the area in which the Sikhs lived, while the southern one was named Haryana, or the Green Place. Whereas the Punjab is largely a dry sandy plateau bounded by the Outer Himalayas, Haryana contains fertile plains, watered by the five tributaries of the River Indus. Its main crops are wheat, rice, sugar cane and pulses.

The state has an area of 17,561 square miles and its capital is Chandigarh. The population is nearly thirteen million and the languages spoken are Punjabi and Hindi. Although the state is not primarily an industrial one, there is a very modern chemical fertilizer plant at Nangal, which cost £10 million to erect and which employs 2,500. A report describes it as 'elegant and efficient, all chrome plate and polished floors.'

Assembly work has been carried on primarily at Ambala, a town just ten miles inside the northern border, where the Hindi language is spoken. J. Lloyd and Eileen Bone (Canada) went here in 1953 and were joined later by Daniel and Evelyn Taylor (Canada 1953), who had been previously in Ludhiana. An assembly was commenced at Ambala in 1954. Harry and Phyllis Aspinall (U.K. 1962) worked here for some time before serving the Lord at Ludhiana until 1974 when they returned to England

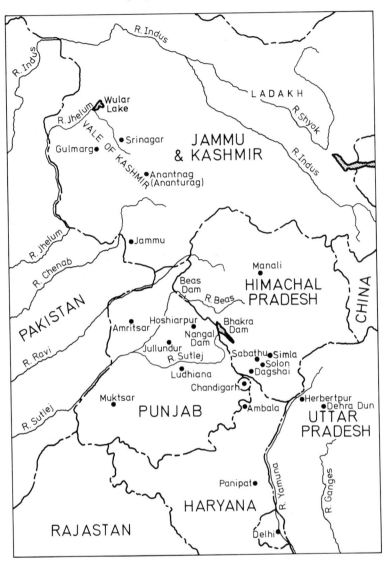

to take up work with the Scripture Gift Mission. Help was also given by V. T. John before his removal to Ludhiana. Miss Lorna Morrison, commended from New Zealand in 1949, moved from Meerut to Ambala in 1971 in order to be free to minister to women there and at Ludhiana and other assemblies.

She involved local people in the distribution of literature in the streets and bazaars. Over the years she has seen lives transformed through the literature and the personal testimony of those who distributed it. A small bookroom has been opened and once or twice a year a tent campaign is held in or near the town. E. Samuel of Kerala took an active part in Ambala until he moved to Meerut, but G. Daniel has now taken up full-time work here.

In 1959 a gospel campaign was held in the capital, Chandigarh and some blessing was seen.

**Mountainous
terrain**
(H. Avery)

Simla   (Indian High Commission)

12

Summer Resort
(*Map page 162*)

Bordered on the north by Jammu and Kashmir, on the east by Tibet, on the north and west by Uttar Pradesh, Haryana and Punjab, the state of Himachal Pradesh is 21,496 square miles in area. It has a population of over four million and the languages spoken are Hindi and Pohari. The country is mountainous but nearly half the people are engaged in agriculture.

It is usually described as a hill state and it is probably best known because of its capital, Simla. This has long been regarded as a very attractive hill station and has been described as the 'hot weather capital,' because it was the practice for the government to migrate there from Delhi in the hot season.

Various missionary societies have attempted the evangelization of the area, but not entirely successfully. Quite a number of assembly missionaries have engaged in service in this state during the present century. Charles J. Wright (U.K.) went to Brancepath in 1900, marrying Martha E. Ogden in 1905, and at a much later date together they gave a number of years at Dagshai, before returning for another spell of service in Brancepath. He died in 1954 and she in 1963. The work at that centre was commenced by Harold Avery (U.K.) in 1934, who laboured there for nine years before removing to Kalimpong. Mary Ward (U.K. 1934) went to this Himalayan town to learn the language of the hill tribes and was joined by her fiancé, William Ward, to whom she was married in 1935. They took over the running of two mission stations while the Wrights were on furlough for two years, but in 1937 they joined Alan E. and

William Ward

Myrtle McKenzie (N.Z. 1934) at New Delhi, where a new assembly had just been formed.

In 1902 G. Harold Watson (U.K.) came to Sabathu to take over a leper hospital which had been started in 1837, and he was joined there by Miss Jessie P. McLaren (U.K.) in 1903, whom he married later that year. Miss Isabelle L. Thomas (U.K.) came to help them in 1935. The Wards returned to Sabathu to relieve the Watsons at that time. During World War II, from 1939, Sabathu became a hill station for troops, so for four years, the Wards had meetings for service men as well as for the 70 to 80 lepers, and some came to know the Lord. Because the McKenzies needed help in Delhi, Mr. and Mrs. J. B. Childs took on the leper work to release the Wards. Very shortly after, however, Mr. Childs died and Janet returned to England to take up work in 'Echoes' Office. Dr. and Mrs. D. John Gilbert (U.K. 1938 and 1939 respectively) then came to continue the work.

The latter had not been long in Delhi before riots broke out following the imprisonment of Gandhi. They found a notice on their gate one morning, 'Quit India or die.' European women were being stripped naked and shot in their gardens. Chinese were locked in their rooms and their possessions burned on the

Teaching Nepalis (B. F. Norman)

streets. Houses were looted and shops broken into. Indian friends risked their lives by bringing food to the missionaries. The Wards returned home in 1945.

Miss Beryl F. Norman (U.K.) took up work at Manali in the centre of the state in 1950. Mr. and Mrs. Donald E. Stanton, commended from Australia in 1962, have laboured in the Simla area for the past twenty years. With his experience in the printing trade, Don has been able to specialize in the publishing of literature and periodicals in English, Hindi and Tibetan, to present the gospel and to provide Bible teaching. Many of his books have a worldwide circulation. His intention is to reach the many Tibetans in northern India.

Floating raft;
craftsman
(Air India)

13

Land of Floating Islands

(Map page 162)

The beauties of Kashmir – the charm of a boat trip from Lake Wular to Srinagar, the amazing rich carpet of mountain flowers at Gulmarg, the orange and apple blossom in the terraced fields on the hill slopes – have occupied pages of description in accounts of the state of Jammu and Kashmir in the very north of India. It is probably the only place in the world, however, where one finds floating islands. Rafts are made and covered with a little earth in which seeds are sown, and the rafts are allowed to float on the river. So that, as one writer remarks, 'not infrequently a man's land may aptly be described as lost, stolen or strayed.' The Vale of Kashmir lies between the Middle and Outer Himalayas, and through it runs the River Jhelum. But the vale is only a small part of a rugged mountainous state.

Jammu and Kashmir, which had earlier been under Hindu rulers and Muslim sultans, became part of the Mogul Empire under Akbar from 1586. After a period of Afghan rule from 1756, it was annexed to the Sikh kingdom of the Punjab in 1819. But in the following year Ranjit Singh made over the territory of Jammu to Gulab Singh and in 1846 he also acquired Kashmir. With the formation of the Indian Republic in 1947, the Hindu Maharajah of the Muslim state acceded to India, but the war with Pakistan resulted in the state being divided between the two countries. There is still a feeling of resentment that the plebiscite promised by Jawahartal Nehru (which would undoubtedly have led to a verdict for Pakistan) was never allowed, (see Alistair Lamb's book, *Crisis in Kashmir*). The state's frontiers with Pakistan and Tibet make it a crucial area

Ladakh—Lama festival   (Indian High Commission)

for India. Physically the Tibetan plateau continues into
Kashmir.

The state has an area of 85,700 square miles and a population
of nearly six million, the majority of whom are Muslims. The
capital is Srinagar, which is located in the vale and is renowned
for its woven shawls and its wood carving. The forests produce
some medicinal drugs, but the chief industry is tourism.

The people live in the more sheltered valleys. Their fields are
small and are carefully levelled and irrigated. Rice and
buckwheat are grown and, in some parts, wheat and maize. The
wilder parts, such as the Indus valley, are not cultivable and are
practically uninhabited. At Ladakh, which is claimed by both
India and Pakistan, and in other parts of the state, polygamy is
said to be common. Among some tribes, polyandry (where the
woman marries all her husband's brothers as well as her
husband) is practised.

As already indicated, the people are Muslims (although the
elements are still identified with gods), and the languages
spoken are Kashmiri, Dogri and Urdu. Little, if anything,
seems to have been done to evangelize this state and there is no
evidence that it has ever been entered by an assembly
missionary. With the exception of P. C. Xavier, who is working
with a medical mission at Ananturag, there is no assembly
representative in the state.

14

Among the Kanarese

Karnataka is one of the larger states and has an area of 74,037 square miles and a population of over 37 million. It is composed of the former Mysore State and what was known as the Belgaum District, the latter having been part of the Bombay Presidency until the reorganization. The capital of the state is Bangalore and the language spoken generally is Kannada (or Kanarese), although Marathi is also spoken in Belgaum.

Belgaum City was the location of the Senior Officers' School of the British Indian Army, as well as of the Army School of Education. It was a typical district of British India, with all the characteristic features described by novelists in the early part of this century, but it was also mixed with the territories of the Indian princes of Kolhapur, Miraj, Sangli, Jamkhandi, etc. It was an area where malaria, cholera and smallpox were prevalent. The population, which was mainly Hindu, included a large number of Brahmins, who were to be found mostly in the learned professions and in senior posts in the government service. There were two main castes among the many existing: the Lingaita, who were merchants and business men, and the Marāthā, who were merchants and business men, and the class houses were of thick mud walls and roofs of country tiles, but the poorer people had to be satisfied with three feet high walls of split bamboo and roofs of grass.

Karnataka is India's only source of gold production. She also mines iron, manganese and silver, but the principal occupation is agriculture.

Rural Indian life
(Tear Fund)

The gospel was first brought to Karnataka in 1820, when missionaries of the London Missionary Society began educational and evangelistic work in the city of Belgaum. They withdrew in 1904 and the work was taken over by the Methodist Missionary Society, and the schools and colleges then established still continue to the present day. It was obviously essential to raise the standard of literacy in order that the people might understand the gospel message and be able to read the Word of God and the educational work was always with these ends in view. Unfortunately, there has sometimes been a misinterpretation of the intention and some have even questioned the need for this activity. Michael Hollies in *Paternalism and the Church*, p. 3, quotes Bishop Whittaker as saying, 'We thought that we were offering them Christ, and they thought we were offering them a school.' The M.M.S. still has a large church in the city and many in the villages, but there are many towns and villages without any Christian witness of any kind.

Work associated with assemblies first began in Belgaum in 1898, when Mr. and Mrs. Villiers F. Hunter (U.K.) and Miss Mary McComas (U.K. 1896) settled there. They were soon afterwards joined by Ebenezer W. McGavin, who married Miss McComas. A number of new workers came in the following ten years and a testimony was established in a number of centres. As the Methodist missionaries of those days were strongly evangelical, an agreement was reached (perhaps somewhat unwisely) that assembly missionaries would not start work in areas already being evangelized by the Methodists. In consequence, the new workers concentrated on work amongst British and Anglo-Indians in Belgaum, and the Marathi-speaking villages to the west and south of the city. Many of the early workers had come to India with the Poona and Indian Village Mission, and some of them already knew Marathi, and were convinced of the need of the villages before coming to the area.

At the time of the terrible famine in Gujarat in 1900, workers in the Belgaum District also quickly established orphanages to care for the children whose transportation Mr. Bird had arranged, and there is no doubt that some of the blessing of later days was due to the loving care exhibited to these poor unfortunates in the hour of need.

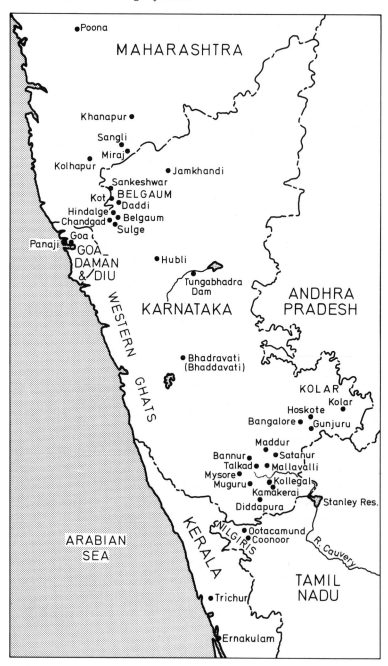

Poona

MAHARASHTRA

Khanapur

Sangli
Miraj
Kolhapur
Jamkhandi
Sankeshwar
Kot BELGAUM
Daddi
Hindalge Belgaum
Chandgad Sulge
Panaji Goa
GOA
DAMAN
& DIU

Hubli

Tungabhadra
Dam

KARNATAKA

ANDHRA
PRADESH

WESTERN GHATS

Bhadravati
(Bhaddavati)

KOLAR
Kolar
Hoskote
Bangalore Gunjuru
Maddur
Bannur Satanur
Talkad Mallavalli
Mysore Kollegal
Muguru Kamakerai
Diddapura
Stanley Res.

ARABIAN
SEA

KERALA

NILGIRIS
Ootacamund
Coonoor

R. Cauvery

TAMIL
NADU

Trichur

Ernakulam

In 1900 William C. Irvine from New Zealand came to Belgaum. He had gone to India in 1897 with the Poona and Indian Village Mission, but later left the Mission and linked up with missionaries who had gone out from assemblies. He associated himself with Ebenezer W. McGavin, who was located five miles outside Belgaum and who had the care of 40 boys who had lost their parents in the famines of 1896–1900, and others who were added subsequently. In 1903 Wm. Irvine married Miss Agnes Kay, who had gone out from New Zealand with the Poona and Indian Village Mission in 1898. They helped in the boys' orphanage, taking over the responsibility in the latter part of 1903 and continued there until 1912. By that time all but three of the original members of the orphanage had either died or moved away. Thirteen were in assembly fellowship and 47 were married, some to girls from Mr. and Mrs. Hunter's orphanage. Over the years the boys had helped with visiting and gospel outreach; some were baptised and helped form the assembly when it was established. Mr. Irvine often used to tell of the time when he had to climb 60 feet down a well to pull out one of the boys who had fallen in. He concluded that the boy wanted to baptise himself.

William Irvine also became known in due course for his literary work. His interest in publishing began in 1908 when he produced a monthly leaflet in Marathi to refute the teachings of false cults. By the following year, a Christian magazine, *Schastra Pradipak,* was being produced regularly in Marathi, while in 1910 he started *The Indian Christian,* a monthly magazine in English, which still circulates all over the world. He wrote a large number of tracts and his book, *Heresies Exposed,* ran into several editions and is still widely used as an exposure of false cults and heresies. He industriously engaged in visiting villages and preaching the gospel.

In 1912 a poor beggar was given shelter and care in the hospital at Hindalge. A few weeks later he was joined by another beggar and so began 70 years of service to sufferers from leprosy. In those days leprosy patients were treated almost as criminals. They were forcibly admitted and detained, forbidden to use public transport or to serve in positions in the community. Sufferers were often caught by the police and confined in leprosy patients' asylums. Treatment was almost non-existent. Chalmogra oil was applied and later injected. The disease could neither be arrested nor cured. In 1950 D.D.S. became available and was widely used, and dramatic results were achieved. Medical research has since provided other drugs, which helped in arresting the disease. But in those early days there was little that could be done beyond giving the lepers care and attention. William Irvine took over the superintendence of the leprosy hospital which grew up at Hindalge. Over the years, Gordon Ritchie, Raymond C. E. Atkinson, George J. Turner, Joseph Gaikwad and others helped, and a minimum staff was maintained to reduce overhead expenses. Later Dr. James W. McMillan and Dr. P. M. Rajput became honorary Medical Officers, and William F. Forward (Aust. 1963) became the honorary superintendent. The hospital now has 80 beds and there are 720 patients in clinics as well. Cases for reconstructive surgery are now prepared at Belgaum Hospital and the operations are carried out at Sankeshwar Mission Hospital.

The Irvines had a fruitful life and ministry and he rejoiced that he was able eventually to see high caste and low caste breaking bread together. He died in 1946 and his widow died in Tasmania in 1963.

Mr. and Mrs. Arthur E. Storrie, who first worked with the Poona and Indian Village Mission, left the Mission and were commended to the work in 1903 by assemblies in Australia. They commenced at Chandgad, twenty miles west of Belgaum

The Western Ghats   (Indian High Commission)

Travelling by an ox cart   (P. Marsh)

City. The name means 'The Fort of the Moon' and many years
ago the Fort of Shivaji Maharaj stood on a small hill: it was here
that Arthur Storrie built the mission bungalow and it was here
that they worked for over 40 years. The district is a beautiful
one, on the Western Ghats, 2,000 feet above sea level. There are
89 villages in the district, and the Storries visited the villages,
preaching and giving medical help. Bears, panthers, cheetahs,
tigers, wild pigs and jackals inhabited the forests and helped to
provide a cacophony of sounds at night. The people are mainly
Hindus but there are some Muslims. The Storries had been
used to the blessing of many, but in 1946 he became blind and
they returned to Australia, where they both died in 1950.

Grace Brayne (U.K. 1926), who worked at Chandgad,
describes some of her experiences in *Indian Reflections*. She tells
of visiting villages by ox cart, travelling at two to four miles an
hour, to be greeted first by a congregation of dogs. Eventually,
she says, p. 14, 'Someone will sweep the earthen floor of the
verandah with a little short brush, making a great dust which
nearly chokes one. A dirty old blanket, which has served as the
only bedding for the household for many a day, is thrown out
and the visitors are invited to sit on it.' There are always those
who need medicine and this provides a contact. The Brahmins
are usually antagonistic and often refuse to listen.

Ernest A. Rimmer (N.Z. 1905) had previously worked for some years in India with a missionary society, and then spent a year in Sri Lanka. In 1906 he joined the de Carterets (N.Z. 1899) at Belgaum and also helped in the work at Chopda with Mr. Horace Mears. As a young man Horace had been a member of a Bible class led by Henry Martyn and his interest was naturally aroused in India from an early age. Commended from Australia in 1901, he took charge of Mr. William Irvine's work at Sulge orphanage during the latter's furlough, before commencing a work at Chopda in 1907. That same year he returned to Australia and married Florence L. Thompson in 1908. Soon after the Mears engaged in work in Khanapur and then helped in the boys' orphanage until their return to Australia in 1926. Miss Cora R. Newport (N.Z. 1904) joined Horace to learn Telugu, but died in 1907. Ernest Rimmer engaged in visiting the villages and winning souls for Christ. Most of those converted were from the lower castes, and he found that there were some who also wanted to add Jesus Christ to the other gods they already had. In 1908 he married Miss Ethel C. Hollands from Godavari and they moved to Kot, about two miles from the market town of Daddi, to commence a new work. They did some medical work in addition to visiting and also started a small day school. Unfortunately his ill-health compelled them to return home in 1909 and he died in 1931.

Arthur Reddell (N.Z. 1899) took up residence at Odmaru, but was unable to remain because of ill-health and had to return home.

J. Herbert de Carteret, like many others, commenced with the Poona and Indian Village Mission, but later joined assemblies. He married Miss Maude Hunter at the time of the Indian famine and they continued in village work in Belgaum until 1910, when they moved to Daddi to carry on the witness and to relieve Mr. and Mrs. Ernest Rimmer. There were 25 villages where Kanarese was spoken and hundreds where Marathi was spoken. For the next ten years they maintained a constant preaching ministry in the villages, although often faced with bitter opposition. They visited fairs and festivals, often camping out, and preached in homes and market-places. A modest dispensary was started, which provided a good contact, as people came from the many villages around. Sometimes there were problems at festivals where 150,000 or more gathered.

Nellie H. Robertson
and orphans

They pitched at the edge of the crowd, but thousands would surround them and not infrequently threaten them. There were no sanitary arrangements and it was pitifully hot. In 1933 they moved to Khanapur and reached out to villages in the south, where people had not heard of Christ. Herbert died in 1943, but Maude continued to help in the orphanage at Daddi. She also helped at Chandgad for a time, before retiring in 1951. She died in 1969.

Mr. and Mrs. Maurice J. Wark, commended from Australia in 1909, also made Daddi their centre for some years, engaging largely in children's work and in conducting a babies' home. They were busily occupied in visiting villages and conducting a dispensary until they removed to Khanapur for a time. Miss Freda Parkinson, commended from Australia in 1933 assisted the Warks at Daddi in the dispensary work before finally joining Dr. Reginald S. Churchward in the hospital in Tiruvalla. She retired in 1944. Miss Nellie H. Robertson (commended from Australia in 1928) continued to help in the orphanage work at

Daddi and moved with it to Khanapur, which had better educational facilities. Miss Nellie Robertson cared for the girls and younger boys. Several of the former boys are going on well and at least one, Ratnaker J. Mirajker is now in full-time service for God. There she is still working after 54 years of service, with only two very short furloughs.

Mr. and Mrs. F. Joseph Brown, commended from Australia, joined the Mears's to work in Marathi at Khanapur in 1904. Like Horace, Joseph had been a member of Henry Martyn's study group. Mrs. Brown found a great encouragement in the work among women and children. Joseph's service ended tragically in his death at sea in 1931. She bravely continued until 1934 but then retired. Miss Jean Thomson (U.K.) also served at Khanapur from 1926. Dr. Cairns and Christine Smith (U.K. 1977) also helped in the work at Khanapur.

An interesting feature of the work at Khanapur was among 400 adults and children of the Criminal Tribes Settlement. This settlement was an attempt by the government to reform the descendants of certain tribes in which crime was a tradition and,

Workers conference at Khanapur: (*back row*): Bill F. Forward; Dr. D. John Gilbert; Ratnakar S. Mirajkar; D. R. Avale; G. Celeste Hull; Heather I. Smith; M. P. Solomon; (*middle row*): Gladys Forward; Nellie H. Robertson; Mrs. Mirajkar; Mrs. Avale; Edna E. Ramage; Jean Campbell; (*front row*): Deborah J. Forward; Venay Mirajkar.

(S. F. Warren)

in fact, almost a religion. The adults were unpromising material, but the children proved to be as responsive and lovable as any other children. Since education was compjlsory among them, they could be given printed and written matter to read or learn by heart (including the Scriptures, of course), in a way that was obviously not possible with illiterate children, and the missionaries took full advantage of the opportunities afforded to them.

Alfred E. Roxburgh (N.Z. 1908) spent two years from 1910 at Daddi and then joined the Storries at Chandgad before going on to help George Henderson (U.K. 1908) at Khanapur and Dr. E. Villiers Hunter at Belgaum. He gave much time to visiting villages and distributing literature, but retired in 1912.

Gordon Ritchie, commended from New Zealand in 1933, and his wife, commended from Australia in 1934, were formerly with the Poona and Indian Village Mission, but then joined assembly missionaries in Belgaum in 1943, helping in work among lepers. In 1945 they moved into the city to engage in Bible teaching and to commence an assembly there, while still retaining an interest in the leper work. Gordon also preached and taught in Chandgad, Hubli, Tambulwadi and Sankeshwar, and Mrs. Ritchie helped in Sankeshwar hospital. A constant programme of village meetings with Indian brethren, encouraging scattered believers and teaching in local assemblies over a wide area, involved so much work that some places were not visited more than once a year.

In 1951 Gordon recommenced the Marathi magazine and the following year they moved to Bombay to work among Marathi-speaking people there. Harold McGregor was at that time introducing his radio broadcasts and Emmaus courses were being distributed. Gordon helped in the production of *The Gospel Steward* magazine and, for a time, supervised the work of *Living Waters* radio programme.

George and Edith (Aust.) Henderson, engaged in preaching and literature distribution in Belgaum, but in 1918 they began work at Sankeshwar, a fairly big market town 30 miles north of the city of Belgaum. Sankeshwar lies in a rural area about a mile from the river Marinkashi. The population of 40,000 is composed of both Hindus and Muslims. There is very little industry and most of the local people are employed in some form of farming, the main crops being sugar cane, rice, tobacco and

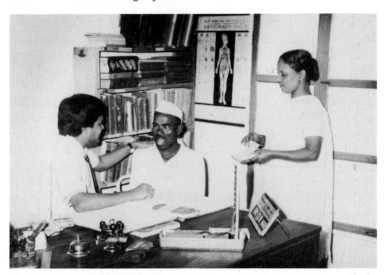

Sankeshwar Hospital—Dr. Dev Danam Mitta   (M. Keyse)

groundnuts. It is little more than a village, but has a high school and an arts and science college. In times of serious drought, the government provides employment in the form of road work. Consequently the main roads in the area are well constructed.

In the early days of the work at Sankeshwar, George Henderson, who later went on to qualify as a doctor, wrote, 'the darkness here is appalling and if we stayed twenty years, we would not see a convert.' When he first arrived at Sankeshwar in 1913, he lived in a tent until it was blown down in a storm. In 1923 he was sold some land for £45 on which the nucleus of the General hospital was built. It later became a compact unit of 33 beds, including a maternity section, operating theatre, X-ray unit, and chemical laboratory. Prior to this, they had opened a dispensary, since Mrs. Henderson was a trained nurse and they prayed four years for a doctor. Then Dr. and Mrs. Dev Danam Mitta joined the staff as a wonderful answer to prayer. After George Henderson qualified as a doctor, the work began to expand. Then, in 1936, the construction of the Silver Jubilee Leprosy Hospital was begun on a plot of land not far away.

Patients came by bus, bullock cart, hand-cart, bicycle and taxi. They were almost invariably undernourished and suffered from intestinal parasites. There was a high incidence of tuberculosis in the area, both pulmonary and abdominal, and diseases of all kinds. There were many opportunities to present the gospel. Patients were always accompanied by several relatives, who heard the gospel preached in the wards, and contrary to George's initial gloomy prognosis, a large number were converted. At least 300 ex-patients were known to be Christians. Some of the story is told in the illuminating book *Bible and Stethoscope,* by Dr. George Henderson.

Dr. and Mrs. Reginald S. Churchward (U.K. 1939) at first joined the Hendersons at Sankeshwar. In 1940 they took charge of the hospital that was handed over to the assembly missionaries at Tiruvalla (Kerala).

The Hendersons were pioneers, who worked under difficult and sometimes dangerous conditions; in fact, plague was raging in the district when the work began. For many years there were few helpers, but ultimately relief arrived. None of those who subsequently came commenced a new work, but they followed up the work which the pioneers had started and proved faithful and capable co-workers. Minnie Begent (Aus. 1928) who for seventeen months helped the Warks and Nellie Robertson at Daddi, married Raymond C. E. Atkinson (Aus. 1926) in 1929. Both were high school teachers in Tasmania and it was through Ray's influence that Minnie was brought to know the Saviour. They served in various capacities in Khanapur and a number of other centres for over 44 years. Ray laboured in the villages and market-places and later became responsible for the business management of the Sankeshwar Leprosy Hospital. Both he and his wife assisted in the medical work there. He also edited a monthly prayer letter for 36 years and a Marathi monthly magazine for fourteen years and because of his fluency in the language he served on the B.F.B.S. Marathi Bible revision committee. He only resigned from this because it involved being absent from his other work.

Ray and Minnie also helped at the children's homes at Daddi and Sulge and saw much blessing. When William C. Irvine retired from the editorship of the Marathi monthly magazine, *Light on the Scriptures,* Ray became the editor. The magazine had a wide circulation throughout the country. After a stroke, he was compelled to return to Australia in 1971, but he was happy to do so, as Ratnakar Mirajkar, whom he had seen grow up and graduate, resigned his post as high school teacher and was commended by the Belgaum assembly to full-time service.

Until his death in 1980, Ray maintained contact with all the full-time workers known to him and helped in the transmission of gifts. Minnie still hears from many of those who were children in their care.

Miss Kathleen L. Peebles worked with the Hendersons at Sankeshwar from its commencement both in medical and village work, for many years before retiring. She died in 1982. Dr. D. John Gilbert writes of her loyal service and utter reliability. Miss Isa B. Jaap commended from Scotland in 1938 joined Dr. and Mrs. Henderson and remained at Sankeshwar. Here she certainly proved the Lord, for she had no mail and no money for three months. She spent some time at Daddi, where the children's home was adapted for hospital work.

Miss Joyce Richards commended from Australia joined the work in 1945 but left a year later to marry Arthur Flack. Miss Beatrice Chisholm, commended from Scotland, joined the work in 1947 and spent a happy period of service there, only leaving to marry George J. Turner in 1950. Miss Edna E. Ramage, commended from Australia in 1948, became Nursing Superintendent at the Leprosy Hospital, with responsibility for organization of staffing and supervision of patients. Dr. James W. McMillan, commended from Australia in 1953, was a welcome addition. He not only undertook the responsibility for the medical work, but also engaged in extensive written ministry and in teaching in the local assembly. Miss Doreen M. Hurrell from Australia, who had been teaching in Ootacamund, joined the work in 1957, when she became Mrs. McMillan. In the same year, Dr. Walter M. Darling came to Sankeshwar and continued there after his marriage to Miss Grace Beattie in 1961. Dr. John Gilbert also spent some time there from 1947. Miss Mary Edwards came in 1955 and Miss Heather I. Smith from Tasmania in 1962, becoming Nursing Superintendent of the S.K.U. Mission Hospital. She helped Kathleen Peebles in village visiting and also became involved in camps and Bible classes for young women. Miriam Keyse, commended from U.K. went first to Khanapur in 1964. When she transferred to Sankeshwar in 1971, she became Superintendent of the general hospital. Those who worked at the hospital never lost sight of their primary role. When asked whether it was really worthwhile to hospitalize patients with intestinal parasites again and again, as inevitably they were re-infected on return to their

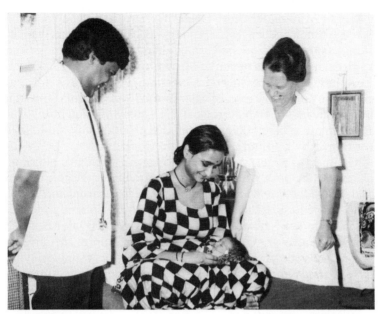

Sankeshwar Hospital—Miriam Keyse and Dr. Dev Danam Mitta

Sankeshwar Hospital—TB ward

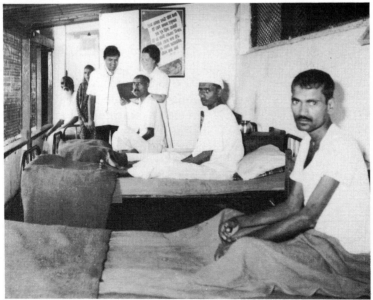

villages, Miriam replied, 'Of course, we hope they will be saved'. When the leprosy hospital was closed, Miriam Keyse, Edna Ramage and others formed a committee to care for the spiritual needs of the patients. Miriam and Edna have served the Lord in village witnessing with blessing. The Leprosy Hospital closed in 1977 because of the shortage of doctors and the hospital work was transferred to the Leprosy Mission hospital at Belgaum. The care of leprosy patients around Sankeshwar was continued by a Community Health programme.

George J. Turner, commended from Australia in 1945 came to help in the boys' orphanage which was under the care of Mr. and Mrs. Maurice Wark and Miss Nellie Robertson, and also in the leprosy hospital at Belgaum, of which he became honorary Superintendent. He was joined in 1951 by his wife, Beatrice from Sankeshwar. George was especially helpful in ministry among the young people in the assemblies. They retired in 1969.

Mr. and Mrs. Ben Gates, also commended from Australia, engaged in village evangelism in the Marathi language at Belgaum from 1952 to 1955. Miss Jean Campbell, commended from Australia in 1968 joined Miss G. Celeste Hull (commended from Australia in 1948) and worked among women and children, before they were led to take up work in Goa.

When William F. Forward was fourteen he nearly lost his life being buried in sand and, at that time, promised to give his life fully to the Lord if he was saved from death. After military service, he entered Emmaus Bible School at Sydney, Australia. While there, a letter to the assembly from Ray Atkinson expressed a desire that a young man from Emmaus should relieve him for furlough. It seemed a clear indication of God's will. William and Gladys Shelford, whom he married in 1963, finally received clear confirmation through an address by T. Ernest Wilson of Angola. The Brisbane assembly commended them and they set sail. The day they landed at Bombay, feeling helplessly incompetent, Bill was asked to preach. Several souls were saved – and all doubts vanished. They spent their first nine months at Khanapur with the Atkinsons and two years studying Marathi with Gordon Ritchie. One day Bill was taken by Gordon to Cumbum in South Andhra Pradesh to meet the believers, only to find that they had sent him three telegrams, asking him to come as A. H. Roberts had died. They spent some years here and Bill travelled around teaching and preaching in Andhra Pradesh, Tamil Nadu, and Kerala. In 1970 a need arose at Belgaum Leprosy Hospital and he became superintendent while Gladys engaged in work among women but gradually they handed it over to Indian administrators, while Dr. Cairns Smith handed over the medical work to Indian doctors. During this time Bill and Gladys proved invaluable in Bible teaching. In 1978 it became clear that the hospital needs were met and that the Belgaum assembly was progressing well. Bill and Gladys accordingly returned to Australia.

The work among leprosy sufferers in Hindalge and Sankeshwar has without doubt been a most fruitful work over the years, and several hundreds of patients have professed faith in Christ. Some of these are now with the Lord; some have backslidden and grown cold; but many of them are now witnessing for the Saviour in their own homes and villages, after being discharged symptom-free. One of the men won through this work is now in full-time service for the Lord and has been most successful in selling Scripture portions. There are other full-time Indian workers in the District. One was once the

Mary Edwards

Ready for study;
G. Celeste Hull
and Beatrice
Turner in
background

laboratory technician at the Sankeshwar General Hospital, and the other the driver for the village leprosy clinic work. Both were commended by the assembly at Sankeshwar.

The orphanage work has also been the means of winning many. Most of those who were brought up in the orphanage are in assembly fellowship today, and some are elders and workers.

Apart from these, results generally have been encouraging. Some have been won through the work among tuberculosis sufferers in the Sankeshwar General Hospital. In recent years there has also been a growing work amongst Telugu-speaking people in three centres in the district, and there have been some encouraging results in the work amongst students and other young people in Belgaum City.

There are now no overseas missionaries at Chandgad, Daddi or Sulge. The property at Chandgad was sold to a believer with an interest in the small group of Christians there, and that at Daddi was sold to another believer, who had two Christian ex-leprosy patients there as caretakers. The property at Sulge was developed as a camp and conference centre. While none of the assemblies in the district is very large, they are growing, and a number of Indian brethren and sisters can minister acceptably in their appropriate spheres. At least three Indian brethren and their wives are also doing real missionary work, looking to the Lord alone for the supply of their needs.

Memory verse
for the day

The greater part of Karnataka was formerly known as Mysore
State. This was a table-land in the angle where the Eastern and
Western Ghats converge in the Nilgiri Hills. It is between 2,000
and 3,000 feet above sea level. The majority of the population
are Hindus, but there are some Muslims.

Mysore City has been described as a miniature of all India,
with temple processions, a palace, a mosque with its minarets,
markets, a mission hospital and a tiger forest nearby. A friend
who met Grace Cole (U.K. 1946) and Beatrice Fountain (U.K.
1946) saw them leaning over the ship's rail with two very
personable young men and gave vent to silent lamentation, but
the two girls came off the ship heart-whole. At Hoskoti they
started language study and then gave themselves to children's
work. They adopted nine orphan girls in the suburb of
Laksumipuram, and were also able to help the struggling
assemblies. For some time they ran a small clinic. Districts like
Chitaldrug, Hassan, Kadar, Shunaza, and others were all
evangelized by missionaries.

In 1953 the two young missionaries were asked by the owner
to vacate the house. But at that time the Perkins's were moving
to Bangalore, and they left a lovely house which they had built,
which was ideal for the children. So Grace and Beatrice went to
Diddapura, where they had a wonderful three years. Miss
Fountain was able to help in assembly visiting.

Mysore City—a miniature of all India   (P. Marsh)

Grace and Beatrice returned to Mysore City in 1957 with their small 'family' of orphan girls. One of the elders of the Mysore assembly found the ideal house. Several of the girls put their faith in Christ. Beatrice Fountain helped at Hebron School for a time. Five of the girls married, and the others are happy in their careers. Whilst there Grace and Beatrice were able to help the struggling assemblies. After 19 years they had to leave their home in Mysore City and were offered a beautiful house on the Nilgiri Hills, 6,500 feet up, far above the heat and dust of the plains.

Bob Glasgow describes Mysore City at festival time, in *Still 500 Million to Reach*, pp. 19, 20, 'in November it was a candelabra, a galaxy of flickering festival lights. Every wall and balcony was outlined by a row of lamps – *divas*, or small earthenware saucer-lamps. The wicks lay in the oil and against the side of the *divas*, giving candles of light along the walls and windows. Above the twinkling city rose the distant ridge of Chamundi Hill, contoured with bright electric lights that sketched the shape of the monster that was slain by the goddess Chamundi.' He goes on to describe the resounding monotony of the Brahmin inside the temple 'as he intoned the return of the great god Rama from exile in the forest to a city that greeted him with a glaze of lights, the *dewali* story.' There are no assembly workers in this great city with all its idolatry and need.

The commencement of Christian witness in Mysore State was in the last century, when Miss Louise H. Anstey came to India with the London Missionary Society. Ill-health forced her to return to Scotland in 1874. She returned to India two years later, however, but this time as an independent worker without a salary, and evidently in fellowship with assemblies. She moved to Kolar when the state was in the grip of a severe famine and opened up a new work in the form of orphanages for 600 boys and girls. Her activities included evangelistic and educational work in Kolar and the surrounding villages, the cost being met mainly out of her own resources. While there she was joined by William A. Redwood (commended from Devon in 1882, by George Brealey and Robert Chapman) and by Annie Macdonald, the future Mrs. Redwood, commended from Glasgow in 1881. They helped in the orphanage until their marriage in 1885.

They were followed in 1885 by Miss Florence P. Bird and Miss Eleanor Stonehouse (later Mrs. E. Lynn) and in 1888 by Ebenezer Lynn. Prior to the arrival of any of these missionaries, Miss Anstey had found the work too much to handle and had sought help in 1880 and 1881 from the American Methodists, who were the only evangelical body in the area. The assembly missionaries gradually left the work at Kolar and in 1890, after they had all left, the orphanages were handed over to the American Methodists free of charge. Difficulty had arisen since two missionary societies had raised objections with William Redwood to an independent mission work being undertaken in an area in which they were already working.

To avoid friction the Redwoods left Kolar and started in Malavalli, then a town of some 8,000 people, situated 65 miles from Bangalore. Job Abran and John Halliday, who had been serving at Kolar with their families, joined the assembly which was started at Malavalli. John B. Gabriel, a Muslim convert from Kolar, followed them in 1891 and undertook pastoral responsibilities there until his death in 1945. At first the people of Malavalli were unresponsive, but Mr. Redwood was able to cure the head official of ulcers and an immediate change of attitude resulted. In the first decade of the work, four schools

John B. and Hannah Gabriel   (T. Patient)

were established in and around Malavalli, including one for the children of Christian missionaries.

The Malavalli Taluk had some 186 villages and small towns, with a total population at that time of 200,000. In *Brethren Missionary Work in Mysore State*, p. 12, Kenneth J. Newton says that Malavalli and Kollegal were the centres from which missionary work in the state radiated. 'From Malavalli it spread to Talkad, Satanur, Maddur and Bannur; and from Kollegal to Kamakerai, Diddapura and Muguru.' A great deal of this progress was due to the Redwoods. To quote Ken Newton again, 'In July 1895 Mr. and Mrs. Redwood with their four

Mysore—idol mask   (P. A. Pritchard)

194

Bangalore—Clarence High School with Arthur and D. Joyce Flack   (S. F. Warren

Living Water   (C. Gilmore

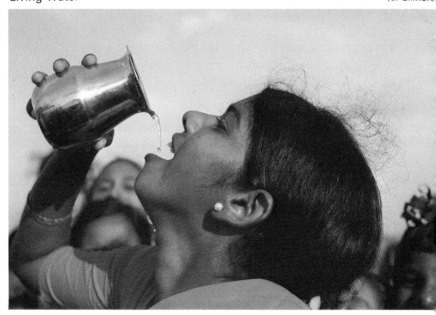

children left for their second furlough in England. In their nine years at Malavalli the foundations of the work had been laid. There were four schools, a small boarding home, preaching tours, medical work and a small Christian community.' Within a few days of the commencement of the journey home, however, William Redwood had died and been buried at sea. His family caried on the work. 'Alfred McD. Redwood was in Bangalore from 1910 till 1960; Walter Redwood in Bangalore from 1913 to 1960; Annie Redwood in 1913 married John Evans from Wales and both worked in the Kanarese field till 1957; Grace came in 1910 to Bangalore and later married Wilfred Wilcox, who was principal of Clarence High School from 1932 to 1951. Mrs. William Redwood herself returned to Bangalore in 1910 and stayed there till her death in 1933.'

Wm. Redwood was indefatigable in evangelism. Besides visiting the villages around Malavalli and preaching in the streets of the town and at the weekly market attended by as many as a thousand people, he visited almost every house. A room was opened in Malavalli where people could go to read the Bible and portions of the Scriptures in Kannada. He also applied himself to the treatment of the sick and suffering. There was no hospital or doctor in the whole of the Malavalli District, so that 100,000 people were without medical assistance. Thus he was kept busy with his dispensary. He opened a school where the sons of Brahmins could be taught English, which proved very popular. In the process of learning English, they also learned much of the Scriptures. Later the government gave him a piece of ground for the erection of a school.

In the years before the Redwoods' first furlough, Mr. and Mrs. Ebenezer Lynn, Miss Florence P. Bird and Mr. Thomas Patient had arrived. The ladies were greatly blessed amongst the women and children, while the men, with the help of Indian brethren, were engaged in village evangelism. On the Redwoods' return, Mr. and Mrs. Lynn, Miss Florence Bird and Miss Agnes M. Clarke moved to Kollegal in 1891.

Kollegal was 22 miles from Malavalli and was the headquarters of another district, and had its own government offices, a small staff of officials and a magistrate's court. At that time, it was a town of 10,000 people. The Redwoods spent some time in Kollegal and attempted to reach some of the hundreds of smaller towns and villages around it and Malavalli. An extract from his own account is quite illuminating. He wrote, 'Much patient plodding is required in visiting and working these villages. They are mostly situated in out-of-the-way parts, with no roads leading to them, and often in feverish jungles where very few will venture. This is particularly true of the villages in the Taluk of Kollegal. Millions of poor heathen in this great empire are born, and live, and die in such unknown places, and never hear the name of Christ. But should they be left to die in darkness because it costs something to reach them? God forbid! We have already reached some thousands of such people. But their hearts are more difficult to reach than their villages. Unlike natives of large cities and towns, these villagers are as heathenish and superstitious as they were a century ago. Their villages are little Sodoms without even a Lot in them. Their moral condition is too terrible to contemplate. In some villages not even one moral man can be found. This is scarcely to be wondered at, seeing that idolatry and the grossest licentiousness are bound up in each other. The marriage tie is only what the man likes to make of it. Many have more than one wife, or one wife and one or two concubines. In some cases, men put away their wives because they are sickly, and take others, sending the poor sick

Malavalli—paddy fields   (T. Patient)

William J. M. Redwood

one adrift to live or starve as she may. Some parents devote their daughters to some deity, which means that they are given up to a life of infamy.'

It seemed evident that more effective work could be done at Kollegal and the tendency was for new workers to settle there rather than at Malavalli, so that it became the principal centre of work and a place where much blessing was seen. In 1892 Miss Emily A. Austin (U.K.), who remained there until 1899, and in 1894 Miss Amelia Braden (U.K.) went to Kollegal. In 1895, Mr. James H. Aston left England, intending to go to the Godavari District but, on hearing of Mr. William Redwood's death, he went to Malavalli instead. Miss L. Lavinia Southgate (later Mrs. George Humphries) went to Kollegal in 1896; Miss Ivason (later Mrs. Aston) and Miss D. Elizabeth Saunders (U.K.), (later Mrs. Buchanan) followed in 1899; Miss Grace H. Cookson (U.K.) in 1900; and Mr. Frank M'Laine (U.K.) in 1901. It was this spate of new workers that caused the work to spread beyond the confines of Malavalli and Kollegal. Mrs. Redwood returned to Malavalli in 1896 and stayed until 1900,

Villagers at the time   (T. Patient)

but her health broke down and she had to spend ten years in England, afterwards returning, nevertheless, to Bangalore to spend 22 more fruitful years of service.

The hospital and dispensary work opened the door for the gospel and the number of patients increased rapidly. But there was another contributory factor. During the years 1898–1900 there was a very severe famine in Gujarat State. H. Handley Bird established himself at Ahmedabad and commenced to gather children (most of them orphaned of both parents) together from the city and neighbourhood. Other workers, including George Humphries, Florence P. Bird and Ebenezer Lynn, went to Ahmedabad. The reception of the Gujarat children in 1900 led to the commencement of the orphanages in Malavalli, Kollegal and Kamakerai in the Karnada field, in the Belgaum District and in Tamil Nadu. Thirty-five boys were settled at Malavalli, a hundred girls at Kollegal, and 27 boys at Kamakerai. The settling of these orphans a thousand miles from their previous homes created a number of problems. As Ken Newton points out, *op. cit.*, p. 16, 'Many of the orphans grew up, were married and regarded the Mission as still responsible for their welfare. Even today some of their descendants try to force the missionaries to help out in times of financial and other crises. Many of the orphans gave a very uncertain testimony to possession of new life in Christ, and although nearly all were baptised, it appears that for them baptism was more a matter of convenience than of conviction. In the Mission they found security and a sense of community, something they, as orphans and outsiders in Mysore State, could not have obtained in the local Hindu community. A more positive and fruitful work has been done in caring for many local orphans, whose lives would have been of privation and shame had not the Mission provided them with a home. Many of these have gone on to be real spiritual helps in the brethren churches.'

The principal founders of the work in Kollegal were the Lynns, Miss Florence P. Bird and Miss Agnes M. Clarke. When they went there in 1891 no one could have imagined the influence they would have in establishing the testimony there. The Birds, of course, were a family of missionaries: in addition to Florence in Kollegal, Handley was in Madras, Howard in China, and Cyril and Mary in Africa. A trained nurse, Florence

George Humphries' first home in India   (*Links,* May 1907)

Kollegal—mission compound   (*Links*, July 1904)

was commended to the work by George Müller of Bristol. She was awarded the Kaiser-I-Hind medal for her service in India, and when she died in Kollegal in 1950, she had completed 65 years in India (60 of them in Kollegal). Ebenezer Lynn, whose sister was a missionary in the Godavari District of Andhra Pradesh, spent 60 years in India and died in 1948 at Ootacamund. Agnes Clarke, also a nurse, completed 47 years of missionary service in India and died in Bangalore in 1937.

Quite early a bungalow was purchased for the station by William H. Stanes, brother of Sir Robert Stanes, and in 1900 a second compound was purchased on the outskirts of Kollegal. When the missionaries moved to Kollegal in 1891, they were able to secure the use of an abandoned travellers' bungalow, which was the rendezvous of the washermen's donkeys. As Mrs. Lynn and Miss Bird were qualified nurses, they promptly commenced medical work – and were deluged with patients. Bullock carts full of patients began to clatter to their doors each morning with the first streaks of dawn, to join the chorus of the braying donkeys. The workers often visited remote villages and it was a small thing for them to ford the Cauvery River waist-deep at night, clinging to the rear end of the bullock cart which was their conveyance, but which had in the deep water developed into a raft instead of a cart. They toiled tirelessly to reach the hearts of the people and were rewarded.

When in 1900 Florence P. Bird went to collect the orphans from the famine-stricken towns of Gujarat, as already mentioned, a dozen or more of the 100 little destitutes died on the way back and the remaining collection of little skeletons was a challenge to the patience and love of the workers. The story spread through the villages and very soon babies were being left at their gate or tied to the hedge. Over 1,200 girls have passed through the home at Kollegal, many of whom were saved, baptised and brought into fellowship. One became Miss Bird's faithful right hand.

Miss Kathleen E. Bygrave (Canada 1901) and then in 1920 Miss Emily Dorling (U.S.A.) joined the workers in the orphanage: the Lord called the latter home in 1960. In 1925 Miss Catharine Duffey (later Mrs. Walter Russell) and Miss Ruth Anderson, both from the U.S.A., joined the Girls' Home from Maddur. Other missionaries in Kollegal included Miss M. Priscilla McClelland (U.S.A. 1941), Miss Anne M. Vanderlaan in 1947, and Miss Violet Hendrickson who came in 1948 to teach but was forced by ill-health to return home in 1951. Miss Vanderlaan took over the responsibility for the hospital work when Miss Bird gave it up in her 80th year. Miss Rachel Hynd (Australia 1939) engaged in village visiting, dispensary and maternity work at Kollegal, Maddur and Talkad. She married Reginald S. Peake (U.K.) in 1945 and retired in 1959.

Ebenezer Lynn worked very largely in the villages around Kollegal and a number of people were saved. He found the greatest response from the depressed classes and discovered that quite a number of these were intelligent, responsible men who, in due course, became leaders in the assemblies. One became a school teacher. Another won his friend for Christ and then taught him to read and the latter became a full-time colporteur. Mr. Lynn also started a school in the leather community – a class who are despised because they handle dead animals.

Mr. and Mrs. Thomas Patient took charge of the orphanage and boarding home at Malavalli from 1900 until their death in 1937 and 1936 respectively. The responsibility was then undertaken by their daughters, Florence and Fanny, until they handed it over in 1947 to John Evans and his wife, Annie who had been residing in Malavalli since 1924. The Evans's returned to England in 1957 and John died there the same year, having spent 47 years in India.

In 1951 the responsibility was taken over by Bert and Elma Overton, commended from Tasmania in 1950. When the Overtons' service in the Kanarese field began there was

Bert J. and
Elma Overton
(E. G. Wagland)

Bangalore Road
(M. Keyse)

abundant talent there. At that time they seemed the least impressive of all the workers but they were to prove some of the most enduring. Before the Overtons arrived at Malavalli, Mr. Evans had been letting the orphanage work run down with a view to closing it down when they retired. Bert, therefore, began with only a handful of boys and a very limited site. From that unimpressive start the work progressed until today there are about 100 children in residence. They now have sufficient land to grow rice, for a small diary herd and a growing chicken farm. In recent years there have been fewer orphans taken into the home, the emphasis being rather to provide a place where children of poor village Christian families could be educated, in the hope that they would become responsible Christian citizens in their villages. Bert also took an active part in building up assemblies in the area and in founding others. The Overtons' home proved a real oasis for many a tired and troubled worker and when Mrs. Lorna E. M. Hill retired from the 'Montauban' missionary home in 1978 Bert and Elma took charge of that work. His orphanage work made him highly esteemed and when he was brutally murdered on the Bangalore road in 1981 over 2,500 attended his memorial service. Elma returned to Australia the same year.

Ronald Greenfield (N.Z.) joined Ebenezer Lynn in 1939 and in the same year married Miss Everel Chandler (N.Z. 1939) who was helping in the orphanage at Kollegal. They engaged in open air preaching, village meetings and literature distribution, until they moved to Diddapura in 1943 to assist Mr. Alfred E. Perkins in the orphanage, returning to Kollegal the following year. In 1951 Ronald assumed responsibility for the printing press at Bangalore, while Rowland H. C. Hill (U.S.A. 1920) was on furlough. The Hills eventually retired in 1952 and the Greenfields in 1954.

Mr. and Mrs. John E. Warburton (N.Z. 1950) spent many years in Kollegal, engaging in village evangelism and helping in the Bible School at Ernakulam. Mrs. Warburton took part in women's meetings and camp work. John also spoke at special meetings and conventions at Kollegal, Talkad, Bhaddavati, Mysore, etc. Blessing has been seen among university students and others and a special effort was made in 1962 to reach Tibetans.

The initial importance given to the establishing of schools

diminished as the government built schools. The efforts of the Malavalli workers in education were not entirely successful, owing to the absence of educationalists among the missionaries, the non-availability of capable national teachers, and the natural reluctance of the people to send their children to school. The last was very evident at the school at Niddugatta, which was closed in 1898 because of lack of pupils. It was later reopened but, after functioning for a short while, was again closed, because the teachers demonstrated a complete lack of any sense of responsibility. The only other school commenced from Malavalli was at Bachanahalli, three miles away. Sathy-asheelappa, one of the early orphans, began work there as a teacher in 1925. There are now 110 pupils, all from Hindu families.

Dispensary work at Malavalli was started by Wm. Redwood. In 1902, Miss Florence K. Gallop, a trained nurse, commended from the U.K., went to Malavalli and operated the dispensary until her marriage to John McIver in 1907. The work was later taken up by Miss Nora A. Hooper (U.K. 1928), who was also a trained nurse, but in 1937 she moved to Satanur, to join the widowed Mrs. McIver in dispensary work there.

In spite of all the educational, medical and evangelistic work at Malavalli, the response (except from the orphans or boarders) was disappointing. In nearly 100 years of activity, only just over 200 have been baptised as believers. Special efforts were made to contact employees at the hydro-electric works on the river Cauvery ten miles away. Frank M'Laine visited the site from 1901 onwards, and Miss Nora Hooper later held women's meetings there, but the response was somewhat disappointing. A new hall was built at Malavalli in 1956, but the assembly is still only about 80 in size.

In 1897 a work was commenced at Talkad, a village of 4,000 people, and an important centre for Hindu festivals. John and Stephen Halliday and their families moved there from Malavalli in 1899, both to engage in preaching and the former to start an English school. The work did not prosper and the Hallidays moved away. In 1901 the work was recommenced with the arrival from Malavalli of Mr. and Mrs. Sidney O. Peake, who stayed in Talkad until their return to England in 1947. The dispensary work done in the village brought about some contacts and the children's work prospered and there were four

Talkad—scene of the Hindu festival (T. Patient)

Sunday schools in the area. Primary schools were built, but the assembly grew slowly. Both Mr. and Mrs. Peake died in 1951. Mr. and Mrs. Reginald S. Peake (son of Mr. and Mrs. Sidney Peake), who had been at Maddur from 1940, moved to Talkad in 1951. The population then was 5,000 and there were 20 in the assembly. The village school of Kukuru was still operating and approximately 800 patients a month were attending the dispensary. A new school was built at Talkad in 1956, but shortly afterwards the Peakes moved to Australia. There is apparently no testimony there today and the mission compound and assembly buildings have been sold.

John C. McIver, commended from New Zealand in 1904 settled at Talkad initially but, after his marriage to Miss Florence Gallop in 1907, they moved to the small village of Satanur. They started medical work and gradually erected buildings, and he systematically covered the entire area on preaching tours. Apart from three years 1926–29 in the city of Mysore, they remained at Satanur until his death in 1932.

Mrs. McIver carried on the work with the help of her daughter, Christina, until the latter's marriage to Wilfred S. Durham in 1938. The following year Miss Nora A. Hooper

Malavalli orphanage members 1930; Nora A. Hooper on the right and Fanny Patient   (T. Patient)

moved from Malavalli to Satanur, helping Mrs. McIver in the dispensary work and engaging in evangelistic work among the children of the district. Following Mrs. McIver's death in 1956 and, at the same time, an increase in the numbers attending the dispensary, the children's work had to be curtailed. A hall was erected by James Stewart in 1939, but was not used and was sold in 1965 for use as an orphanage.

In 1918 Mr. and Mrs. James Aston, who had previously resided at Malavalli and Kollegal, began a work at Maddur, a station on the Bangalore-Mysore railway. Two Indian families went with them from Malavalli. In 1922 they were joined by Miss Ruth Anderson and Miss Catharine Duffy. The Astons returned to England in 1924 and Misses Anderson and Duffy left Maddur the following year and the work ceased. The only known convert during the seven years' work was a Brahmin girl, whose children subsequently followed her step of faith. From 1925 James Stewart, who was located at Bannur, continued to visit Maddur in an attempt to keep this strategic centre open.

At Bannur, fourteen miles from Malavalli, Mr. and Mrs. James Stewart commenced work in 1921. They engaged in village evangelism and he visited every village for miles around.

A primary school was opened, but very few converts were seen and no assembly started.

Earlier reference has been made to Kollegal. There is still a large number of girls in the home, but the orphanage work has naturally disappeared. The hospital also closed in 1966, although Miss Anne M. Vanderlaan continued a weekly dispensary. Schools were opened at Siddenopura, Satyagala, Mullur and Haruvanapura, as well as on the mission compound itself. Nearly 600 pupils were taught and many have been reached with the gospel. Ebenezer Lynn's preaching tours were very extensive. In 1893, for example, he did 464 visits for preaching in 106 villages. A large number of people were led to the Saviour. One advantage of work in Kollegal was that there were established home industries connected with the silk trade for which Kollegal was famous. Despite difficulties over the years, the assembly of 200 is active and spiritually alive.

Soon after George Humphries arrived in Kollegal, he became interested in commencing a work at Kamakerai, a village eight miles away. Twenty-seven orphans were settled there. When Mr. Humphries returned from furlough in 1904, he was accompanied by two new workers from New Zealand, Edward Buchanan (who was destined to be his successor in Kamakerai) and Alfred E. Perkins, who began the work at Diddapura, where Charles Auchan also laboured. When George Humphries died in 1907, Edward Buchanan took over the responsibility for the orphanage. In 1909 he married Miss Dora E. Saunders and they continued at the orphanage as well as itinerating in the villages. Thousands of gospels were sold at festivals and many people were saved and baptised. There was great blessing from the meetings by V. D. David, the first high caste Indian to confess Christ. Mrs. Buchanan died in 1923 but Edward married Miss Catharine Murphy from Belgaum in the following year. She started a small dispensary, which proved a help to many. In 1945 they were glad to welcome Mr. and Mrs. Murray Mackay (U.K. 1939 and 1944 respectively) to join them. In 1951 the Buchanans moved to Coonoor to take charge of the rest house, but Mrs. Buchanan's ill-health compelled them to return home in 1952, where she died the following year. In 1954 Edward married Miss Eva Rolston and they returned to India in 1962, only to leave the same year owing to the deterioration of Eva's health. She died in 1963, followed by him in 1970. For his work

Wilfred S. Durham and Murray Mackay

Reginald S. Peake

he had been awarded the Kaiser-I-Hind medal, the highest civil award in India.

The work at Kamakerai followed the pattern in other centres, with medical work (in which many lady missionaries helped), elementary schools, evangelistic work, including preaching tours to hitherto unreached areas in the hills, and the orphanage operated for the Gujarati boys. One new feature was the establishment of farming projects by Edward Buchanan. Land at Yeddahalli and Hannagallidoddi, within ten miles of Kamakerai, was granted by the government for the Gujarati orphans when they married. About twenty families settled there and Mr. Buchanan helped them to put this land under cultivation. When he left India for a time in 1952, however, interest declined and families moved to Kamakerai and either sold the land or left it idle. He also encouraged the Christians to breed silkworms and many of the believers today are working in the silk industry. Quite a number of missionaries spent some time at Kamakerai, including Miss Amy V. Mills (U.K. 1923–66), Mr. Leslie W. Bowen (N.Z. 1929–31), who died at the early age of 25; Murray Mackay (N.Z. 1939–56) who married Miss Ethel Harding in 1945; Miss J. Alison Rout (N.Z. 1940–41); Miss Dinah P. Padfield (U.K. 1956–65); Mrs. David J. Roberts (née Smith) 1954–70, and Eric F. Bullock (N.Z. 1953). There are now over a hundred in assembly fellowship. Albert E. Aiken (N.Z. 1930) joined the Perkins at Diddapura but then went on to Kamakerai in 1932 to join the Buchanans.

In 1910 a work was commenced at Diddapura, a small village in a fertile plain where there were no large towns but, on the other hand, many villages. Alfred E. Perkins (N.Z. 1904) had spent a year at Kollegal before joining Wylam H. King for two years at Gunjuru, near Bangalore. In 1906 he married Miss Amy C. Greatorex and they helped in the boys' orphanage at Malavalli and in the work at Gunjuru, until they moved south, first to Kamakerai in 1907 and then in 1910 to commence a new witness at Diddapura, twenty miles from Kollegal. They were confronted with poverty, disease, filthy conditions and idol worship. Within four miles were 33 villages and, with simple medical means and consistent visiting, they presented Christ to the people. A paper in Kanarese was started for the Christians in the area. Those who believed and were baptised were completely ostracized in the villages and often turned out of their homes. An English-speaking assembly was started in 1916. The coffee plantations provided a good response to the preaching and one group in 1920 offered to convert their temple into a meeting hall. Disturbances arose later in the propaganda regarding independence for India. In one village the head man fined everyone who ate or drank from anything touched by Christians. But the government literacy programme facilitated the work and the Perkins taught many to read. A coffee plantation foreman bought two acres of land to give the produce to the Lord. Then 25 believers were baptised at Doddagajanua in 1926 and an assembly started there, but this group was taken over by the Wesleyans. Later another assembly was started, but differences arose over caste problems. When the Perkins returned to New Zealand in 1946 the work quickly faded. They returned to India four years later and meetings began again, but they had to retire in 1954, and he died in 1959 and she in 1960.

They moved again to Mysore City in 1957 and since then there has been no resident missionary at Diddapura. Miss Marietta Middleton (U.K. 1919–28) and Mr. A. Aiken gave help there at earlier dates. The believers there are poor and

Exercising elephants

Mysore—Maharaja's Palace (R. Glasgow)

Bombay—street dwellers   (M. Browne

illiterate and many are widows, but the financial aid given to them has not produced a strong assembly.

In 1910 Mr. and Mrs. Frank M'Laine moved to Muguru. At the commencement he wrote, 'Work commenced in simple faith in the living God, our needs for the work being supplied by His loving hand, our desire being the honour and glory of the Triune God in the salvation of precious souls and the establishment of a church which shall be to the praise of God.' Within two years a school was begun at Kanhalli. Other schools were opened at Tagapura in 1915, Muguru in 1921, and Melhalli in 1923. Then, following the arrival of Mr. and Mrs. Rowland H. C. Hill (U.K. 1920), schools were begun in 1923 for caste children in Muguru, for the Panchamas in Kanhalli, and a night school was also opened in Muguru. In the same year an assembly hall and a dispensary were also opened. It was a great loss to the work when the Hills moved to Bangalore in 1925, and most of the school work began to decline. Helen M'Laine died in 1939, and Frank returned to England the year following.

A priest and his wife were the first converts at Muguru. They were baptised in 1911 and participated in the communion service three days later. The village *panchayat* forbade them to use the village well, and soon afterwards an attempt was made to burn down their thatched-roofed hut. It was not until five years later that more converts were baptised. In 1922 a group of 40 pariahs offered to become Christians if the assembly would pay off their debts: their offer was not accepted! Almost all the converts were Hindus. Up to 1962 there had been 43 baptisms.

Miss Amy V. Mills moved to Muguru in 1932 and continued there until her retirement in 1966. She was a tireless worker and fearless in presenting Christ to officials and to groups gathered in the open air at Hindu festivals.

One writer refers to Miss Amy Mills, who spent some time here. 'Amy Mills of Muguru had never intended becoming a banker but, when the money-changers kept back one-eighth of the face value of the silk cheques, two annas in the rupee, her indignant sympathy for the poor of the land stirred her to cash their silk cheques for nothing. Amy Mills was an evangelical missionary from England. She did not want to become a financier but, when money-lenders accepted jewels as security and returned false jewels after the debt was repaid, she became a money-lender. She also built a threshing-floor and hired it to

Wylam H. and Eva M. King, Crawford J. Tilsley (standing) and Marjorie King (later Mrs. Tilsley)

poorer farmers for a percentage of the grain. She gave this food to others in even greater need.' This surely was practical Christianity.

Bangalore, the capital of Karnataka, is a large business city, with a population of over half a million. Kannada, Tamil and English are spoken but the first is predominant. At the turn of the century, Wylam H. King was converted in Bangalore, while serving in the British army. Soon afterwards, as he indicates in *If Ye Ask I will Do,* he read a book on the life of George Müller and was profoundly impressed with the principle which Müller followed in his work at Bristol of trusting God to supply all the needs of himself and the large number of orphans for whom he had made himself responsible. When Wylam King was drafted back to England, he met for the first time believers associated with brethren assemblies, and unhesitatingly threw in his lot with them. In 1902 he returned to India as a full-time missionary and demonstrated in practice the principles enunciated by Müller. An extremely impressive speaker, Wylam always painted a glowing word picture of the Lord's

Outside 'Bethesda', Bangalore
(P. A. Pritchard)

work in India. His life was characterized by prayer and complete trust in God. Both he and his wife laboured long, in and around Bangalore, among the Kanarese people, and both died in Bangalore in 1952.

Alfred McD. Redwood, the elder son of Mr. and Mrs. William Redwood, had been exercised about serving the Lord in Arabia, but was unable to do so on medical grounds. In accordance with his father's dying request (as he said in *Echoes of Service*, 1936, p. 24), he returned instead to India in 1910 to become a full-time missionary in that country. He settled in Bangalore, taking a particular interest in the British civil and military station located there at that time. His gifts of leadership and Bible teaching quickly developed and there was considerable blessing among English and Anglo-Indians. A local assembly was formed in Fraser Town, a suburb of Bangalore. This grew rapidly in numbers and Bethesda Chapel was built in 1918. In 1970 there were over 150 in fellowship. He was gifted as a speaker and was much in demand. Being keen on encouraging others in Bible study, he was joint author with J. H. Todd of

Bangalore—Alfred and Maria M. Redwood; John and Annie Evans; John Redwood; Wilfred and Grace Wilcox; Walter J. M. and Jean F. Redwood; Nancy Redwood.

Australia of a systematic course of Bible study. It was a correspondence course and covers in a most helpful way the whole of the Old Testament. The authors were not able to proceed with one on the New Testament. He will be remembered by many as the editor of *The Bible Student*. He had to leave India in 1960 and the magazine ceased to be issued. Under God many in various parts of the world owe him a great debt of gratitude for having imparted to them a love for the Scriptures.

Mrs. Wm. Redwood, who had returned to Malavalli in 1896, moved to Bangalore on the arrival of Alfred in 1910 and stayed there until her death in 1933. His younger brother, Walter J. M. Redwood, joined him in Bangalore in 1914 and similarly retired in 1960. Both brothers had a great interest in the dissemination of Christian literature and in 1926 they opened a bookshop in Fraser Town. Later this was moved to larger premises and literature was sent out to many parts of the world. A printing press was purchased and this was developed into a prosperous business according to *Indian Realities*, p. 60. A million and a quarter copies of various sized publications in six languages were produced annually at the press and distributed throughout India. Two Kanarese magazines, *Kavalagaranu* and *Bala Mitra* were printed there, as well as *The Bible Student*. In 1934 the assembly Kanarese Hymnbook was published and it has run into several editions since. The press was sold in 1939 and most of the proceeds given to the Kanarese Workers' Conference for the establishment of another press, which was begun almost immediately, with Rowland H. C. Hill responsible for its running. The Scripture Literature Press, as it was called, has continued to produce Christian literature in both English and Kannada. Over a million pieces of literature and a number of new publications are issued every year.

Alfred and Walter Redwood will be remembered by many in connection with Clarence School at Bangalore. The school was Alfred's vision and he was able to secure cooperation in getting the school established. It opened in 1914 with seventeen children. There were times of real financial crisis when it was thought that the school would have to be closed. Yet, as Walter testified, the miracle always happened and they were saved from ruin. In 1931 it was decided to close the school because of lack of finance, but on the day the letter was to be issued, an offer of help came from Mr. Wilfred Wilcox of Breeks School, Ootacamund. He was a tireless worker and excellent disciplinarian. Apart from his heavy responsibilities at Clarence School, he ran four Tamil elementary schools. His efforts raised

Clarence High School, 1955   (E. N. Horton)

the school to high school status and its influence over the years has been incalculable. There were nearly 600 pupils and many who were won for the Lord while scholars there are now rendering useful service for Him, not only in India but also in other lands to which so many Anglo-Indians have migrated. Wilfred Wilcox took an interest in the Tamil population of Bangalore and at one time was looking after six Tamil Sunday schools with over 400 children. This work lapsed, however, after he left India but there still remains a strong and vigorous Tamil assembly at Richard's Town.

Arthur and Joyce Flack (Australia 1946 and 1945 respectively) took up work in Bangalore and, in due course, he became head of Clarence School, which still continues. Many of those attending the school are of Hindu background but a continuing feature of the school's policy has been that parents of children seeking admission have to sign an undertaking not to object to the Christian teaching which is part of the curriculum. He married in 1946 Joyce Richards who had been working in Sankeshwar. Both were involved in the local assembly and in assisting Indians who are serving the Lord. Joyce returned home in 1981 because of ill-health. Arthur hopes to retire as soon as a successor is found. Miss Emma N. Horton qualified as a teacher in Canada, but had long felt drawn to the mission field. Eventually, after an Inter-Varsity Christian Fellowship Missions Conference, at which Ebenezer G. Vine was the speaker, she received an invitation from Eric Willy to join them at the Breeks Memorial School at Ootacamund. In 1952 she transferred to Clarence School as headmistress of the kindergarten section, and worked with Mr. and Mrs. J. Stewart McNaught, Mr. and Mrs. Clifford A. Wilson (Australia 1951), Mr. and Mrs. Ian T. Hall and Mr. and Mrs. Eric F. Bullock. Others who helped at the school were Stewart Simpson (Australia 1966) from 1966 to 1969, and John H. Martin for a period as principal.

Mr. and Mrs. Rowland Hill, who came to Bangalore from Muguru in 1925 to work among Kannada-speaking people, commenced a day school and Sunday meetings at Akkithim-manahuli. An assembly was established and continued to grow: its numbers being swelled by Christians from Malavalli and Kollegal areas who had moved to Bangalore to obtain employment.

Misses B. and E. Napper and Mr. and Mrs. R. Crookson, all commended from Australia in 1904 worked in Bangalore and in villages in the neighbourhood until their return home for health reasons in 1915. Miss Elizabeth McIntosh (Australia 1906) served the Lord in Singapore before visiting the city in 1909. There she found openings for service among English speaking people and engaged in visiting and tract distribution before returning to Singapore in 1911. Mr. and Mrs. J. Stewart McNaught (Australia 1949), both school teachers, engaged in educational work in Bangalore and Trichur (Kerala), conducted a Bible school and also helped in teaching ministry and in the orphanage work. They returned to Australia in 1965 and Stewart is fully engaged in ministry in that country. Mr. and Mrs. David J. Roberts (Australia 1954 and 1955 respectively), both worked at the Scripture Literature Press and in literature distribution at Bangalore until 1971. He also undertook village evangelism in association with national workers.

The Emmaus work was in the hands of Mr. and Mrs. Eric F. Bullock. Eric went to India in 1950 to fill a teaching post, but was commended to full-time missionary work by New Zealand assemblies in 1953. The following year he married Miss Ruth

Early view of the factory   (C. L. Lucas)

Kjarsgaard from Canada and set up home at Malavalli until they moved to Bangalore. Ruth commenced girls' rallies, which were much blessed. Eric undertook the preparation of radio messages in Kanarese for the *Living Waters* broadcasts. He takes part in Bible Schools and in village evangelism.

The Gospel Recording Centre at Bangalore was the responsibility of Mr. and Mrs. Calvin L. Lucas. Calvin (N.Z. 1964) supervised production of the records and of simple players. He married Miss Elaine Simpson (N.Z. 1964) in 1965 and they were engaged in the local assembly work in a teaching ministry among young people. She has been working with Arthur Flack, Lewis Samraj, M. T. Thomas and D. Benjamin. He conducted drives with a team in villages around, often travelling over rugged mountain trails, but always found an encouraging response. Eleven thousand record players and 60,000 records in 160 languages were distributed in many centres. They recorded 400 Indian languages. Because of ill-health and family responsibilities they returned home in 1980.

Mr. and Mrs. Vay C. Vivian (N.Z. 1967) spent some time in Bangalore to study Kanarese. Miss M. Gwen Nicoll (N.Z. 1931) joined the Redwoods at Bangalore to help in the literary and printing work. She also taught at Hebron Girls School at Coonoor. Miss Jean Fleming (N.Z. 1918) married Walter J. Redwood in 1918 and was identified with his work until their retirement in 1960.

So many of the Lord's servants have laboured in Karnataka that space forbids giving details: if the above seems to be little more than a list of names, dates and places, it should be appreciated that every name represents a life sacrificed to the cause of Christ and that each individual could justifiably claim a book adequately to record the service accomplished.

15

In the Footsteps of Thomas

According to the historian Eusebius, the apostle Thomas landed at Cranganore, a quiet coastal town between Trichur and Alwaye in A.D. 52 and founded churches in seven places. After attempting to evangelize other areas, he was finally martyred at Mylapore near Madras in A.D. 72. The Mar Thomas Church claims to owe its origin to the apostle. If he did not evangelize Travancore in the first century, it seems clear that Pantaenus of Alexandria came in A.D. 180 and that later a body of Christians came from Antioch in the fifth century, who were probably responsible for the establishment of the Nestorian community.

The area in which these early endeavours took place is now known as Kerala. This state combines the two former states known as Cochin and Travancore and also British Malabar, formerly part of the Madras Presidency. Kerala has an area of 15,002 square miles and is renowned for its teak industry, but it also exports tea, rubber and coconut oil. The Western Ghats lie on one side of it and the Arabian Sea on the other side. The languages spoken are Malayalam, Tamil and Kannada and the capital is Trivandrum. The population is over 25 million. Sixty per cent are Hindu, twenty per cent Christian and twenty per cent Muslim. It is the most literate state in India with 67%.

Merchants from Asia Minor began trading with this area in the first and second centuries and many settled down in Kerala and married Indians. Their descendants, however, still refer to themselves usually as Syrians. In the fifteenth century Francisco de Almeida seized control of the west coast from Diu

Hunger for literature   (R. Duff)

to Cochin and in 1509 this hold was strengthened by Alfonso de Albaquerque. Jewish traders who accompanied the early Portuguese fleets found, to their amazement, synagogues of black Jews still following the faith of Judaism – evidently descendants of earlier merchants who had settled in the country. One writer says that 'The Phoenicians who sailed from the Gulf of 'Aqaba to Cochin brought Jewish traders. Tradition says that some of the Jews settled in Cochin at the time that Nebuchadnezzar sacked Jerusalem, and it is even more certain that Jews settled in Kerala after Jerusalem fell to Rome in A.D. 70.'

In the first half of the sixteenth century, the Jesuits (with Portuguese approval) endeavoured to bring the whole of the Syrian Church under the domination of Rome. Fortunately, Dutch rule superseded that of the Portuguese and this saved the Syrian Church from further pressure and persecution. It did, however, suffer oppression later under a Hindu Rajah and then under Typu Sultan, a Muslim invader. It is said that 10,000 Christians were martyred when they refused to deny that Jesus was the Son of God. Subsequent British rule brought peace and prosperity to the Syrian Church.

Krishna Menon, who at one time was the chief lieutenant of Jawahartal Nehru, was a product of Kerala, and other well-known individuals have originated in this state. Politically, the state has a strong communist tendency and did, in fact, have a communist government in the early 1960's. There is a strong sense of state autarchy and there are indications of a drive for a fuller autonomy. Yet the people find it difficult to adjust to changes or to new concepts. Dick Wilson, in *Asia Awakes,* pp. 93-4, points out that they 'almost starved when rice was short and yet failed to take advantage of the nutritious fruits and vegetables all around them, or the fish which their neighbours bring in from the sea – because they were not accustomed to such foods.'

Anthony Norris Groves called at Cochin, then Kottayam, 'the celebrated centre of the labours of the Syrians,' before going on to Quilon, where he wrote, 'I am just entering Quilon

In a Cochin shipyard (Indian High Commission)

by the backwater. I have never seen such lovely scenery, yet man, as Heber says, is vile.' He found the Syrian community in dire need of a spiritual awakening. Nevertheless, the existence of this nominal Christian community is doubtless one factor in the growth of assembly testimony in Travancore.

The Syrian Church plainly needed a revival if its witness to Christ was to be of any real value, and this came through an Indian named V. D. David, later referred to as Tamil David. He was born of Christian parents at Tirunelveli in 1853. His father died while he was a child and he grew up self-willed and independent. At eighteen he ran away from home, robbing his mother of her savings and, despite having been educated in a C.M.S. high school, lived for some years a profligate life in Colombo. His mother never ceased to pray for him and eventually persuaded him to return home. Thinking it would be a help if he married a Christian, a godly girl was found in a C.M.S. boarding school. To her utter disappointment, she found that her husband had no interest in religion. She set herself to pray for him and managed to persuade him to give up drink and to take a post as a teacher. A measure of reform took place, for he earned respect for his industry as a teacher.

A tract was the means of arousing in him a concern for his soul, and he turned to his wife to discover the way of salvation. Her prayers were answered and he now developed a great longing to know the Scriptures and to bring others to the Saviour. Every day he committed to memory a chapter of the Bible, and before long he commenced preaching in the streets and witnessing to the people. At first he saw little blessing, but ultimately he became a great revivalist.

He visited the U.S.A. and Britain, but the greatest impact of his preaching was made on the Syrian Reformed Church in missions conducted in 1895 to 1897. There is no doubt that Tamil David was a chosen vessel. His dynamic preaching swept thousands into the kingdom. Edwyn H. Noel, an assembly missionary in Travancore, estimated that about 30,000 came to know the Lord at that time.

Many of the new converts were eager for instruction in the Scriptures. J. G. Gregson, an army chaplain, was invited from North India to give a month's meetings on the Word of God. Gregson laid stress on deliverance from the power of sin, and the attainment of a life of victory over sin. He taught believers' baptism and the observance of the Lord's Supper. His ministry occasioned considerable exercise on the part of the new converts and created a desire to study the Word and to follow its precepts.

The Syrian Church could not meet the needs which were being felt, and it was amongst these spiritually hungry souls that Volbrecht Nagel and H. Handley Bird were to exercise so much influence, and see the beginning of assembly testimony in Travancore. Nagel had gone to India as a missionary from Germany and was originally connected with the Basle Mission, but had severed the connection on conscientious grounds. He was surprised to find that others had the same convictions as he had. After meeting H. Handley Bird and Thomas H. Maynard, he and his wife enjoyed the closest fellowship with assembly missionaries. He had moved into the Cochin State and was engaged in evangelistic work in Kunnamkulam in 1896. Here a Syrian priest named P. E. Mammen came into contact with him in 1898 and, as a result, left the Syrian church and was baptised by Handley Bird. When Mammen returned to his home in Travancore, he and a small company of believers met on the following Sunday to remember the Lord in the breaking of bread. This was the beginning of assembly testimony in Travancore.

From this small beginning the testimony rapidly increased. Whilst Volbrecht Nagel, H. Handley Bird and William H. Stanes were a great help during their visits, none of them virtually resided in Travancore. The establishment and development of assembly testimony in the early days was essentially the work of Indian believers. A number of gifted national brethren were raised up by God, many of whom had previously been members of the Syrian Church and who had been brought to a knowledge of salvation through the preaching of Tamil David. The memory of P. C. Varkey, F. E. Numby, C. T. Mathai, E. J. Jacob and others is still revered by believers in Kerala, especially by those who attended the great conventions of 5,000 or more at which many of the speakers were Indians.

It was Nagel's practice to preach in an area and to form an assembly of the converts. As soon as an assembly had been established, he moved on to another area. Thus, as already mentioned, he left Cannanore to work at Kunnamkulam in the face of much opposition. A strong assembly was soon formed, converts from Hindus, Syrian Christians and Roman Catholics

Cochin refinery   (Indian High Commission)

being linked together. But his main work was among the needy
outcastes.

He moved on to Parur in 1900, where he was later joined by
Arthur V. Thynne, and four years later to Cochin, a large city
with a cosmopolitan population, so that Indians, Europeans and
others came to the meetings and much blessing was seen. Here
the Nagels were joined by Miss Margaret Gordon (later Mrs.
Roch), Miss Maria M. Dunn (later Mrs. Alfred McD. Redwood)
and Miss Charlotte C. Sundgren. An assembly was established
at Cochin, which Nagel left in the hands of an Indian worker.
Moving on to Trichur in 1906, he acquired a compound of some
sixty acres. Here he was joined by Mr. and Mrs. Wilhelm A.
Kocher, Miss Frieda Burchardt, Miss Clare and Miss
Katherine Diegel, all from Germany. A large orphanage for
girls was erected, a number of huts for poor widows, cottages for
the poor and outcastes who had been ejected from their homes
on their masters' estates when they professed faith in Christ.
Rehoboth, as the place was appropriately named, was
transformed from a wilderness to a beautiful garden, producing
fruit and vegetables for the orphanage. A school was established
and, since it was three miles out of town, the children in the
immediate area flocked to it, including Roman Catholics,
Jacobite Christians and Hindus. Many were brought under the

sound of the gospel and within the sphere of Christian influence. In a short space of time, a large and active assembly came into being. Nagel returned home to Germany on furlough in 1914 and was unable to return, and died there in 1921. His son, Gottley Nagel, went to Angamally in 1931 and was extremely active, but he died in three months.

Volbrecht Nagel was possessed of the gifts of evangelist, pastor and teacher and was greatly missed. House visiting, open air preaching and congregational preaching occupied most of his time. He spoke Malayalam fluently and attracted large numbers in the open air and at other meetings. An excellent hymn-writer, he would often inspire fellow-travellers with his singing. He has often been referred to as the second Samuel Hebieh.

News of the blessing in Travancore created intense interest in Britain and Australasia and from 1901 new workers began to arrive to strengthen the work. Among these was Edwyn H. Noel, who first joined Mr. and Mrs. Nagel while learning Malayalam. He discovered that Kerala was among the most populous states in India and was particularly impressed by the need of the outcastes. Itinerating in Kunnamkulam, Parur and

From left to right: (*back row*): Josephine J. C. Mitchell; Charles J. V. Rolls; Harriet S. Nagel; Edwin H. Noel; Emma K. Kocher; (*middle row*): Miss M. Gordon; Valbrecht Nagel; Julia Noel; Wilhelm A. Kocher; Miss Maria M. Dunn; (*front row*): Frieda Burchardt; Charlotte C. Sundgrer.　　　　　　　　　　　　　　　(*Links,* May 1912)

Puthupally, in each of which there were indigenous assemblies, and in central Travancore generally, he covered vast areas on foot. The outcastes became the special object of his concern. Roads were few and paths were rough or non-existent. Meetings were usually held in school buildings which were little more than mud huts. He lived frugally and all he had was given to the poor among whom he laboured. Sometimes he would receive the gift of a few small eggs or some home-grown tapioca.

He moved south to Kumbanadu in 1905. There he entered into the labours of Tamil David, H. Handley Bird and Volbrecht Nagel. There were many assemblies who needed help and many Hindus who were ready to listen to the gospel turned to the Saviour. He walked hundreds of miles, visiting homes and preaching the gospel. Charles J. Rolls, who had previously been in Ceylon and then in Coimbatore, relieved the Noels at Kumbanadu in 1912–13 and again in 1918–20 and also took part in ministry in various other centres until his retirement in 1921.

In 1909 Edwyn Noel married Miss Julia Shirtliff, a qualified nurse who had been commended from New Zealand in 1907 and who had stayed with the Nagels at Trichur and Parur. They made their home at Kumbanadu. The same year Edwyn started a Bible school for evangelists, while Julia commenced medical work among the women. He spent a great deal of time with Indian brethren in evangelizing the area and had campaigns with P. C. Varkey and K. V. Simon when many were converted and baptised. Schools were recommenced in many centres to enable people to learn to read. By 1918 there were 30 assemblies with 2,000 in fellowship in the area, and there were thirty Indian evangelists shepherding and preaching. A Bible depot was opened, which distributed over 12,000 Bibles, New Testaments and gospels. There were also 2,500 children in the schools.

In 1919 George A. Black of New Zealand joined them and a vigorous visiting programme was introduced, although they experienced a considerable amount of opposition. Antagonists, for example, beat drums during meetings and threw pigs' entrails over the preachers afterwards. One evangelist was kicked and trampled on, Bibles were stolen and burned, and every possible obstacle was placed in their way. Yet large numbers were saved and hundreds were baptised. Conventions attracting thousands were held in thatched *pandals,* and hundreds of thousands of tracts were distributed.

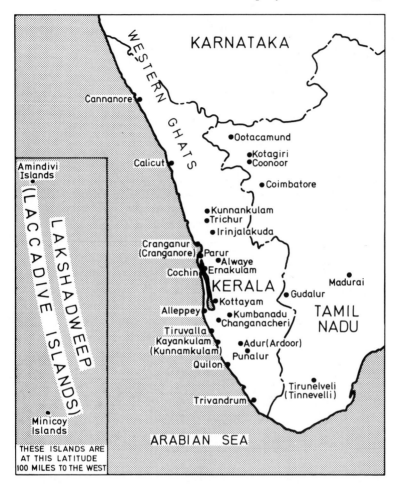

George Black moved to Irinjalakuda in 1920 to help in the boys' orphanage and to build up the assembly. In 1922 he married Miss Agnes E. Moraine (N.Z. 1921), who had joined Mr. and Mrs. J. M. Davies (U.S. 1920) at Parur. In 1923 they moved to Puthupally, where they spent fourteen years and found abundant opportunities for evangelizing in the market places and at festivals. Agnes started a small dispensary which attracted large numbers. George visited many tea and rubber plantations and preached the gospel to workers. Believers were baptised at Pambadi, Kottayam, Changanacheri and Pandalam. In 1937 they transferred to Alleppey, where he engaged in

itinerant evangelism and preaching, and helping at Ardoor, Trivandrum and Kumbanadu. They retired because of ill health in 1946 and George died in 1962 and Agnes in 1967.

In 1936 the Noels took over the printing press run by Alex Soutter and removed it to Kumbanadu. When Edwyn Noel died at Kumbanadu in 1943 over 4,000 attended the funeral. Julia Noel continued with the medical and printing work and work among women, ably assisted by Miss Mai commended from New Zealand in 1913.

Other brethren helped in this fruitful field, including P. T. Thomas, whose well-informed mind was dedicated to the service of God, K. G. Thomas who was known for his evangelistic fervour, P. C. John who was an ever-ready helper and guide, P. V. Varkey (the son of P. C. Varkey) who was greatly used in laying the foundations of assembly work in Travancore. Familiar with his Greek New Testament and able to handle the largest audiences, Frederick E. Numby was called the Spurgeon of Travancore and even in his last days at Cannanore, where he was brought up, his ministry was still blessed to many. K. V. Simon, small of stature but an intellectual giant, was a master of Sanskrit, Syriac and other languages, and his monumental work on Genesis was highly esteemed. C. T. Mathai had the energy and driving force of a strong leader and was invaluable in training young men; unfortunately he died at the early age of 40. E. J. Jacob, never very robust, gave himself unreservedly to the work and was valued as a shepherd and hymnwriter. How many there were in those days, whose lives and ministry made an impression for God.

Charles J. Rolls (N.Z. 1910) had a very helpful period of ministry among Syriac believers.

Trichur became a centre of spiritual activity, following the building of the Rehoboth girls' orphanage at Nellikunnu. Mrs. Nagel and Miss Josephine C. Mitchell (U.K.) continued there for several years. Miss Maria M. Dunn, commended from New Zealand in 1905, joined the Nagels at Parur in order to learn Malayalam, and worked among women and children in their homes and in the market-places. When the Nagels moved to Trichur, she continued in the work with Miss Margaret Gordon until the latter retired in 1913. She then moved to Trichur and in 1914 married Alfred McD. Redwood (from the U.K.) and

Near Trivandrum

shared in his work at Bangalore. Miss Charlotte C. Sundgren also commended from New Zealand in 1905, joined the band of workers at Parur but in 1907 went on to Trichur to help in the orphanage, and the evangelistic work amongst women and girls in which Miss Mitchell was engaged. In 1909 she took over responsibility for the orphanage and was encouraged by the conversion and baptism of many of the girls. Miss Alice B. Mai, in 1913, also helped in Trichur. She was a great visitor and walked many miles to visit scattered believers. She helped at the boys' home at Irinjalakuda in 1918, and in 1920–22 took charge of the school and orphanage at Trichur during Miss Sundgren's furlough. Many were saved through her faithful visiting. She returned to New Zealand in 1934 to look after her parents and died in 1966. Miss Edith C. Wallace was led to Trichur in 1932. Miss E. Sisley Putwain joined in the orphanage work in 1940, and the last ten years of Charlotte Sundgren's life were given over to the care and spiritual well-being of the girls. There were problems of food shortages and increasing prices of grain and, at the same time, there were several outbreaks of cholera and smallpox. But the work progressed and many were saved. She was called home at Ootacamund in 1951 following an operation, but her last thoughts were for her girls.

Edith Wallace took over full responsibility for the orphanage in 1951, during a period of testing with food rationing and isolation, but many girls were saved at this time. She and Phyllis

N. Treasure worked together at Kunnamkulam for some years. Phyllis Treasure heard the Lord's call to serve Him while still a child and she received a final indication when hearing Edith Wallace speak at a missionary conference. For some months in 1963 Edith, Phyllis, and Mr. and Mrs. J. Stewart McNaught worked at the orphanage at Nellikunnu. Then the McNaughts accepted an invitation to teach at Lushington School and Miss Wallace went to Irinjalakuda to look after the boys' orphanage. At the same time Edith and Phyllis continued visiting and personal evangelism among women. Edith retired in 1980 after more than 40 years' service and Phyllis was left in charge at Nellikunnu. While her main work is at the orphanage, she conducts Bible studies for students, teaches in Sunday school and gives help in the local assembly. Lack of leadership in some of the assemblies in Kerala has led to a number of problems.

In 1920 Mr. and Mrs. J. M. Davies of U.S.A. arrived to begin many years of labour in Kerala. Before very long they made Trichur their centre and Mr. Davies was able to move out from there over a much wider area, as Mr. Nagel had before him, exercising a ministry that proved effective and fruitful in building up assembly work in an ever-widening circle. His gifts as a preacher and expositor resulted in a solid work.

Mr. and Mrs. Alex Soutter also arrived in 1920 and quickly found a sphere of service, which included the supervision of the

J. M. Davies and family

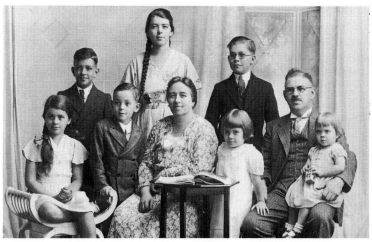

boys' orphanage at Irinjalakuda, a work which Mr. and Mrs. Wilhelm Kocher of Germany had had to relinquish in 1915. Indian evangelists were carrying on a steady and progressive work in Kunnamkulam, Trichur and Irinjalakuda and Cochin, as well as in Angamally and Parur in the north of the province, and the message was being spread through towns and villages. J. M. Davies and Alex Soutter found themselves happily yoked in service with a group of national brethren whom Mr. Nagel had taught in the Scriptures. T. D. Lonappen, who was one of them, continued his witness for God interruptedly until his 99th year. E. I. Jacob, C. T. Mathai, E. P. Verghese and others were proving their value to the assemblies and in witness to the unconverted.

At Tiruvalla in 1930 Dr. V. Verghese purchased land and built a small hospital. As a medical student he had been blessed through the ministry of George Müller and had given his life to Christ. He served in the Indian Medical Service and, on retiring, wished to do something to help others. When he became too old to continue the hospital, he wished to hand it over to a missionary who would carry it on as a Christian hospital. It was quite a small hospital, with only sixteen beds, and it stood in six acres of land. Subsequently Dr. Verghese informed Mr. Gordon L. Fountain that, if a doctor would take it over and run it as a Christian medical mission, he would waive all conditions. Missionaries in the field considered that this was of the Lord and a trust was formed for the purpose.

Dr. R. S. Churchward had been relieving Dr. and Mrs. George Henderson at Sankeshwar in 1939, and it seemed evident that he should take over the responsibility at Tiruvalla. At that time there were 25 beds in the hospital. So many were coming for treatment that it was obviously necessary to enlarge the wards and to extend the nurses' living quarters to accommodate additional staff. In 1941 a men's general ward was erected, followed by a ward for women, the cost of the latter being largely met by Dr. Verghese and his family as a thankoffering to God for His goodness during 60 years of married life. This addition meant that the number of patients could be increased to 60. A grateful Indian planter, whose son had been brought through a serious illness, met the cost of the erection of two private wards, which proved an inestimable boon. Since then, further expansions have taken place, so that

Preparing a winnowing area   (M. Brown)

the main hospital now has 300 beds, while three branch
hospitals together can accommodate another 150 in-patients.
Over 10,000 inpatients a year are admitted and nearly 50,000
new outpatients are treated. There are over 1,500 operations in
the theatre and many minor ones in the casualty department. All
inpatients hear the gospel message regularly. In 1943 the
responsibility for training nurses was undertaken, involving
more buildings and additional staff.

Dr. Reginald S. Churchward took over responsibility for the
hospital in 1940. Mrs. Churchward left India in 1956 to be with
the children in U.K. but Reginald continued in the work until
his retirement to U.K. in 1960. In the early days, P. V. George,
author of the widely circulated book, *The Unique Christ*, was
closely associated with him in the work and Dr. Eric Rea helped
for a time. Many others have given loyal service there, including
Miss Freda Parkinson, Miss Pauline Hodgkinson, who was also
a great help in the Sunday school and in women's work in the

assembly, Miss A. Kathleen Elliott (commended from Australia in 1946), who retired in 1953, Mr. and Mrs. Don C. Adams, who also helped in the orphanage and in Bible teaching for students. Dr. and Mrs. Brian Smith (commended from Australia 1960), who retired in 1971, were also involved in training and Bible teaching of Indian nurses.

Dr. and Mrs. E. Gilmour Davies (commended from U.K. in 1956 in his case and from Canada the same year in the case of his wife, Lila) succeeded Dr. Churchward in 1956 and found themselves faced with all the types of case of western hospitals plus a variety of tropical diseases and complaints. Dr. and Mrs. K. John had left for further training in the U.S.A.

Miss Muriel E. Pitts and Miss Mary C. Miller (both commended from the U.K. in 1950) first joined Miss Edith Wallace at the orphanage at Nellikunnu, Trichur, to learn Malayalam, but later moved to Tiruvalla Hospital to relieve Miss Joyce M. Howes and Miss Kathleen Elliott. They found themselves in charge of a nurses' training school as well as the day-to-day nursing service and supervision of branch hospitals. Mary took over the responsibility for the administration and the nurses' education, and Muriel took the remainder. Miss M. Joyce Stuart (U.K. 1949) (now Mrs. John Whitehead) came to help for a while, and also at Kunnamkulam and Irinjalakuda.

Dr. E. and Lila Gilmour Davies

Miss Mary Bardsley, who had been working in the Godavari District, came in 1955, and in 1956 Miss Mavis G. Smith (now Mrs. D. C. Adams). Miss Elinor Shaw (Canada 1967), also gave help at the hospital. As the work expanded, more Indian nurses joined the hospitals, including Mrs. Annamma Zadaria, who became the first Indian Nursing Superintendent, Miss Pam Gabell (now Mrs. Culliam), Miss K. Joseph (now Mrs. Itty), Miss P. S. Annamma, Mrs. S. Chacko and Miss Elinor Shaco. There were tremendous opportunities for gospel witness among the patients. Miss Pitts and Miss Miller both retired in 1968. The assembly at Tiruvalla is 170 strong.

There has been a flourishing assembly at Kumbanadu for many years. Gordon L. Fountain (commended from New Zealand in 1933) joined the Noels there after spending a short time with the Nobles to learn the language. He helped with groups of Indian workers in evangelization but, after marrying Dr. Christine Vine (from U.K.) in 1936, they made their home at Alleppey, a seaport and the second largest city in the province. Dr. Fountain commenced a dispensary and they started to build up the small assembly, finding the greatest response from the depressed classes. A new hall was acquired and the assembly grew rapidly. In 1939 they moved to Muttampalam, a new area near Kottayam, and engaged in visiting and pastoral work and Sunday school teaching. In 1942 they moved alongside the hospital at Tiruvalla, and Christine helped in the hospital, while Gordon supervised the schools with 140 teachers and 3,000 children. Many young men were helped through the Bible schools. In fact, the greatest factor in the growth of the work was the regional Bible schools at Kottayam, Ernakulam, etc. In 1952 they moved to Nanthancode, near Trivandrum, and there devoted themselves to strengthening the assemblies and engaging in open air preaching. Several new assemblies had been started by ex-Bible school students and were growing healthily. A Bible school was started at Trivandrum and the students were proving a help to the local assemblies. In 1956 they returned to Kumbanadu, and Gordon travelled widely, visiting many full-time workers and dealing with problems in assemblies. After a full life of service, they retired from the field in 1967.

Gordon Junck, commended from New Zealand in 1934, also went to Kumbanadu to engage in study with the Noels and then

Gordon and Dr. Christine Fountain

joined Gordon Fountain at Kurianoor, continuing there after the Fountains moved to Alleppey. In 1937 Gordon Junck married Miss Norah Ardrey (commended N.Z. 1937) and four years later moved to Calicut, the largest city in Malabar. In 1942 they made their home at Kotagiri in order to establish an assembly there, while still helping at Calicut. He often assisted Mr. William C. Irvine in the editing of *The Indian Christian* and, on the latter's homecall, Gordon became editor. At the same time he became increasingly involved in preaching and teaching in many parts of the country. In 1959 he turned his attention to the north of India, where assemblies and missionaries were fewer, and engaged in ministry in Bible schools and in the setting up of the Delhi Bible Bhavan (Institute), which was sponsored by brethren from the U.K. and intended to provide accommodation and systematic teaching for young men in North India. Mr. Junck retired in 1960, Norah having returned home five years previously.

William T. Noble, commended from New Zealand in 1931, joined Alex Soutter at the boys' orphanage at Irinjalakuda to learn Malayalam and in 1932 moved to Kumbanadu to join the Noels and to engage in visiting villages with the gospel. In 1933 he married Miss Annie Kristensen (N.Z. 1931), who had planned to go to India to join her fiancé, Leslie W. Bowen. Although he died, she went ahead with her plans and joined Mr. and Mrs. John Evans at Malavalli and then, later, the Soutters at Irinjalakuda to help in the orphanage. She moved with the Soutters to Kumbanadu and was married there. She and her husband returned to Irinjalakuda, but made visits from there to Ernakulam and Cochin to help the assemblies there. In 1938 they moved to Cannanore on the Malabar coast. It was there in the 1890's that Volbrecht Nagel had worked with the Basle Mission, but the Nobles were the first assembly missionaries to undertake a personal witness in that very neglected area. They ministered to assemblies over a wide area until their retirement in 1951. Bill was called home in 1962.

Eric C. and Mary Phoenix (Aust. 1933), who had been working in Sri Lanka were invited to South India in 1946. They took up residence near Cochin in order to contact the naval base. Many officers and men were converted and a work was established. They also moved around ministering until they retired in 1965. Max S. Liddle, commended from New Zealand

Trivandrum—baptism
at assembly
(M. Brown)

Arthur S. G. Vine   (N. W. Dickson)

in 1959, joined the Fountains at Kumbanadu before marrying Miss Helen Vincent (N.Z. 1959) in 1960. In the following year they moved to Pathanamthittah, where there was no assembly, and reached out to the people at fairs, festivals and conferences. In 1965 they moved to Trivandrum, where there were two assemblies and found many opportunities for preaching and teaching and working among students. For a period they relieved the Fountains at Kumbanadu and gave help in the Bible school and assemblies, as well as teaching in Madras, Ootacamund, and other towns. In 1972 they settled in the hills at Coonoor and Max helped at Lushington School, while Helen became matron of the Hebron girls' school.

George W. Payne, commended from New Zealand in 1950, went first to Tiruvalla for language study. In 1951 he married Miss Bettie Graham (N.Z. 1950), who had joined Mrs. Julia Noel at Kumbanadu for language study. They made their home in Adoor and visited villages with Indian believers and also market places to preach the gospel. They helped in teaching small assemblies and holding Bible schools in Adoor and Kunnamkulam. From 1960 George helped in Madurai Tamil Bible School as well as in those at Ernakulam and Kottayam, while Bettie gave help in the hospital. They returned to New Zealand in 1966.

Miss Phyllis M. Shirtliff, commended from New Zealand in 1950 joined the fountains for language study, and engaged in meetings, camps and study groups for women and girls. In 1953 she undertook the promotion of Emmaus courses and also produced additional courses. In 1964 she had a stall in the centre of Kumbanadu for the Emmaus work and in the following year started a bookroom. Bible schools for women were greatly appreciated and in 1970 women commenced an outreach from Quilon.

Miss E. Sisley Putwain was commended from New Zealand in 1940 to help Miss Sundgren in the orphanage at Trichur. In 1943 she married Arthur S. G. Vine (U.K.) and they made their home at Kurianoor, where she helped in the training of Indian girls, while he engaged in village evangelism. They moved to Punalur in 1945 and helped in building up 30 assemblies in the area. In 1949 they moved to Tiruvalla and engaged in visiting villages and forest areas. Arthur also helped in the Bible school at Kottayam. The gift of a car in 1951 helped in taking teams of young men in village visiting and door to door evangelism until they moved to Tamil Nadu in 1954.

Kerala has produced a not inconsiderable number of capable Indian brethren, such as A. T. Mathew of Gudalur, V. P. Jacob, who is labouring at Bangalore, Samuel Thayil of Kollegal, M. F. Cherian who commenced the Tamil Nadu Bible School at Madurai, Poulouse Thudian at Cannanor, who has a radio programme, and many others whose ministry is being blessed.

Despite all the work that has been done in Kerala, there are large areas where there is still no witness for Christ, and prayer is needed that labourers will be raised up before it is too late.

16

The Country's Centre

Occupying practically the central area of India, Madhya
Pradesh is the largest state, being 171,223 square miles in
extent, and having a population of over 52 million. Eighty per
cent of the people are Hindus, the remainder being Muslims,
Christians, Sikhs and Buddhists. During British rule the area
was known as the Central Provinces and was ruled by a
governor, assisted by a legislative council. It is completely
landlocked and has no ready access to the sea. The capital is
Bhopal and the language generally spoken is Hindi.

The state mines a certain amount of coal and there has been a
serious attempt at industrialization. At Bhopal the Indian
government has constructed a colossal plant for the manufacture of heavy electrical machinery. Unfortunately the
capacity and the equipment installed are patently beyond any
demand which will be made in the foreseeable future. Indeed,
Keith Richardson has described part of it as 'the most fabulous
collection of metal-cutting and shaping equipment that I have
ever seen assembled in one place.'

There has been a gospel witness in the state for a very long
time, but the assembly testimony is of comparatively recent
date. T. A. Kurian served for some years at Sagar, where a
number of Hindus were saved. Cal Din cared for the assembly at
Bilaspur and reached out to the villages around.

A. James and Grace Rowberry (U.K. 1945) went to India
initially under the auspices of the Oriental Missionary Society,
but on a visit to Delhi, they met the McKenzies and went into

assembly fellowship and were acknowledged as assembly missionaries. James helped Alan E. McKenzie while Grace went to Kashmir to assist in a school for missionaries' children. He later joined her there. When partition came, fighting broke out and the school closed. The Rowberrys then spent a short time at Varanasi with Alex Smyth and others, starting a new assembly at Kripa. This work is now cared for by Mr. Shankar.

In 1953 the Rowberrys moved to Nagpur (Maharashtra) to relieve the Stokes for a time. A witness was then started by a few believers at Jabalpur, 175 miles north of Nagpur. Help was obviously needed there and both the Rowberrys and the Stokes moved there, being joined later by Osmond Peters. They travelled widely over this central state, distributing literature and contacting believers, sometimes walking all night, wading through floods, and completely exhausting their strength. Mr. and Mrs. Silas Fox were a great blessing there. Justus Samuel,

Bhopal—heavy electrical industry   (Indian High Commission)

T. G. Samuel and others at one time arranged intensive Bible study for young men and for workers from various states.

At Jabalpur the assembly was initially made up mainly of military personnel, but subsequently others moved in, including Mr. and Mrs. V. Gordon, an able and faithful couple. Mr. Gordon is a government employee. Large numbers of men and women are reached by God's servants in this centre. A number of brethren have been commended to full-time work by the assembly, including T. Devdas who works at Jabalpur: Mr. and Mrs. Gell, who are at Jammu; M. P. Solomon, who is in Belgaum district; and a young man, Alex, jailed in 1968 for gang fighting, who was converted in jail and studied to secure his B.A. and, on release, came to help in the work. Basil James helps in the work among university students.

Land has been secured for a new hall for the assembly and a start has been made on the building. Jim Rowberry and other brethren have services in the prison and have seen remarkable results from the preaching. Grace has travelled miles on foot, by cycle or rickshaw in order that hundreds may hear the gospel. At one time she had 40 children's meetings a month as well as a Sunday school in her home. Because of ill-health she has now

T. A. Kurien and David B. Burt at Sagar convention

Sanchi—the Great Stupa   (Indian High Commission)

Jim Rowberry and Alex at baptism

had to return home leaving James to oversee the completion of the new hall.

The work done by Bakht Singh in a number of Indian states (although not particularly in Madhya Pradesh) cannot be ignored. J. H. Kane gives a fair comment in *A Global View of Christian Missions*, pp. 122–3, when he describes Bakht Singh as 'India's outstanding evangelical church planter.' He says that he 'is the leader of a dynamic indigenous movement which is probably the fastest growing group in India. The three hundred assemblies, patterned after the Plymouth Brethren, are entirely self-supporting, self-governing and self-propagating. A special feature of the movement is the great Bible conferences attended by thousands of Indian Christians under tents or in the open air. Eating, sleeping, and living conditions at these conferences are purely Indian, very simple and most economic. The ecclesiastical accoutrements, so necessary in the West, are completely missing. The preachers live by faith, supported by the freewill offerings of the Christians.'

Bombay—"The gateway to the west"   (Indian High Commission)

Trombay, Bombay—Canada-India Reactor   (Indian High Commission)

17

Gateway to the West

The third largest state in India, Maharashtra, has an area of 118,832 square miles. It has been suggested by many that it should be divided into two and that a new state of Vidarbha should be carved out of its eastern part, but it seems unlikely that this will happen now. It has a population approaching 63 million, most of whom speak Marathi, although English is also in common use. The capital is Bombay, frequently referred to as 'the gateway to the west.'

It is a state with great potentialities. The cotton lands of the Bombay Deccan are a source of considerable prosperity, and the city of Bombay commands two 'gates' through the Ghats. Poona, which was formerly the hot-weather capital of the Bombay Presidency, stands near the crest of the Western Ghats and commands one of the gaps leading to Bombay. The rivers near Bombay have been harnessed to supply electric power to the city's cotton mills. The trade flowing through the port is very considerable and Bombay is virtually the nerve centre of Indian commerce. Textile, chemical and light engineering industries provide employment for large numbers. The state has a reasonably stable government and the possibilities for development are almost limitless.

Yet Maharashtra is a state with a grievance. Two-thirds of the people employed in Bombay, for example, belong to other states. It seems to be a disadvantage in Maharashtra to be a native Maharashtran, and the sense of frustration is building up to resentment. Bai Thackeray says, 'Basically we are not against southern Indians. We want to see local people get a fair chance and an opportunity of jobs now monopolized by foreigners.' It is significant that the Shiva Sena movement, formed to protect the interests of the native minority, helped the local Congress Party to defeat the popular Krishna Menon at the 1967 general election, although the electorate had previously returned him with enthusiasm. Since that time, feeling has become very much stronger. Situations of this kind obviously affect the manner of approach in Christian witness if offence is not to be caused.

Bombay, which is built on an island, has a magnificent natural harbour and is one of the busiest seaports of the east. Its international airport at Santa Cruz now handles jumbo jets from various parts of the world. The rising skyscrapers and the countless flyovers and its cosmopolitan population make it one of India's most modern cities.

Assembly witness in Bombay commenced in 1932, when H.Handley Bird and a few believers met in the home of Mr. McAffee to break bread. Unfortunately this witness did not last for long, but it was recommenced in 1934 when H. Handley Bird took up residence in the city and opened his flat for the purpose. Within two years it became necessary to hire a hall in the centre of the city to accommodate the numbers coming to the meetings. Mr. Bird gathered around him young men to whom he offered residential accommodation and to whom he became a spiritual father. He used to bring them together daily for Biblical instruction and would secure jobs for those who were unemployed. Despite his age and frailty, he was an indefatigable open air preacher and would frequently walk through the streets carrying sandwich boards bearing gospel texts. Harold Avery joined him in Bombay later.

He invited Wilfred S. Durham, then serving the Lord in Bangalore, to join him in the work in Bombay, and when Handley died in 1938, his mantle fell upon Wilf. He had laid a solid foundation, and the testimony prospered through the ministry of Wilfred Durham, and George White and of business brethren like Peter E. Perry. From 1942 to 1947 the assembly, which had moved to its present location at Queen's Mansions, saw a great deal of blessing in the salvation of scores of Allied Servicemen stationed in or passing through Bombay: many of these are now serving the Lord in various parts of the world. It

G.L.S. Press: office; bindery department; Mercedes letterpress machine; editorial department

was during this time that Wilfred Durham commenced the literature ministry which developed in 1942 into the Gospel Literature Service.

The G.L.S. supplies gospel literature in ten major languages in India. It has 275 titles in books and booklets and 91 in tracts (in fifteen languages). In the war years it was difficult to get tracts from Britain, so this work was started. In 1942 Wilf was a trained printer and in 1948 he was able to obtain some additional equipment from the U.K. He was joined that year by Mr. and Mrs. William E. Thompson and in 1949 by Mr. and Mrs. Ian T. Hall (all from U.K.) and in 1950 by Miss Amy N. Liddell, who had previously been engaged in children's and Sunday school work. The work expanded rapidly and Miss I. D. Gordon and Miss E. Gordon also gave help. Wilfred died suddenly in 1951 at the early age of 39, but Mrs. Christine Durham (U.K. 1938) still carries on the work. In 1961 more machines were added and additional premises acquired. Since then more machines have been installed and the work continues to grow.

William E. Thompson landed in Bombay in 1943, having been converted on a troopship en route. He was soon brought under the teaching of Wilf Durham and gained an appreciation of New Testament principles. With a vast influx of servicemen to the north-east, many being converted to Christ, the need for literature both in evangelism and teaching became paramount. Bill Thompson was attracted to the work of G.L.S. and gave all his spare time to it until he was transferred in 1946. On demobilization he joined an assembly and took training in printing and in 1948 married Dorothy Fenton. They were commended in 1948 and went to Bombay. When Wilf Durham suddenly died in 1951, Bill had to take over. The press grew dramatically using primarily the ministry of Indian teachers like Bakht Singh and Jordan Khan. In 1969 Bill had to return to U.K. for the sake of the family.

G.L.S. continues to grow. An important feature of the work has been that the printing work is now not only a viable business but is able to make a growing contribution to publishing work in the vernacular and in particular to encourage creative writing by nationals which is so essential for future Christian work in India.

The English-speaking assembly has now 150 members. In 1940 a new testimony started in the Marathi-speaking industrial sector of the city, in which not only Wilf Durham, but Miss Grace Brayne and Miss Esther R. Burnett laboured for a time. That work is now maintained principally by P. L. Patoley, who was converted through Mr. Durham, and who was commended to full-time service in 1952. He has also been the means of establishing Marathi assemblies at Ambernath and Dharavi. Mr. and Mrs. Gordon Ritchie helped in these for some time. Stuart R. Stokes went to Bombay in 1935 as a bank official, and shortly after his arrival he was baptised by H. Handley Bird. He immediately became active in assembly fellowship and service, and was Superintendent of the Bombay Sunday School for three years till he was transferred by his bank to Calcutta. For a short time he continued there till he was called up for military service; he held a commission in the Indian Army and in various spheres in and outside of India he maintained a steadfast witness for the Lord. On his release from the Forces in India in 1947 he associated himself with Gordon Junck at Kotagiri. He married Esther Burnett and they helped in the work at Nagpur from 1949 to 1963 when they went to Lonaula. They went to Nagpur at the invitation of an Indian brother from Kunlu, T. A. Kurian. There are reasons for thinking that the history of assembly work at Nagpur may go back well before the Indian Mutiny. In 1966 they moved to Poona where they remained until after a brief visit to Goa they retired to U.K. in 1971.

In 1953 another testimony was started at Bandra, a predominantly Roman Catholic suburb, initiated by Mr. and Mrs. Harold McGregor, who had come to Bombay in 1952 to help in the gospel literature work. He and his wife went to India in 1939 and 1940 respectively with an interdenominational mission, but they severed their connection with the mission in 1948 and joined the assembly at Delhi, being later commended to the work by New Zealand assemblies. They spent some time at Ranikhet (Uttar Pradesh), but had to leave because of the high altitude. They started a hostel where fifteen young men could live and engage in systematic Bible study. This assembly prospered through work in the area and also through the ministry of the Living Waters Broadcast, which Harold launched that year, and through the Emmaus courses a few years later. The Bandra assembly moved into its own spacious hall in Santa Cruz in 1969. There is a large Sunday school, and the assembly is led by local brethren, all of them business men.

The McGregors retired for health reasons in 1968.

Mr. and Mrs. Alexander J. McLeay (N.Z. 1966) came to Bombay to join Mr. Harold McGregor in the Living Waters Radio Broadcasts. He was a qualified electronics technician and upgraded the equipment. In 1967 he visited Dr. Edward S. Short at Narasapur to modernize his equipment and to enable him to produce more and better Telugu broadcasts from there.

Telugu assemblies were also formed at Worli, Chembur, Chatkopar and Santa Cruz. The Worli assembly is the parent group and commenced functioning in 1962: it is composed mainly of working-class people from West Godavari. They have no full-time workers, but the brethren are very active in gospel work. Ministering brethren like S. Prabhudas from Andhra Pradesh visit them periodically to give help. Until Harold McGregor left Bombay in 1968 he gave part of his time to Bible teaching in these groups. After the McGregors left, the McLeays undertook full responsibility for the broadcasting work. In 1970 the Far Eastern Broadcasting Company opened a new station on Seychelles, and messages are now readily heard all over India.

In 1967 an assembly was established in its own premises at Thana, the industrial hub of the Bombay region and 25 miles north of the city. There is an excellent Sunday school and an active outreach to the outlying villages, particularly among the Marathi-speaking people. The work is maintained by brethren working in offices and factories. Gordon Ritchie gave considerable help to this assembly.

A Tamil-speaking assembly was started at Dharavi in 1951 and a Malayalam-speaking assembly at Sion in 1966. The latter received accretions, *inter-alia,* from young men coming from Kerala in search of employment. It has a full-time worker to assist in the work, but the Dharavi assembly is maintained by brethren working in mills and factories.

Bombay and its suburbs still present opportunities for evangelism and church planting, but there is a need for more full-time workers if a serious advance is to be made. There is also a very great need for able teachers of the Word to visit these assemblies from time to time. Alfred H. Chote, J. M. Davies and William Walker have given appreciated ministry over the years, but able teachers from overseas could make a valuable contribution, particularly if those who have served in India in

G.L.S.—despatching
literature at Worli

the past, could visit Bombay and other cities. There is, of course, a financial problem, because funds cannot be exported from India, but that should not prove insoluble.

The attractive hill city of Poona, to which the state government moves in the hot season, has been the scene of gospel witness for many years. A number of earlier missionaries started their service with the Poona and Indian Village Mission, but others have also worked in the city and surrounding area. Mr. and Mrs. Hubert T. Kimber of Australia served the Lord here from 1949, spending most of their time assisting in the small assemblies in the area. They had previously been with a Mission and had joined the assemblies. Mr. Kimber was used in a teaching ministry in many parts of India. They retired in 1958. Mr. and Mrs. Stuart R. Stokes also spent some time in the work here. Dr. Sundesaran has been a great shepherd and a gifted minister in Poona.

Mr. and Mrs. Gordon Ritchie moved to Poona from Bombay in 1958, when there were a million Marathis there. They concentrated on cottage meetings, usually conducting at least ten a month. Later they engaged in special teaching meetings for evangelists and teachers in Andhra Pradesh, as well as Bible camps in Belgaum and a Bible-selling mission to Goa. In 1969 they moved back to Bombay and spent a year in meetings in and around the city, where there were then thirteen assemblies. They retired to New Zealand in 1970.

Miss Eileen V. Garrard (Australia 1962) is engaged in village work, Bible school teaching and outreach to women and girls in the Poona area. She also has a Bible study programme for

Amy N. Liddell

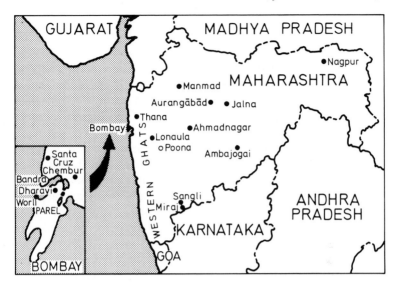

college students and teachers and meetings for nurses. She is heavily involved in camp work and organizes camps and conferences for Bible teaching. A qualified school teacher, she has schools in villages and trains potential girl leaders, as well as helping in the local assembly.

In 1971 K. M. Mathai, Harold Suttle and D. Awale joined together in Aurangābād and started as assembly. The testimony steadily increased and in 1976 Mr. and Mrs. B. G. Mridude were commended to full-time service in the assembly. The gospel is being consistently carried to nearby places and another assembly was commenced in New Aurangābād in 1978. The work is also progressing at Jalna, 40 miles away.

At Manmad the assembly started in 1965 through the work of P. R. Awale and H. Suttle, and the hospel is being taken to many of the surrounding villages and towns. P. R. Awale and A. H. Ingles are now responsible for the work and the testimony is progressing.

Miraj is a railway junction, where D. Awale used to visit and preach the gospel. In 1963 K. S. John, who is serving on the railways, was transferred to Miraj and slowly the work prospered and an assembly was established. In 1972 D. Awale went to Ambajogai to preach the gospel and then in 1974 people were touched by the Lord. These became the nucleus of an assembly at Sangli and the work has continued to progress. Through the ministry of P. L. Patoley, there are also two small assemblies at Ahmadnagar.

Lest it should be deduced that conditions are comparatively easy, it may be as well to glance back a few decades. In *Indian Realities,* p. 1, W. C. Irvine quotes a happening in 1937 'of a man being sacrificed to propitiate the rain god in Gurnpur, where drought is prevailing this year. The victim was decoyed from another village. In chains, with his forehead smeared with ash and vermilion and with a garland round his neck, the man was paraded through the streets to the accompaniment of the beat of drums, and shortly after he was beheaded with a sharp axe before the village temple. The head was placed reverently by the villagers before the deity.' On receiving the news of the human sacrifice the police seized the body and arrested 25 persons, including the headman of the village, the perpetrator of the crime, and the priest who officiated at the ceremony.

18

A Landlocked State

(Map page 260)

Manipur is a relatively small state of only 8,628 square miles. It is completely landlocked and borders on Burma. The mountains between India and Burma form a continuous curve from the north-east of Assam to Cape Negrais. The Patkoi Hills in the north broaden out into the Naga Hills and to enclose the Manipur Plateau. Then the Lushai Hills and Chin Hills run south from Manipur. It is, therefore, a fairly mountainous state and altitudes vary from 2,500 feet to 10,000 feet.

Most of the people are farmers and the main crop is rice. The population is over a million and the people are of Mongolian origin and the language used is Manipuri although Hindi is becoming prevalent. There are, however, 40 tribes, each of which has its own dialect. The largest tribes are the Hama, Patte, Thankhual, and Kuki, all of whom are nominally Christian, but there is no obvious sign of a new life in the vast majority of cases. Tribes such as the Koms, Annal, Chiru and Waring have never heard the gospel, and since the villages of the interior can be reached only on foot, it may be long before the message reaches many of them. Ninety per cent of the population is Hindu. The capital is Imphal and other main towns are Ukhrul and Moirang.

Christianity was brought to this area by American missionaries in 1874, but their activities were limited to the northern parts of the state. In 1909 Presbyterian missionaries entered the southern part. Other missionary societies followed.

Assembly work had its beginnings in Churachandpur in

Children receiving medical treatment   (R. Duff)

1968, with the arrival of C. F. John. At Imphal, the capital, Thangliensing Sungte, who belongs to the Hama tribe, commenced in 1975. His wife, Rebecca, is also a very able worker and they have been able to present the claims of Christ to many in the few years they have been in the city. Assemblies have been established in Imphal, Churachandpur and at seven other centres. Most of the members of the assemblies are from the Kuki tribe. There are seekers in other villages and the Sungtes are reaching out to them.

There is a very great need for literature and for Sunday school materials. There are many problems associated with the work. There is a lack of transport in the hilly regions. Roads are narrow and can only be traversed by jeep or by walking. This restricts visiting village assemblies.

The Manipur assemblies sent T. Jamthang Kuki to the Delhi Bible Institute for two years' study and since 1975 he has been serving the Lord in Manipur as a full-time evangelist.

At Churachandpur the English high school still has 300 pupils.

19

State Within a State

The end of British rule in India left the country with quite arbitrary borders between states and not unnaturally, when independence came, pressure built up for adjustments to be made on the basis of language. 'Nehru had consistently argued that India was now one nation, but as prime minister of an independent India, he was obliged to recognize the force of the "local nationalisms" within the country to the extent of agreeing, against his real wishes and better judgment, to the redrawing of state boundaries by the criterion of language.' By the 1960's the process of reorganizing the country into 'linguistic states' was well advanced, although representations are still continuing in regard to some areas. It was thus that it was decided in 1968 that the new and autonomous state of Meghalaya should be carved out of Assam to cater for the special needs of the Garo, Jaintia, Khasi and other tribal peoples. It is really a state within Assam, however, and very much dependent upon its agriculture.

Meghalaya is a relatively small state, covering only 8,660 square miles and the population is over a million. Its capital and administrative centre is Shillong, which, of course, is the capital also of Assam. It is essentially a tribal state and the languages spoken are Garo and Khasi. Its physical features are very similar to those of Assam, but it is situated at 3,000 to 10,000 feet above sea level. It is drained by the Brahmaputra and its tributaries, but while there is a marshy belt, the alluvial lands farther from

the river are very suitable for the growing of rice. In the area of the Garo Hills, oranges and other fruit trees are also cultivated.

Apart from Shillong, there are no large towns or cities. The state is not very densely populated and most of the people live in the villages which spread through the valley and into the hills.

The gospel was brought to the state by the Baptist Missionary Society and the first conversion recorded was as long ago as 1859. Sixty per cent of the population is nominally Christian. There are no assembly workers and no assembly in Maghalaya.

20

A Baptist Stronghold

(Map page 260)

Nagaland is a small state of only 6,368 square miles. It is a land of hills, some rising to 12,600 feet. It is another landlocked state, bordering on Burma. The Nagas insist that they are a distinct race. Phizo, their underground leader, says, 'We are not Indians and will never become Indians.' Some, in fact, have turned to China for arms and equipment for use against India. The Indian forces met with armed resistance from the Nagas almost as soon as the republic was formed and at one time, although there are few more than three quarters of a million Nagas in India, the Indian army had 40,000 troops pitted against the rebels. One group is demanding a completely independent Nagaland (see V. Elwyn's book, *Nagaland*). Nehru ultimately agreed that they should have a state of their own and this was formally inaugurated in 1963. But fighting broke out again in 1968. As Dick Wilson says, *op. cit.* p. 233, 'There is a religious element in this tangled dispute, since 60 per cent of the Nagas are Christian converts. British missionaries have been most active among the hill tribes, and have tended to become involved with them politically as well.' No doubt this is one of the contributory factors in the government's reluctance to admit any new missionaries.

The capital of the state is Kohima and other towns are Dimapur, Mokokchung and Tuensang. The people have a Mongoloid origin. The main languages are Assamese and a local Naga dialect. Most of them are farmers, cultivating paddy.

Dusting of paddy crop   (Indian High Commission)

The first Christian missionaries were Baptists who came in 1871. They reached most of the towns, but there are many villages in the interior which have never heard the gospel. The Baptist churches are well organized and will not allow visiting preachers to preach unless they carry recommendations from Baptist leaders, comparable to assembly 'letters of commendation.' The Baptists claim that 90 per cent of the population is Christian, but 60 per cent would probably be a more accurate figure.

An assembly was commenced at Dimapur in 1974, as a result of the labours of Alex Abraham. Others could be started in some of the remaining towns if workers were available. There are over a dozen tribes in Nagaland and each tribe has its own dialect. Workers are needed to reach out to such.

At the risk of repeating what has already been said, we venture to quote James and Marti Hefley regarding the conditions in Nagaland. In *By Their Blood*, pp. 152–3, they say, 'The greatest Christian advances have been made among the Nagas and other tribal peoples of North–east India with a background of pagan animism. In the 1920's over a hundred thousand were baptised under the direction of American Baptist missionaries. The Hindu majority of India resented and feared such a large conclave of Christians in one area. After independence there were incidents of discrimination, ... An influential missionary had already encouraged the Nagas and their kinsmen to think of organizing their own nation. A Christian tribesman formed a revolutionary government. The alarmed Indian government banned all foreigners from the area and sent in troops. The hostilities have continued for thirty years, with many killed on both sides. Reports persist that Chinese communists are supplying arms to the Christian rebels and promising to help establish a Naga nation. The unrest has spread to predominantly Christian tribes along the borders of Bangladesh, Burma, Laos and Vietnam.'

21

The Princely State
(*Map page 142*)

Formerly part of the Madras Presidency, Orissa is located on the Bay of Bengal and is bordered by Bihar (with which it was once linked) and West Bengal on the north and by Madhya Pradesh on the west. The River Mahanadi, which flows by Sambalpur and Band, bisects the state from west to east. It covers an area of 60,178 square miles and its main towns are the capital, Bhubaneswar, Cuttack, Puri and Berhampur. The language of the state is Oriya. The population is over 26 million, of which 1.7 per cent is Christian.

It has the distinction of being the first state in which one of the former princely rulers of an Indian state has made a 'comeback'. In 1967 the Maharajah became the chief minister of Orissa, when he led the Swatantara Party to victory in the Orissa elections.

At the same time, it is a state with problems. It is one of the areas in which in 1966–67 there were cases of actual starvation. Difficulties are also being created by the increase in population. Despite all the publicity on family planning, the state's population is rising at what is regarded in some quarters at an alarming rate. Between 1960 and 1970, for example, the number of school children quadrupled and it is understood that this was repeated in the following decade. The percentage of literates is only 26. The strain on teaching staff, buildings and educational materials is quite serious, but a greater problem is the lack of employment which already exists.

In the capital of Bhubaneswar, a town of idol worship, where

School-children   (R. Duff)

Kuraput District—buying record players and receiving free gospel
records
(C. L. Lucas)

there are more than 200 Hindu temples, T. M. Sebastian and M.
S. Thomas started an assembly testimony, but work is not easy.
In the coal mining town of Talcher, M. Selvanayagarm has
established an assembly, a good percentage of the members
being Tamils. A small assembly is also functioning at
Sambalpur and A. C. Jacob gives his full time to the work. Only
1.5 per cent of the population is nominally Christian.

In 1968 the State of Orissa passed a law imposing a penalty of
one year in prison or $1000 fine for missionaries convicted of
converting minors, women or untouchables. If 'force, fraud or
exploitation of hunger' are used, the penalty can be doubled.

22

Country of the Five Rivers

(Map page 162)

In the north-west of India, bordering on Pakistan and hemmed in by Himachal Pradesh and Haryana, the state of Punjab is now only 19,445 square miles in extent – roughly a third of its size before it lost territory to Pakistan and Haryana. Its name is derived from a Persian word meaning 'five rivers', referring, of course, to the Jhelum, Chenab, Ravi, Beas and Sutlej. It is largely a dry sandy plateau, part of the extensive Punjab Plain and bounded by the Outer Himalayas. The population is over sixteen million and its capital (which it shares with Haryana) is Chandigarh, and its languages are Punjabi and Hindi. It is partly industrialized, the chemical factory at Nangal, for example, having been erected at a cost of ten million pounds and employing 2,500 people.

Mahatma Gandhi was very critical of some of the conditions in the Punjab (and, of course, in other states as well). He wrote in *Young India* in 1925, 'Some of the national habits are bad beyond description, and yet so ingrained as to defy all human effort. Wherever I go this insanitation obtrudes itself upon my gaze in some shape or another. In the Punjab and Sind, in total disregard of the elementary laws of health we dirty our terraces and roofs, breeding billions of disease-producing microbes and founding colonies of flies. Down south we do not hesitate to dirty our streets, and early in the morning it is impossible for anyone, in whom the sense of decency is developed, to walk through the streets, which are lined with people performing functions of nature which are meant to be performed in

Amritsar, Golden Temple   (R. Duff)

seclusion and in spots which human beings need not ordinarily
tread. In Bengal the same tale in varying form has to be told; the
same pool in which people have washed their dirt, their pots,
and in which cattle have drunk, supplies drinking water. These
are not ignorant people; they are not illiterate; many have
travelled even beyond the borders of India.'

Arthur and Rita Stedman (N.Z. 1952) were instrumental in
starting the testimony in the capital. After labouring in other
parts of India, they moved to Chandigarh in 1961. At that time it
was a city of 100,000 and by means of door to door evangelism,
distribution of literature and finally a tent campaign, they were
able to commence a small assembly in 1962 with regular
meetings in the bookroom. For the next six years they were
engaged in a strenuous programme of colportage work, visiting
Muktsar and other centres and selling thousands of Gospels.
Arthur visited many large fairs and bazaars with a team of

Ludhiana—
distributing
gospels
(S. F. Warren)

Ludhiana—
main road;
Harry G. Aspinall
on bicycle
(S. F. Warren)

Ludhiana—
Harry G. Aspinall
outside
gospel hall
(S. F. Warren)

distributors. The war between Pakistan and India restricted activities and meetings considerably, but after hostilities had ceased, the work went on again. Amritsar was another target for the literature team, and gospel campaigns and tent missions were held in Chandigarh and other centres. Rita helped at times at Hebron Girls' School. Many were converted. One Sikh wanted gospels for each of the 300 men in his section of the army. The Stedmans returned to New Zealand in 1969.

The work at Chandigarh suffered greatly from the loss of the Stedmans and of Lewis Samraj, who had to return to Bangalore to care for his family. A small group of believers is carrying on, but full-time workers are badly needed in this important city.

The work at Ludhiana was started by V. T. John of Kerala, who moved there from Ambala about twenty years ago. In 1965 he was joined by Mr. and Mrs. Harry Aspinall and Mr. and Mrs. Daniel Taylor (Canada 1953). The latter laboured at Ambala from 1954 to 1965. In 1978 V. T. John moved to Chandigarh. Dr. Nambudripad, who is director of the C.M.C., cares for the Ludhiana assembly. Dr. Nambudripad has a remarkable testimony. He came to U.K., a high caste Hindu, in 1956 for post-graduate medical studies in neuro-surgery, studying in Scotland and Bristol where, through the reading of God's Word and influenced by the life of a Christian nurse, he came to Christ. When he made the news known to his family in India two members came to England to take him back. Though subjected to many forms of coercion he has stood firm in his faith and has been widely used throughout India as a speaker. The Ludhiana Christian Medical College has attracted numbers of Christians of all denominations from all over India, and many joined the assembly, which has a fine hall. Dr. Margaret A. Ingram (later Mrs. George N. Patterson) was at Ludhiana for several years, as well as other assembly workers.

Farther north at Jullundur is a small assembly, which is helped greatly by a brother from South India, who is a bank employee but spends his spare time serving the Lord. Some progress has been seen here.

23

Home of the Baronies

The second largest state in India, Rajasthan has an area of 132,149 square miles. Prior to independence, it was known as Rajputana and comprised a number of feudal baronies, but these have all been merged into one state. The Rajputs were of colourful and legendary fame and gave their name to the group of native states and to the whole region. It is an extensive plateau, sloping towards the Ganges Valley on the north-east and drained by tributaries of the Ganges. In the centre lies the Aravalli Range and it is bounded on the south by the scarp of the plateau which forms the Vindhya Range. Part of the country is a sandy waste, with hills and waterless valleys – the Thar desert. It is a land of contrasts, of bitter cold and searing heat, of lush wheat fields and arid desert. Millet, wheat and barley are grown and considerable areas are forested. Cotton and woollen goods are still made and Rajasthan's handicrafts are known all over the world.

The capital city is Jaipur and the languages spoken are Rajasthani and Hindi. The population is sparse by comparison with that of some other states being just over 34 million. The majority are Hindus, but there are also Muslims, Jains, Sikhs and Christians. Eighty nine per cent of the population is Hindu and the number of Christians is extremely small. To the Hindu it is wrong to take life. At one temple, rather surprisingly rats are regarded as sacred and devout Hindus feed them with grain! Literacy in Rajasthan is only nineteen per cent, as compared with 67 per cent in Kerala, for example.

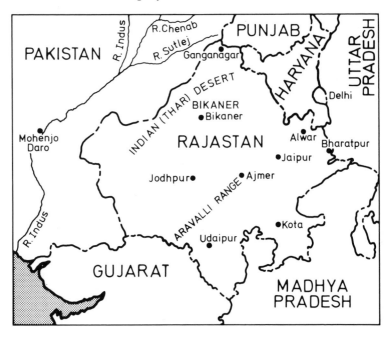

Although assemblies were established in many centres in South India over a century ago, very little was done by them to reach other parts of India. It was not until 1960 that any brethren from the southern assemblies penetrated into the north-west frontier state of Rajasthan – 1500 miles from Kerala.

In 1960 a young graduate from the Hindustani Bible Institute at Madras went to Kota and commenced distributing literature. He held meetings on his first Sunday, but trouble broke out the next day. The house at which he and other Christians were living was surrounded by a mob of people who were opposed to the gospel. Tracts and gospels were burnt and the young man himself was beaten up. They were threatened with death if they persisted in preaching, but the police intervened to save further trouble. In the first month six believers were baptised and an assembly was started. Opposition continued, but souls were saved and added to the assembly. After a year, M. A. Thomas remained at Kota, but Philip Abraham moved to Gwalior in Madhya Pradesh, K. C. John moved to Jaipur and Paul Kant to Ajmer.

After two years another brother, V. M. Dorairaj, joined them to acquire a knowledge of Hindi and then moved to Alwar in the north-east corner of the state. Alwar was the headquarters of a princely family during British days and is well known for its palaces, museum and armoury. Unfortunately Mr. Dorairaj was martyred by opponents of the gospel in 1966. Then T. J. Joseph and K. S. George went to Rajasthan, and the former took Dorairaj's place in Alwar. Here he found a young nurse from Kerala working in the hospital. Before long she resigned her appointment and married him, and they have been serving the Lord in Alwar ever since. The assembly goes on well.

K. S. George went to Bikaner in 1965, a border district adjoining Pakistan, and deep in the Thar desert. During the war with Pakistan, he was often in danger, but the Lord protected him. He was able to start an assembly there in 1966.

George David in 1963 and later T. V. Cherian went to Jodhpur (population 319,000), and C. L. Jose went to Ganganagar. In 1972 T. S. David, commended by the Kota assembly, moved to Lakheri. Assemblies have been commenced in all the places where these brethren are working.

In Kota and Alwar (population 213,000 and 100,000 respectively) a serious attempt has been made to raise the level

Jaipur   (P. Marsh)

Jaipur   (P. Marsh)

of literacy. Many schools have been started, where Hindu children are taught the Scriptures each day. In Kota a small Bible school is also functioning in Hindi and English. About 200 have been baptised at Kota since the work started. Many have moved to other places for employment, but this has only spread the testimony. The assembly at Kota numbers over a hundred, and that at Jaipur has 50 members. Assembly halls have been built at Kota, Jaipur, Alwar and Bikaner.

In view of the importance of Jaipur, the modern capital, known as the 'pink city' of Rajasthan, with its textile and railway industries and obvious commercial significance, the assembly would benefit from full-time workers able to teach and to evangelize the area. K. C. John went there in 1961 for several years, but help is still needed. Ajmer is a large flourishing town, with food and textile industries and a railway workshop, and is clearly a strategic centre. Its population is 262,000. Paul S. Kant went there in 1961 for a few years and an assembly was established, but much more could be done.

M. A. Jos worked for some time in Bharatpur, and help is still needed. Udaipur, with a population of 163,000, is a city of lakes and island palaces, but with a tremendous spiritual need. T. V. Cherian worked there from 1969 and was followed by Mr.

and Mrs. M. G. Samuel in 1977. There are still large numbers of villages in Rajasthan which have not heard the gospel and there is no one to go.

In the bombing of Frankfurt am Main during the war, one of the casualties was the somewhat imposing St. Mark's Church. The roof had gone, the walls were shattered and the interior was completely ruined. From the gaping hole that was once a door, the charred and burned pews, the dust and debris from the walls and roof, the myriad fragments of coloured glass from the windows, all presented a picture of unrelieved destruction and destitution. The pitiless weapons from the sky were incapable of distinguishing church from factory. St. Mark's was forsaken and derelict.

Yet amazingly, amidst the chaos and confusion of rubble, one piece of sculpture thrust itself in stark splendour against the unclouded heaven. There, above the shattered remnants of the high altar, was Thorwaldsen's superb statue of the Christ, completely intact. Despite all the devastation and the pall of forlorn hopelessness which seemed to hang over the desolate building, the statue was unharmed. All else had been reduced to crumbling ruins, but the Christ was intact. Irreparable damage might surround it, but the statue remained in all its perfection.

One who picked his way through the shapeless heaps of rubble might ultimately have stood to gaze with admiration upon the wonder of the sculptor's work, almost miraculously spared to display its perfection. But a closer examination would have revealed that the statue had not been entirely exempt from the agony the church had suffered. It was almost perfect – *but the Christ had no hands!*

Is it not still true? *The Christ has no hands.* It is ours He is pleased to use to achieve His purposes. It is ours He takes up to do His will. *The Christ has no hands.* Are they ours for which He waits?

> 'Take my hands and let them move
> At the impulse of Thy love.'

In states like Rajasthan, with such large cities with only one worker, the need is urgent.

Sowing rice   (Tear Fund)

Madurai—Temple tower
(S. F. Warren)

Mt Zion chapel
(S. F. Warren)

Ootacamund—missionary picnic

(P. A. Pritchard

Reading the Word

(Tear Fund

24

The Valley of Rice

(Map page 260)

Located in the eastern Himalayas and bounded by Tibet, Bhutan, West Bengal and Nepal, Sikkim is a small state of 2,745 square miles and the population is roughly 345,000. The state religion is Mahāyāna Buddhism, but a large proportion of the population is Hindu. There are also some Christians and Muslims.

Sikkim became an Indian state in 1975 and it is inhabited primarily by the Lepchās, who are indigenous to Sikkim, the Bhutas, who came from Tibet, and the Gorkhalis who came from Nepal. The languages spoken are Sikkimese, Bhuttia, Lepchā, Khaskura and Nepali. Originally under Tibetan rule, the country was ruled from the 14th century by the Namgyal dynasty, but has lost parts of her territory from time to time. The East India Company, for example, acquired the Darjeeling district in 1839.

It is a land of great variation in altitude, climate and vegetation and it has a great variety of birds, butterflies and flowers. It is extremely fertile and is known to the Sikkimese as Denjong, the Valley of Rice. The economy is mainly agricultural and the principal crops are rice, maize, millet, oranges, ginger and soyabean. Coffee, zinc, lead, silver and gold are mined, and there are a number of small industries.

The Church of Scotland Mission began work in Sikkim in 1886 and established some elementary schools. The Free Church of Finland about 80 years ago also conducted schools and organized industrial work in rugs and cloth. According to

Alexander McLeish in *The Frontier Peoples of India*, p. 133, 'Missionaries reside at four centres and number two men, one married, and four simple women workers. There are about thirty Indian workers. It will be seen, therefore, that the whole work is confined to a small area only and that there is great scope for extension, specially through really efficient Indian workers. A church might well come into existence in Sikkim which would carry the gospel to the closed lands on its frontiers.' There has been apparently no attempt on the part of assemblies to commence a work in this state, despite the obvious potentialities.

25

The Tamil Country

Tamil Nadu is a state of 50,333 square miles, with a population of over forty eight million. The Tamil language is universal in this state. The state occupies most of the southern foot of the peninsula, only a relatively narrow strip being left to Kerala. Its capital, Madras, is almost on the border of Andhra Pradesh, and has a population of three million. Among other large towns are Vellore, Kanchipuram, Cuddalore, Thirwarur, Rajapalaiyam, Nagercoil and Madurai, but it is Madras which is best known.

Assembly work in the state virtually dates back to A. N. Groves' first visit to India in 1833. It was then that he was urged to go to the Tirunelveli area to help a German missionary named Rhenius in his difficulties with the C.M.S. At that time he met John C. Aroolappen, who had been converted through C. T. E. Rhenius, and the young man travelled with Groves through south India, translating for him where necessary. Obviously Aroolappen imbibed from the older man those principles of service which the latter followed personally and, when he left Groves, he implemented his mentor's principles.

He was only seventeen when he first met Groves, and when he launched out into full-time Christian service, he refused any salary, but earned his living by agriculture. Other converted Indians gathered around him and they built a village, which they called Christianpettah in North Tirunelveli (now part of Ramnad District), where they worked, worshipped and preached. A printing press was set up and Aroolappen translated a number of tracts. In 1859 he wrote that 'five

Tamil Nadu artisans   (Indian High Commission)

hundred had renounced idolatry, but 172 only learn and hear
attentively.' Fourteen native elders were working with him and
there were thirty village stations with 673 persons under
instruction. He engaged constantly in itinerating and bazaar
preaching and ran several outstations with schools.

When the 1859 revival broke out in Ulster and the north of
England, he and others gave themselves to prayer that it might
spread to India. Extraordinary scenes followed. Many believers
publicly confessed their faults and, deeply exercised, searched
the Scriptures. There was a great putting away of open sin.
Hundreds were converted and many went out to preach the
gospel. As in Ireland and America, as in the Welsh revival of
1905, and other occasions, there were strange happenings,
physical prostrations, dreams, visions, speaking with tongues,
and other outward signs, some of which seemed to be
counterfeits of God's work, but there was unquestionably as real
a visitation of the Holy Spirit as in the 1859 revival in Ulster.
For five years these remarkable manifestations continued, but
they did not spoil Aroolappen. When he died in 1866, it was
with the words, 'For me to live is Christ, and to die is gain', on

his lips, and he left behind him to carry on the work his son and twenty converted men. To this day there are Christians in Christianpettah.

Unfortunately, when Aroolappen died, his son invited the C.M.S. to take over the assemblies he had founded, but many of the believers were unhappy about the changes in the form of service, and in 1895 H. Handley Bird was invited to visit the area to ascertain what he could do to help.

In 1896 Mr. and Mrs. Thomas H. Maynard settled in Tirunelveli and soon afterwards started a boarding school for boys in Ramanathapuram at a site which they subsequently named Mount Zion. The village which grew up there is situated on the borders of the Ramnad and Tirunelveli Districts, lying about 100 miles north of Cape Comorin, the southern tip of India, about nine degrees from the equator and almost at sea level – the hottest part of India. Rainfall is scanty, crops are poor and people work hard to wrest a living from the soil. Yet this place was destined to become one of great spiritual blessing and the scene of the labours of many missionaries, in succeeding years. Later on, meeting-rooms were built in ten villages and schools were maintained in 21 villages.

By 1900 the Maynards had been joined by Miss Marian Darling and Miss Minnie L. Teague (U.K. 1898) and later that year by Mr. and Mrs. Frank A. Rose (commended from Australia and U.K. in 1899 and 1901 respectively) and Alfred Young. Because of a famine in north India, H. Handley Bird decided to send a hundred orphan boys from Gujarat to Mount Zion. Buildings had to be erected to house them and a boarding school was erected on a bare granite spot, which was formerly the site of a Hindu temple. When the boys arrived, they were in a terribly emaciated state and some of them did not survive. Their arrival augmented the numbers in the small school they had already established. Thus a village came into being, with its own post office, schools, orphanage, dispensary and assembly. But work was not confined to Mount Zion. It was a centre from which the missionaries visited numerous villages over a wide area, preaching the gospel and helping assemblies and schools. There were 124 villages within ten miles of Mount Zion. New workers came and launched out to establish centres in other parts of the district. Able ministers and preachers from the large Mount Zion assembly visited at least twenty village assemblies regularly. Now there are no foreign missionaries there and the work is in the hands of Indian brethren alone.

In addition to caring for the orphans and teaching them trades, Mr. Maynard was continually engaged in visiting villages, sometimes conducting as many as six meetings in a day at different villages, as well as selling thousands of Scriptures and distributing a countless number of tracts. He was usually accompanied by a faithful Indian helper named C. N. Ramaswami. Many Tamils professed faith in Christ and were baptised. Baptism, of course, was the crucial point with believers in India. There was always great opposition to this from Hindus, and when a convert was baptised, it almost inevitably involved active persecution and often physical suffering. The work was arduous. The nearest railway station was 40 miles away and a bullock cart (not the most comfortable of conveyances) was the only means of transport to visit the

Tamil Nadu Pongal festival   (Indian High Commission)

villages. Disease, such as cholera, smallpox and typhoid were rampant and, for superstitious reasons, the majority of the people were opposed to being inoculated.

George and Frances Hill (U.K.) both felt the call to the mission field, but were hindered by ill health. Eventually the doctor agreed to their going and in 1931 they joined the team at Mount Zion. They long recalled their first experience on arrival at their destination. They were taken to a bare, whitewashed room, with a rough mud-brick floor. The room contained two wooden cots, a small roughly-made table and two wooden chairs. They were warned not to put their cases on the floor because ants would come through the floor and attack them. They were also informed that the furniture was only on loan until the village carpenter could make some for them. When they had survived the initial shock, they discovered that the conditions were quite normal and that it was wise to forget the comfort and luxury of home in England. Miss Edith Bates, who later became Mrs. A. George Phair, joined the work at the same time and phlegmatically adjusted herself quickly to the conditions.

Miss M. Winifred Dickson, commended from Belfast in 1948, joined Miss Annie Watson at Ilanji near Tenkasi, but then moved to Sankaranayinarkovil, where Miss M. Eccles (Tillie) was working (also commended from N. Ireland in 1946). Miss Josephine Lacroix, commended from Pondicherry in 1947, joined her in the work there in 1951, visiting villages by bullock cart and talking to women about the Lord. They had regular dispensary work in Sankaranayinarkovil. Winifred and Josephine moved to Mount Zion to relieve the Hills and were fully employed in the orphanage and dispensary, but found some time to visit the many small assemblies in the area. In 1961 they moved to Tiruchirapalli (then Trichinopoly) 150 miles north, where P. I. Jacob had laboured.

Among others who worked at Mount Zion for a time must be numbered Augustus and Grace Morling, who first went to India with the Baptist Missionary Society in 1930 and 1933 respectively and saw much blessing in a number of fields, not excepting the Mountains of Death, near Salem (so named by the hill people because of the high incidence of malaria and blackwater fever there). In 1949 they met Mr. Henry T. Gander and in the following year moved to Mount Zion, later

The Nilgiris   (P. A. Pritchard)

transferring to Ilanji. They were subsequently invited to Bangalore to help with the Tamil assembly there. In 1951 Mr. Morling started *Sthanabathy* (Ambassador), a Tamil periodical, and also undertook the preparation of radio programmes for F.E.B.A. When Dr. Billy Graham went to India in 1956, he was asked to record all his messages in Madras and Palayankottai, and these were later relayed to the ten largest cities in South India. Augustus also established a Tamil publishing house and handed over 25,000 books to Indian elders. Unfortunately they had to retire in 1968 because of ill-health, but are still able to work among Indian immigrants in Britain and to provide cassettes for use by Indian nationals throughout the world.

Mr. and Mrs. Frank A. Rose, who gave such valued help at Mount Zion, settled at Vadamalapuram and engaged in a varied ministry through dispensary, school and village work and saw many brought to the Saviour before they retired in 1935.

Mr. William T. Revell (N.Z. 1905) also joined the Maynards in 1905 to learn Tamil and then engaged in preaching and visiting in Solapuram and Christianpettah. There were over twenty day schools in the area and local Indian brethren were engaged in teaching and in other outreach. In 1911 he moved to Vadamalapuram and continued in literature distribution and preaching. In the following year, he married Miss Emily H. Russell (U.K. 1909), but she died within two months. For a time he relieved Mr. and Mrs. Henry T. Gander at Naraikkinar in the same district, where they had gone in 1910. In 1916 he married Miss Dora M. Annear and they made their home at Kadayainallur, where they built a hospital and a small dispensary. Dora engaged in a very fruitful medical ministry and soon gained the confidence of the village women, while her husband was using his motor-cycle to reach surrounding villages, teaching and preaching and training local brethren to carry on the work. Miss Annie Watson joined them there in 1920. In the same year the Revells returned to Vadamalapuram to supervise the school work in the absence of other missionaries and then in 1922 went to Mount Zion to relieve the Youngs for a couple of years. Following that, they returned to Kadayainallur and, at the same time, supervised the work at Naraikkinar. Wilfred A. and Hilda Munnings, commended from Canada and U.S.A. respectively, went to Naraikkinar in 1952 and began learning Tamil, in preparation for taking over the responsibility

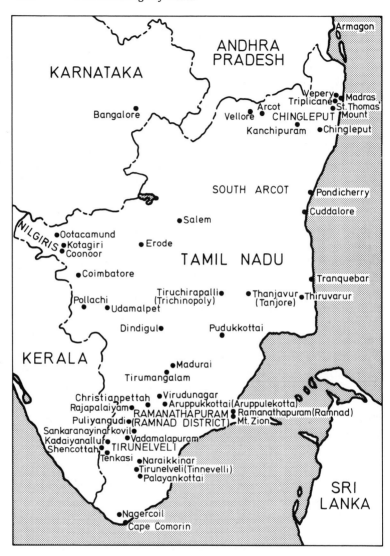

for a number of schools. In 1953 Dr. R. E. Harlow suggested that they should undertake the translation and distribution of Emmaus courses. They did this in addition to running the schools. Then they were able to transfer the school work to Mr. and Mrs. Samuel Dharmakkar in order to be free for ministry in the local assemblies. Subsequently, they took over the running of the Beaulieu Home at Coonoor and gave help in ministry in various places until their retirement in 1969.

A gospel coach was built in 1935, large enough to take a tent and enable Will to take a number of Indian brethren with him to carry when they were distributing literature and preaching the gospel. His labours were blessed and several assemblies were established. Subsequently, centres were established also at Virudunagar, Sankaranayinarkovil and Tenkasi. In 1942 the Revells moved to Pondicherry, but found conditions were difficult because of political unrest and differences between the French and Indian authorities. A jeep, fitted with an amplifier, was acquired and proved a great help in village preaching. Ronald Appleby (U.K. 1949) joined in the work but after a short while moved to Vadamalapuram and then to Puliyangudi in Ramnad District. In 1956 the Revells moved to Bangalore and then to Ilanji before returning in 1960 to Vadamalapuram. Mrs. Revell died the following year and William moved to Virudunagar to live with Tom Brown (who had been commended from N.Z. in 1929) until his own death in 1966.

The work at Vadamalapuram owed its development to a number of missionaries. Apart from the Maynards, the Revells and the Roses, Miss Jessie L. Treweek and Miss Bertha Townley were commended from New Zealand in 1914 for this work. Bertha engaged in work among the children in the orphanage and boarding school and in visiting women in the villages. Within three years Mrs. Rose's health failed and Bertha took over the responsibility of the school, with the assistance of Jessie Treweek. There were many difficulties but they proved God's sufficiency. In 1924 Bertha married Mr. Ernest V. Brewerton and went with him to Malaysia to work among the Tamil-speaking Indians there.

Jessie Treweek gave help to the Revells in the schools and in visiting women in the villages. Later she went to Kadayainallur, where a witness had been commenced, and devoted herself to visiting the villages and distributing literature. She often camped out with Indian fellow-workers in the course of the visiting programme. During the absence of Mr. and Mrs. Frank Rose, she took charge of the school. With others, she visited a number of festivals at Sankaranayinarkovil and sold large quantities of literature there. She spent a year relieving Mr. and Mrs. E. Brewerton in Malaysia, but returned to India in 1934 and went to Naraikkinar to relieve the Ganders. Here she took charge of the boarding school with 70 girls, as well as operating three day schools.

Thomas T. Brown had joined Will Revell at Kadayainallur to learn Tamil. There he distributed thousands of tracts and sold Scripture portions in the markets and at festivals in the villages around. He spent some months in 1933 at Pondicherry, where a new hall was being built, and also gave assistance at Mount Zion. In 1936 he married Jessie Treweek and they made their home temporarily in Naraikkinar, helping with the school work and village visiting. But they moved to Virudunagar the following year to start a new work in a town with 80,000 inhabitants. They placed the Scriptures in every house in the town and district and also distributed 40,000 tracts, in their first year. They acquired a new hall in 1940 and the work grew rapidly, and the literature distribution had a profound effect.

Mrs. Brown died in 1942, after twelve months' illness. Tom continued at Virudunagar, while periodically providing relief at Mount Zion in the school and other activities. He made many pastoral and teaching visits also to Nadurajapuram, Kadayainallur, Ilanji and other centres, and helped Indian brethren start new assemblies at Rajapalayan and Aurpuhottai. He spent much time encouraging local believers and instructing them in Scriptural principles. A new work was started at Shencottah and also at Tirumangalam, among those saved being a temple priest, a doctor and his wife, two teachers, a retired police officer and some excise officers. Team witness was quite a feature at that time and, on one occasion, 50 brethren went as a team to evangelize Tenkasi, which then had a population of 40,000. In 1973 many of the older missionaries rejoiced as Aroolappen's great grandson baptised 25 converts, which 500 people watched. After a long and fruitful life of service, Tom Brown died in 1974. He was a most disciplined man and told S. F. Warren when they were travelling together in South India that the messages he gave each day in several centres were always based on his morning reading for that day. At his homecall he was found with his Bible and *Echoes Daily Prayer Guide* open on his chest.

Among other helpers at Vadamalapuram were Mr. and Mrs. David J. H. Hill (N.Z. 1949), who heard the call to India through Miss Myrtle E. Talbot when she visited their assembly.

Coonoor

Mrs. Hill was the daughter of Mr. and Mrs. Ernest V. Brewerton of Malaysia and her mother had previously worked in the area. They engaged in the school work at Vadamalapuram, where there were then 230 girls in the boarding school, and Joyce was able to help in the orphanage. They were also involved in literature distribution and in the sale of Scriptures. Quite a number of the girls in the school were saved. After helping for a brief period in the Missionary Rest Home, they set about strengthening the village assemblies. For a while in 1953 they gave help at Ootacamund and Coonoor and in 1956 settled at Pondicherry, where the Revells had so faithfully proclaimed the gospel. During the last months of the latter's ministry there a number had been converted, including several Customs officials. The Hills assisted the assembly in putting up the new Bethel Hall in 1957. They also produced radio programmes in Tamil and helped in the Emmaus correspondence courses, as well as giving practical help in maintenance at Ootacamund. They eventually returned to New Zealand in 1961 to engage in secular employment.

Miss Kathleen McNaughton, commended from New Zealand in 1950, spent a year on the staff of Hebron High School at Coonoor, and then went to Vadamalapuram to learn

Outside Madurai
gospel hall

Tamil. She married Ron Appleby in 1952 and they gave assistance first at Mount Zion, before moving the following year to Dindigul, 40 miles north of Madurai and having a population of 100,000. There they helped in the Emmaus work, conducted meetings among children and adults, visited festivals and generally engaged in village evangelism. Because of Kath's ill-health, they were compelled to return to New Zealand in 1955, but went back to India in 1960 for a year, before transferring to Fiji to continue working among Indians there.

Miss Ruth M. Taylor, commended from New Zealand in 1935, joined the Revells at Kadayainallur to learn Tamil and to engage in work amongst women and girls in the villages. Dogged by ill health from the start, she was advised by other missionaries that she would never stand up to the climate and the strain and might as well return home at once. With characteristic determination, she carried on for over 40 years of fruitful service for God. She was never a good patient: she once discharged herself from hospital while still suffering from typhoid fever. With a clear vision of the regions beyond, she set aside prospects of a good New Zealand marriage, to give herself completely to the Lord's work. Mastering the Tamil language, she developed the qualities of a good all-round missionary. A good nurse, counsellor, visitor, youth leader, open air meeting enthusiast and Scripture distributor, she proved equally at home with hospital nurses as with dejected women prisoners, as acceptable to religious Hindus as to needy Anglo-Indians. She adopted several Indian girls, for whom she cared and to whom she gave a Christian upbringing. Her 'adopted' daughters have always thanked God that her love embraced them in their deep need. Unrivalled in hospitality, she maintained an open house day and night. There was always room for another mattress on the floor.

In 1943 she undertook the supervision of the school at Vadamalapuram, which then had 82 students, but she also found time for medical work in the dispensary and for visiting the villages with the Scriptures and holding open air meetings. In 1948 she moved to Sankaranayinarkovil, but still maintained an interest in Vadamalapuram.

In 1952 she moved to Madurai, which then had a population of 800,000, and where there was the largest Hindu temple in south India. The temple of Meenakshi had four towers, 160 feet high, and dominated the whole city, and a large number of temple prostitutes were always to be found in its precincts. Ruth commenced meetings for women, a Sunday school in English, another in Tamil, and weekly meetings for the nurses at the government hospital. Later, she added to her programme regular meetings for women at the local prison. The small assembly, founded by M. E. Christian and his family, was very active and had several outreaches, and Indian brethren also started a small Bible School in 1955. A new hall was built and a large number of unconverted started to attend the assembly meetings. At the rededication of the temple in 1963, there were 400,000 visitors to Madurai and 40,000 tracts were distributed among them. As in many parts of India, there were disturbances in the early 1970's, with riots in many places, but the unrest led

Madurai

to a desire to hear the gospel and often 150 women would be listening to the missionary's message. Miss Ruth I. Warner (N.Z. 1960) joined Miss Taylor in 1962 and they worked together in the city. Ruth Warner decided to give more time to the preparation of material for national workers to use in their meetings and also to the training of Indians in children's evangelism. Workshops were held for Sunday school teachers. In 1972 she became Teacher Training Secretary for the Tamil area of the Christian Education Evangelical Fellowship of India, giving her many opportunities for training Indians in children's evangelism. At a major crusade in the city in 1975 there were 6,000 at the meetings, and both Ruth Taylor and Ruth Warner took part in the follow-up of converts.

Among the interesting features of the Madurai area, Bob Glasgow, *op. cit.*, p. 75, describes one of the less attractive. 'The burning ghat near Kurrukhalpalti, south of Madurai, did not cremate its bodies very well, for the people were poor and could not afford much fuel. The stream beside the ghat was dry all the year, except during the monsoon, so that what we saw in the heat of May looked like a dry ditch with femurs and skulls and smaller bones bleaching in it. The local custom was that once a year on a known night a local priest would take one of the skulls from the valley of dry bones and walk around Kurruk village

Tiruchirapalli—P. I. Jacob baptising Hindu convert (M. Browne)

Tiruchirapalli, near Bethany Gospel Hall—fakir collecting alms (M. Browne)

Tiruchirapalli—toward the Hindu Temple   (M. Browne)

with a candle burning inside the skull. The villagers shut themselves inside their houses for very fear on that night, for they believed that if they saw the light inside the skull they would go blind.'

M. E. Cherian went to Madurai in 1943 and found many young believers in need of teaching, so he started a short term Bible School there in 1956.

Miss Jocelyn E. Cameron, commended from New Zealand in 1958, joined Ruth Taylor at Madurai. During language study at Ootacamund, she was able to help Mrs. Lorna E. M. Hill at 'Montauban'. In 1960 she married Kenneth R. Pullenger, who had been commended from New Zealand in 1957, and they made their home at Madurai, assisting in Bible school teaching, Bible class and Sunday school, and in village evangelism. They even held meetings on the roof of their house. In 1964 they took over the Emmaus work from the Munnings and shifted the office to Madurai. In 1966 they had outstanding campaigns, 10,000 people attending some nights. Indian helpers were added to the Emmaus staff and soon over 100,000 courses were sent out. Demonstrations and riots later hindered the work and Kenneth was faced with serious difficulties at Madras, where he had gone to help at a stall during a festival. They eventually retired in 1968.

Kenneth R. Pullenger Emmaus Home Studies

Minna A. Noschke—selling gospels   (D. J. H. Hill)

Many others, including Miss Minna A. Noschke (U.K. 1921), Miss Amy E. Wharton (U.K. 1924) and Miss Grace M. Stalley (U.K. 1936), gave help in the schools at Mount Zion and the area. The boarding schools at Naraikkinar, Vadamalapuram, Mount Zion and Kadayainallur are now the responsibility of Indian brethren. The 23 village schools in the area were gradually taken over by the brethren: the government continues a grant in aid in respect of these, but the capital expenditure is the responsibility of the brethren, and is often a serious problem.

Edward J. and Rosalind Honeyman met at the Bible Training Institute at Glasgow. Soon after they heard Mr. and Mrs. George Hill at a missionary conference and, as a result, went to Mount Zion in 1967. Ten months later the Hills returned to the U.K., leaving them in charge of the orphanage with twenty boys. Ted developed the agricultural side so that the boys would have a trade when they left school. He also built a 40-bed hostel at Vadamalapuram. They returned to the U.K. in 1970, leaving the orphanage in the care of A. Paul Vasan and a committee which he had formed.

There was a dispensary at most of the stations in the area for many years, but there was no missionary doctor. In 1954 Miss

Noschke suggested that medical work at Vadamalapuram would bring a crowd for the local Christians to evangelize. The population of the area was mainly descendants of the original converts at the first orphanage and they were still using educational and medical work and the children's home as means of evangelization. Obviously these people would have a predisposition to listen to the gospel message and the hospital would bring them to the centre. Ultimately, Dr. Rhona M. Oliver came and the work then began immediately to expand. Others came to help, including Miss Kathleen Owen from 1955 to 1956, Miss Alison McGregor from 1956 to 1965, Miss E. Alberta Feil from 1960 to 1980 and Mrs. Revell from 1960 to 1961, as well as Mr. and Mrs. W. Alexander Munnings, Dr. Shobha Linton, Misses Tillie Eccles, Wilma G. Farringdon and Elsie M. Phillipson. Elsie gave help subsequently at Dindigul, Ilanji and Shencottah before settling at Tenkasi.

E. Alberta Feil, commended from New Zealand in 1959, joined Ruth Taylor at Madurai to learn Tamil, before going on to relieve Alison McGregor at the hospital. She also undertook visiting of women in the villages. She tells of one high official

Vadamalapuram—
patients arrive
(S. F. Warren)

commenting that it was not until he had seen the treatment his wife received at the hospital that he realized the true character of Christianity. The number of patients steadily increased and each one was spoken to personally and many trusted the Saviour. Miss Josephine C. Mitchell went to Angamally in 1908 and spent many fruitful years there.

Assembly work in Tiruchirapalli (Trichinopoly) started in 1948 when P. I. Jacob, who was in secular work in Malaysia, resigned and went with his family to work for the Lord in Tiruchirapalli. He had a sound knowledge of Tamil and commenced regular meetings in his new home and in the homes of friends. A few were saved and a small assembly started in his home. M. Winifred Dickson and Josephine Lacroix joined the work here in 1961, by which time the assembly had grown considerably and they were able to give help in many of the activities. Over the years the assembly had been helped by the ministry of A. Leonard Goold, Silas Fox, Alex Smyth, Kevin H. Osborne, Arthur S. G. Vine, J. M. Davies, Dr. E. Gilmour Davies, John H. Warburton, J. Stewart McNaught, Charles Wigg, Alfred H. Chote, Tom T. Brown, A. Jim Rowberry and William Walker. Visits were paid by Winifred and Josephine to Tanjore and Pudukkottai. Dr. Joseph Mathuram exercises a profitable ministry in the assembly and in cottage meetings.

Tiruchirapalli—Bethany Hall   (M. Browne)

Ootacamund has proved a fruitful field for quite a number of missionaries. Alfred H. Chote, commended from New Zealand in 1952, joined Thomas T. Brown at Virudunagar to study Tamil but moved to Bangalore two years later. In 1955 he married Miss Valda Duske (commended from New Zealand in 1954), and they made their home at Aruppulekotta, which then had a population of 50,000. There was a small assembly there and they were able to help in teaching other assemblies in the vicinity. In 1960 they moved to Ootacamund and engaged in itinerant preaching and teaching over a wide area. Meetings were held in halls, pandals, homes and in the open air. Together with Indian brethren, Alfred visited festivals, fairs, tea plantations and schools. Much literature was distributed. In ministry it was customary to have three sessions a day of an hour and a half each. In camps and Bible schools, they were also able to instruct and encourage Indian workers.

To provide missionaries with some respite from the plains in the very hot weather, rest homes were acquired in the Nilgiris at Ootacamund and Coonoor and many workers have given help here. The property is on a commanding site, 7,500 feet above sea level high above the valley where is Hebron School. Mr. and Mrs. C. W. Thomson (N.Z. 1910) spent some years here, Mrs. Thomson also acting as matron of the Hebron Mission School for Girls. They retired in 1942 and he died in 1951 and she in 1962. Mr. and Mrs. Stewart P. Collings (N.Z. 1962) also gave two years' help at 'Montauban' at Ootacamund and at 'Beaulieu' in Coonoor.

Miss M. Gertrude Mosley (N.Z. 1920) joined Mr. and Mrs. Edward Buchanan at Kamakerai (Karnataka), visiting women and engaging in assembly activities. Ill-health compelled her to return home in 1925, but she returned in 1930 to help at 'Montauban' until 1936. She came back once more in 1949 to assist Miss Myrtle Talbot at the rest homes, but in 1955 joined Mrs. Marjorie Webb at Rajahmundry in the Godavari in village visiting and literature distribution. After four years in Bangalore, she retired in 1960 and died in 1973.

Miss Myrtle E. Talbot (N.Z. 1932) spent six months at 'Montauban' before becoming matron of Breeks School for Missionaries' Children, but she returned to 'Montauban' in 1938 and served there for over 20 years. During the war, the home was opened as a leave centre for troops and over a thousand soldiers enjoyed its facilities and some hundreds were saved in consequence. In 1950 'Beaulieu' at Coonoor was added to take the overflow of guests. Failing health restricted Miss Talbot's activities in her later years and she retired in 1960 and died in 1966.

The third largest city in India is Madras, and of its population of over three million, about 200,000 profess to be Christians, although many are without a true knowledge of Christ. The city was formerly the premier presidency town of India, a power in the land when Bombay was still a tributary to a foreign king, when the site of Calcutta was merely a muddy wilderness, and Karachi did not exist. It has a long history. A. C. Rose writes, 'A mile or two southwest of the city, rising abruptly out of the level land, is a hill known as St. Thomas' Mount, the reputed site of the martyrdom of the once-doubting apostle in A.D. 68. The most southerly suburb of Madras is still known as San Thomé in his honour. A colony of Christians known as Syrians has existed on the west coast since A.D. 400, thought to be the fruit of the labours of missionaries from Persia. According to the Anglo-Saxon Chronicle and also the testimony of William of Malmesbury, King Alfred sent two ambassadors, Sighelm and Athelstone, in A.D. 883, with alms for Rome and instructions to continue their journey to St. Thomas in India.'

"Montauban", 1923

But it was material, rather than spiritual, considerations that led the English to Madras in the 17th century. Cheap and excellent muslins and printed calicoes lured Francis Day, the East India Company's agent, to abandon Armagon, 60 miles to the north to establish himself in the territory of the Naick of Chingleput. There he built a 'factory' at Madraspatram and enclosed it with a battlemented wall, naming it Fort St. George.

'The town is a mixture of ancient and modern, east and west, crowded slum and healthy suburb. Coconut palm plantations and terraced ricefields persist, bordered by buildings and modern roads. The ramshackle bullock-cart wanders about in the path of the electric tramcar, and the limousine with its closely curtained windows slides past the comfortless junks, both laden with purdah women. The fishermen launch their crude catamarans and sail out into the path of great liners and other ships. The old fort remains, an appealing relic of the past. Its stout bastions and gates, which withstood the French cannonade, are now merely ornamental, but they enclose ancient buildings and modern barracks. Prominent is the tall, severe spire of the Church of England building which, in troublous times, was a mark for enemy gunners.'

In such surroundings the work of evangelism has been carried on for over one and a half centuries. It was here that Henry Martyn looked his first on India's appalling need, and soon after wrote in his diary, 'Now let me burn out for God!' Most of the major missionary societies are represented in the city. At the turn of the century, a young Englishman named F. Howard Oakley, an accountant of 'exclusive' background, went to India with the intention of maintaining himself by secular work while serving the Lord. After a brief stay in Bangalore, he moved to Madras and commenced to practise his profession in that city and continued there until his death in 1961. He contacted a few like-minded believers and they began gathering together on an 'open' basis, to remember the Lord, and for prayer and ministry. The early meetings were held in the home of one of the believers. Later A. C. Rose of the Madras Railways joined them. He was an able speaker, writer and Bible scholar, who lived in Madras for about 25 years, during which he identified himself with the assembly and all its activities.

In 1888 Sir Robert Stanes had asked George Müller if he could recommend a young missionary to come out to

Madras—
H. Handley
Bird's house
(M. Brown)

Coimbatore to help in the assembly work. In 1923, H. Handley Bird, who had come to India in 1888 at George Müller's suggestion, and had worked in various places in South India, including Tirunelveli, Coimbatore, Coonoor and Cochin, although he knew no Indian language, decided to move to Madras. He hired a large house in the centre of the city and used it primarily as a hostel for young men coming to the city for study or work. He lived with the young men, training them and teaching them the Word of God. He even found jobs for them. When there was a cholera epidemic, he personally cleaned the toilets and latrines lest his young brethren should contract the disease. Although a cultured and dignified man, he paraded round the streets with sandwich boards with gospel texts. Many of the young men who lived with him 60 years ago became leaders in assemblies, and his name and memory are still revered.

A room in the house was set apart for meetings and it was here that the assembly met. Other accommodation was reserved for visitors to the city, who were thus able to help in the work. H. Handley Bird conducted Bible studies at 8 a.m. each day and, when he was away, he ensured that Jesse Webb, J. M. Davies or someone of their calibre took his place. The studies commenced with Genesis 1 and went through the whole Bible, a chapter a day. They proved of such blessing that many believers in the vicinity took advantage of them. Later, Silas Fox became a regular visitor and held special meetings once or twice each year. A. H. Roberts, who regularly attended the Bible studies, became a full-time worker. T. G. Samuel also laboured to maintain the assembly witness in Madras and to expand the work.

The premises leased in 1923 soon became inadequate for all these activities and for the assembly needs and in 1926 a larger hall was acquired capable of seating a hundred people, but this soon had to be extended. Mr. and Mrs. William A. Kimber (U.K. 1925) joined H. Handley Bird in the work. Miss M. L. Teague from Tirunelveli, who knew Tamil, and Miss H. Elsman (U.S.A.) moved to Madras and started witnessing among women and children. The latter also had a work among nurses in English. Miss Gladys M. Hughes-Games came to Madras in 1924, having been commended from U.K., and proved a valuable addition. Hundreds of students who attended Bible classes or assembly meetings over the years have been saved. Indian brethren began to make their contribution, and when Mr. Bird left, they took on the responsibility he had carried.

He left for England in 1931, making it clear that he would not return to Madras because the work was well-established and the assembly could carry on without him. A. H. Roberts took over the responsibility for the hostel and the assembly elders assumed the responsibilities of the assembly. Evangelization was given a prominent place, and house meetings, open air meetings, Sunday school work, young people's work, etc. were carried on assiduously.

For some years there was only one assembly, but many members travelled long distances. Occasional meetings were held for the breaking of bread in a number of other places for the benefit of those who were unable to travel so many miles to the meetings. In due course, however, a plot was purchased at Vepery in 1956. A Sunday school was started in Triplicane in a Hindu locality and the Sunday school soon had 100 children from Hindu homes. Gospel meetings were started and by 1955 an assembly was established there. The work prospered and there are now several mature brethren carrying on the work, and there are ten assemblies in Madras.

An important feature of the work at Madras is the Assembly Bible and Training Institute commenced in 1974 and which was originally located at Poona, but in 1978 was transferred to Madras. Courses are for eight academic months, divided into two semesters. There is also a condensed course for workers. Accommodation is restricted to 20 students. Over 60 past students are now serving the Lord full-time in various states in India. Max S. Liddle (N.Z. 1959), who was principal 1974–76, worked first in Kumbanad, where he married Miss Helen Vincent in 1960. Later they moved to Partharamthitta, where they engaged in systematic house visiting. They also gave help in Trivandrum (Kerala), Coonoor and Madurai, but returned to New Zealand in 1977. Other lecturers have been Silas C. Nair, Victor J. Sunderaraj, K. V. Samuel, George David, Lewis J. Samraj, J. Stewart McNaught, Alfred H. Chote, William Walker, A. James Rowberry, R. S. Mirajkar, Peter G. Ferry, Alex Smyth, G. D. James, Fred G. MacKenzie and many others.

In Royapuram another assembly started in the early 1950's, the nucleus being drawn from the original assembly. Many people were converted and added to the church. Local brethren also commenced a work in an industrial suburb of Madras and an assembly was formed there. Despite all that has been done, there is a realization that the work has not kept pace with the increasing population, and the assemblies are exercised about this matter.

Ian E. McCleary (N.Z. 1958) took up residence initially at Narasapur and then at Rajahmundry in Andhra Pradesh and engaged in teaching and visiting surrounding districts. In 1961 he married Miss Jennifer Whitehead (N.Z. 1961), but the following day went down with hepatitis and they had to return to New Zealand for a while. When they came back in 1963, Ian

Madras—Bible study group   (C. Redit)

Madras—singing grace before breakfast   (C. Redit)

commenced lecturing at the Hindustan Bible Institute at
Madras, many of the members of the staff of which were in
assembly fellowship. He still maintained a close association with
the assemblies and gave help wherever possible. In 1972 he left
H.B.I. and became field director of a theological extension
course for training nationals in Bible study.

Miss Colleen Redit (N.Z. 1964) went to India to join Ruth
Taylor and spent some time at Madurai, Bangalore and
Coonoor. In 1965 she commenced the distribution of milk
powder (provided by Christians in New Zealand) to the needy
in Madras. In 1966 she moved to Madras to work amongst
women and girls, and to participate in counselling women
students at the Hindustan Bible Institute. Later she added
house and hospital visiting, classes for nurses, rallies, and
training women as leaders. Considerable political unrest
developed in Madras. Also, in 1970, over 10,000 liquor shops
opened after years of prohibition and the need for spiritual help
increased accordingly. In 1973 permission was granted to place
a Bible showcase in the main Madras railway station, where it is
seen by thousands every day, and translations in twelve
different languages make it possible for all to read and
understand.

The Hebron High School for Girls and the Lushington Boys'
School, both originally staffed by assembly teachers, were
amalgamated in 1974. The junior school was transferred from
Coonoor to Ootacamund and the old Hebron property sold.
There are about 250 boys and girls at Hebron from all parts of
the world, half of them being children of missionaries and half of
business people of European and Asian origin. The school is
headed by Jonathan and Sue Ingleby. Ron Russell (now a
retired missionary) chairs the council, and Una Marshall
(Australia) looks after the senior girls' hostel a mile away. Whilst
the staff may miss some of the experiences of the missionary
who is mixing with unconverted villagers every day, their work
is no less essential and the presentation of the claims of Christ to
these young people has not been without effect.

Lushington takes its name from C. M. Lushington (a
brother of the then Governor of Madras), who in the 1820's
sited his home on a lovely hillside which had been recently
purchased from the Todas of Manjackalmund. Over a century
ago, Dr. Pope, later head of Bishop Cotton's School at

Lushington School

Bangalore, ran a school at Lushington, but the present one is on the site of its namesake's former residence and opened in 1961. Rupert T. S. Darling, the first headmaster, paints vividly the picture of the troubles, difficulties and blessings of the first few years. Initially there was a close association with Breeks School nearby and Mr. Fox, the principal of Breeks, taught at Lushington. Many have given help there over the years. Alex Smyth and Bob and Heather Glasgow were there in the 1960's. Miss Elizabeth A. Brohn (N.Z. 1959) first went to Koyyalagudem, but moved to Nidadavolu in 1960 to join E. Joyce Harding. Later, she took up teaching at Lushington School, whilst also helping in the hospital at Ootacamund. She returned to New Zealand in 1963 and married Robert A. Hamill.

On the hill above Lushington School is a village of the Toda tribe, with its crawl-in entrance and smoke-filled huts, which has intrigued anthropologists for years. A large round stone stands there, which a Toda youth must lift before he is considered a man and is allowed to marry.

How many workers there were during the years. G. R. Daniel, associated in his early days with Bakht Singh, gave

Breeks School   (P. A. Pritchard)

himself to a wide ministry and saw quite a number of assemblies founded. J. Sundaram, who was greatly helped by Gordon Junck and A. Leonard Goold, left his profession as a school teacher to become a full-time servant of Christ and was blessed in preaching, particularly to children. C. N. Ramaswami, converted through W. H. Stanes, accompanied H. Handley Bird to Tirunelveli and was greatly used in ministry with A. C. Rose, Alfred Young, Henry T. Gander and William T. Revell. J. C. Aroolappen's grandson. Thurgiah shepherded the flock at Christianpettah for a long time. Then there were P. V. Verghese, P. T. Thomas, K. V. Simon, P. C. John, K. G. Thomas in the south of Tamil Nadu, and Matthai Achen in the north of the state. All of them, labourers who will be recognized of their Master one day.

   In 1953 Mr. and Mrs. Arthur Vine moved from Kurinoor to Coimbatore, Vadamalapuram and learned Tamil for bilingual outreach to town and country. Mrs. Vine had excellent opportunities with women in the town. Open air meetings and literature distribution helped build up the assembly and a new hall was built. In 1958 they moved to Dindigul and two years later opened a small bookshop there and endeavoured to build up the small assembly. Countless villages remained un-evangelized. They retired in 1962 and Arthur died in 1981.

Miss Alison M. McGregor, commended from New Zealand
in 1956, joined the Vines at Coimbatore to learn Tamil, while
helping there and at Vadamalapuram in the hospital. In 1959
Mr. and Mrs. W. A. Munnings gave help in Vadamalapuram
and a good group of the nurses were trained to go out into
the villages as midwives and dispensing assistants. The work
opened up homes and hearts of villagers, and Indian brethren
like Sundaram and C. V. Samuel were able to take advantage of
the opportunities for preaching and teaching. In 1962 Alison
moved to a new centre at Pullangudir, where medical work was
started, and then in 1963 to Tenkasi to relieve Miss Elsie
Phillipson. The following year she returned to Vadamalapuram
with Dr. Rhona M. Oliver and Miss Minna A. Noschke. Alison
eventually returned to New Zealand in 1968 to care for her
mother.

The work has prospered in many cities and towns in the state.
When Mr. and Mrs. C. V. Samuel were first commended to
full-time service, they went to Madurai and were able to help
the assembly there from 1950 to 1953. They then moved to
Dindigul where, in the early days, there was opposition, but the
Lord blessed the work and souls were added to the assembly.

During the days of Sir Robert Stanes and H. Handley Bird in
Coimbatore there was a small assembly in the town, but when

Todas, 1905

Western Ghats from Elsie M. Phillipson's balcony   (S. F. Warren)

they moved, the work turned 'exclusive'. But in 1945 T. T. Zachariah was led there and many came to the Lord through his preaching and an assembly was re-established there. In nearby Pollachi there is another assembly where T. T. Verghese is labouring. At Udamalpet another assembly is cared for by G. K. Thomas.

In 1953 K. V. Samuel was commended to full-time service at Madurai. After helping in the work there for three years he moved to Erodey, where his witness was blessed and an assembly was established. P. Johns was commended to the work by this assembly. K. V. Samuel later moved to Salem, where another assembly has been founded.

There are also live assemblies today at Tirunelveli, Tiruchirapalli, Ramnad, Kanyakumari, Tanjore, S. Arcot, etc.

Tamil Nadu has been the scene of much blessing, but the need is still tremendous, and the Indian brethren, who are now primarily responsible for assembly activities and testimony, need the constant support in prayer of those in the west.

Agra—Tāj Mahal (M. Browne)

314

Punjabi village—running for gospels

(S. F. Warren)

East meets West

(C. Gilmore)

26

A Neglected State

(Map page 260)

The smallest state of India, Tripura in the north-east, is only 4,035 square miles in extent and has a population of just over two million. The capital is Agartala. The languages spoken are Bengali and Tripuri. Half the population are of Mongolian stock and half are tribal.

It is a Hindu state of great antiquity and was ruled by Maharajahs for 1,300 years before its accession to the Indian

Farming in Tripura   (Indian High Commission)

Union in 1949. It became a Union Territory initially, but was converted into a state in 1972. The main crops produced are rice, wheat, jute, cotton and sugar-cane. Sixty-five per cent of the land area is covered by forests, so that farming is restricted.

There is no assembly in the state and no assembly worker.

27

Where Buddha Started

In 1833 the then Bengal Presidency was divided into two parts, one of them becoming known as the Presidency of Agra and later as the North-West Province. In 1877 the two provinces of Agra and Oudh were placed under one administrator still as the North-West Province and Oudh. In 1902 the name was again changed to the United Provinces of Agra and Oudh, shortened in 1935 to the United Provinces. At independence, however, the states of Rampur, Banaras and Tehri-Garwhal were merged into the United Provinces, this name being changed in 1950 to Uttar Pradesh.

This state is in north India and is bounded on the north by Himachal Pradesh, Tibet and Nepal; on the east its neighbour is Bihar, on the south Madhya Pradesh, and on the west Rajasthan, Haryana and Delhi. Delhi is administratively separate and is a Union territory. The state is 113,677 square miles in size and its population is 111 million; it is thus larger in size and population than Britain. Of the population 84 per cent are Hindus and fifteen per cent Muslims, and there are smaller numbers of Sikhs, Christians, Jains and Buddhists. The common language is Hindi. There are eleven administrative divisions and the capital is Lucknow. The state has quite a number of universities – Allahabad, Agra, Varanasi, Lucknow, Aligarh, Roorkee, Gorakhpur, Varanasaya Sanskrit Vish-wavidyalaya, Uttar Pradesh Agricultural University, Phoolbagh Kanpur and Meerut.

Agriculture is the principal industry and occupies 78 per cent

of the work force. Food grains, sugar cane and oil seeds are the chief products. Uttar Pradesh is one of India's main producers of sugar. Textiles, paper and chemical industries provide employment for many, and there is also an oil refinery and an aluminium smelter. In 1854 Mr. and Mrs. W. Ziemann, Van Gerpen and H. Hoppner came from Buxar, Bihar, to commence visiting of the city and district of Ghazipur. A. Sternberg, who also helped in the work, described the city as 'surprisingly populous'. Visits could last about a month and the Word was preached daily and literature distributed. They found the inhabitants to be unusually quiet listeners. Eventually a mission house was purchased near the city to facilitate further contact but there is no evidence that a permanent assembly work was established at that time.

Lucknow, the capital of the state, is a neat garden city, with many monuments recalling the Moghul-Hindu history and culture. There is a small assembly, which was started by E. T. Thomas about twenty years ago. It is still hoped to obtain a central place of meeting and thereby to expand the work. For the time being, activities are confined very largely to personal work in and around the city and in the distribution of literature.

Varanasi, Banaras, previously known as Kashi, has been described as India in miniature. In *The World and the West*, p. 34, Arnold J. Toynbee defined India as 'a society of the same magnitude as our Western civilization, a whole world in herself.' That might well have been said in measure of Banaras. The heterogeneous population comes from all parts of the sub-continent. The city's premier industry is the weaving of the famous Banaras saris. It was in this university city that Buddha preached his first sermon and where he called upon his disciples to spread his message abroad.

To the Hindu, Varanasi is the most sacred city in India. It was founded in 1200 B.C. and millions of worshippers come here to bathe in the sacred river Ganges and to worship in the many temples. One writer says, 'Whoever bathes in the Ganges at Benares and drinks Ganges water there, having at the same time due regard to the needs of the priests, may be cured of the worst

Meerut—sugar cane   (Indian High Commission)

Varanasi—bathing in the Ganges   (R. Duff)

Varanasi—evangelist K. John witnessing to Hindu holy man on the
Ganges   (M. G. G. Harvey)

diseases. Consequently upon Benares are deliberately focussed all the maladies of the Hindu millions. Again, whoever dies in Benares goes straight to heaven. Therefore endless sick, hopeless of cure, come here to breathe their last. There are no latrines along the water-front. The people prefer to use the sandy places at the water's brink among the bathing stairs. Thus one typhoid or cholera carrier may, during his stay, infect 10,000 persons. The river banks are dried sewage. The river water along the banks is liquid sewage. The faithful millions drink and bathe in the one, and spread out their clothes to dry upon the other. Then, in due time, having picked up what germs they can, they go home over the length and breadth of India to give them further currency, carrying jars of the precious water to serve through the year.'

The Hindu University is one of the largest universities in Asia. Kripa Sankar, a native of Banaras who was redeemed from Hinduism, started assembly work here in 1975. There are many earnest seekers after truth there.

Allahabad, the home town of Pandit Nehru, is located at the confluence of the Ganges and the Yamuna and is a sacred bathing place for Hindus. Mr. and Mrs. P. A. Mammen gave up their secular employment and, after training, came to Allahabad as commended workers in 1976. There was only one family of believers at that time, but an assembly has now been established in the city. Again, in Rae Bareli, a district with about two million people, there was no assembly. But after working with the Mammens at Allahabad, Mr. and Mrs. P. A. Samu moved to Rae Bareli in 1978 in the hope of establishing an assembly.

The work at Herbertpur at the foot of the Himalayas very largely revolves around the Mission Hospital. Dr. Geoffrey D. Lehmann came from an English engineering family and he graduated in engineering, with the intention of entering the family business. But he heard the call of God to medical work in North India, took a medical degree and went to India in 1934. When he saw the high incidence of eye diseases, he went to Canada and qualified as an eye specialist, returning to Herbertpur with his wife, Monica, to engage in this particular work. In doing so they have never lost sight of their primary responsibility to win souls for the Lord Jesus Christ and Geoffrey and Monica have been a blessing to many. They have now retired although Geoffrey still makes prolonged visits to

Herbertpur Mission Hospital   (E. Kuhn)

Dr. Geoffrey D. and Monica Lehmann   (E. Kuhn)

India. Dr. and Mrs. Peter F. M. Warlow, who were also at the hospital, returned to the U.K. in 1966.

Miss Esther Kuhn (U.S.A. 1961) joined the hospital as a nurse with a heart for the poor hill people. The hospital has an intensive evangelistic programme and reaches out to the villages around. There are many scattered believers in the surrounding areas without any pastoral care. In 1967 Emmanuel Raj from Tamil Nadu was led to settle at Dehra Dun, 25 miles from Herbertpur, and gave help in the evangelistic work. Ten years later he married Beulah Pannuraj, who gave up a lucrative job to become a full-time worker with him. They held Bible classes in their home, engaged in visiting and teaching and finally established an assembly at Dehra Dun. They subsequently purchased a property and developed a bookstore, reading room and libraries, and other activities. A garment factory has been started where poor and handicapped men are taught a trade to enable them to earn a living. There is also a hostel for young men to assist the poor and needy and to help students learning a trade or seeking employment. They cared for 100 children in three hostels and Esther Kuhn moved to Dehra Dun to assist in the work in 1975. They now have 459 children, 100 under fifteen years of age who come from remote Himalayan villages and Tibet. There are 300 baptised believers in the assembly. Breaking of bread and other services are also held in Kishanpur, Dakpathu, Panahpur, Hashiarpur etc. Miss Jean Fletcher (U.K. 1980) joined as a nurse and is rendering help in much of the work. Miss Connie Freeman continues with daily clinics and also in Sunday school work.

Alan J. Linton (N.Z. 1952) early became proficient in Hindi and Urdu. After helping in Delhi, he moved north to Meerut in 1956 and, in the same year, married Dr. Shobha Gulati. They distributed thousands of tracts and Scripture portions, particularly at fairs and festivals, and also engaged in Emmaus work with Miss Lorna Morrison. By literature distribution, tent meetings and open air meetings, they reached out to the surrounding area and some people were saved and added to the assemblies in the state. An assembly was started at Meerut, but in 1970 the Lintons had to move away because of their need for more accommodation for the Emmaus work. They later returned to New Zealand, but in 1978 Mr. and Mrs. E. Samuel moved here from Ambala to care for the assembly and to spread the message to a wider field.

Dehra Dun   (E. Kuhn)

The work at Kanpur was commenced by H. H. Max Jahn (U.K. 1949). An assembly was started but, after his homecall in 1967 and the transfer of many believers, particularly of those working in the Air Force, the work came to a standstill. In 1972 K. L. John of Kerala took up the work and the assembly has been revived.

Agra is the city of the Tāj and is situated on the banks of the Yamuna. Mr. and Mrs. M. A. Jos of Kerala were commended to the work here and a small assembly is functioning. Mathura has been described as a seat of ancient culture, but it is also a city of great need. Mr. and Mrs. A. Varghese moved here in 1978 and an assembly has been commenced.

28

The Region of Cholera's Threat
(Map page 142)

As a result of the India Independence Act of 1947, the Province of Bengal ceased to exist. The territory of Cooch-Behar State was merged with West Bengal in 1950 and the former French possession of Chandernagore became part of the new state in 1954. Two years later certain parts of Bihar State were also transferred to West Bengal. East Bengal, which was predominantly Muslim, had been transferred to East Pakistan, or Bangladesh. West Bengal is bounded on the north by Sikkim and Bhutan, on the east by Assam and Bangladesh, on the south by Orissa, on the west by Bihar and on the north-west by Nepal. Its total area is 33,921 square miles and its population is over 54 million. The capital is Calcutta and there are 15 districts, excluding Calcutta. The language spoken is Bengali.

Although the state is largely sacred, it has several important industrial areas. It has a number of major irrigation and power schemes under construction or actually in operation. It also has large coal deposits. Agriculture is one of the largest industries, wheat, oilseeds, rice, tea and jute being the main products. There is also a flourishing fishing industry. Steel, automobile, locomotive, aluminium and fertilizer factories employ a large number of the population.

Seventy per cent of the population are Hindus, twenty per cent are Muslims and the remainder are made up of Christians (including R.C.s), Buddhists, Sikhs, and Jains, the Christians being less than one per cent of the population.

The state has at least one unfortunate distinction. A World

Near Jamshedpur—paddy field   (R. Duff)

Health Organization report of 1939 said, 'In India, the region of endemic cholera falls within the state of West Bengal, with its nucleus in Greater Calcutta and dominantly in the *bustee* population, ill provided with even elementary sanitary facilities. The cholera situation has great significance, not only to West Bengal and all of India, but to the world at large.' After 44 years the situation has scarcely improved.

West Bengal has been the scene of the devoted labours of many missionaries over the years, including those of the Baptist Missionary Society and the Church of Scotland. Not far from Calcutta is Serampore, which was the centre of the work of William Carey, Joshua Marshman and William Ward in the last decade of the eighteenth century. The work of many missions has been centred in Calcutta, but none perhaps as well known as the work of Mother Teresa, who now presides over what has been described as 'the most flourishing religious order in Christendom.' Agnes Gonxha Bajaxhiu was an Albanian, who went to Calcutta in 1928, when she was only 18, to join the Irish Loreto sisters in their teaching convent. When she picked up a woman from the pavement who had been attacked by rats, she concluded that religion needed a more practical side and founded her own order. There are 40,000 lepers in Calcutta and Mother Teresa's Missionaries of Charity are almost the only people caring for them, and her order is the only body with a refuge for dying destitutes – Nirmal Hriday by the side of Kālī's temple. Although she is a Roman Catholic, there is no doubt that her work has affected the general attitude to Christianity in the city of Calcutta. It is perhaps significant that the only really comparable work – that of Charles de Foucald's Little Brothers and Sisters of Jesus – is also Roman Catholic.

Conditions in some parts of Calcutta are completely deplorable. One writer describes many of the homes as made from 'a confusion of packing cases, corrugated iron, cardboard, straw matting, odd bricks and wads of newspaper', and, when constructed, giving only enough room to squeeze inside. Geoffrey Moorhouse describes somewhat better homes in his book, *Calcutta,* p. 85, 'The huts are made of wattle, they have tiled roofs, they have mud floors. They are so congested that there is no more than an arm's span in the dirt-track lanes that separate one row from another. And open drains run down the middle of each lane, so that you tend to walk down them at the straddle.' There is no electricity, and a standpipe provides water for 125 people.

He says of the sewerage of the city, *op. cit.,* p. 88, 'Along the whole thirty miles length of Greater Calcutta, there is not much even remotely modern sewerage. Instead there is what they call the service privy. This is a small brick shed with a platform above a large earthenware bowl and it is usually wholly exposed and unprotected from flies. It is supposed to be emptied daily by Calcutta Corporation but it is sometimes weeks. Even with the service at its best, the bowl has usually long since overflowed across the surrounding ground. It represents the beginning of cholera, of every other gastro-intestinal disease in creation, with smallpox and tuberculosis thrown in as well. For the stinking mass around the *bustee's* privy is washed straight into the ponds and tanks of water in which the people clean themselves and their clothes and their cooking utensils. Every year, when the monsoon falls, the incidence of cholera in Calcutta rises from its

Calcutta scenes   (S. F. Warren)

service privies.' For many in Calcutta their only home is the side-walk where a plastic bag can be a status symbol. Many are born there, and when morning comes some blankets do not move for their owners have died there.

Some readers will doubtless turn over the page rapidly lest their thoughts should be disturbed by the repellent and undesirable, but are they really justified in ignoring what is happening to their fellow-men or the conditions the Lord's servants have to face? Is it really appreciated, for example, that 'starvation and famine really mean a man who dies with a stomach containing undigested grass; a child whose body has started to split open with lack of food, so that its liquids begin to trickle out; a fisherman who is so weak that a dog begins to eat him before he is dead; a crowd which goes scavenging among poultices full of blood and pus and scabs in the hope of finding something putrid but edible there too.' Is it realized that the picturesque rickshaw man has to pull his rickshaw and run at least twenty miles a day to make enough to live?

There are two assemblies in Calcutta, one cared for by Mr. Shenoy and the other by Ken W. Smith and Sunil Chakravarthy. The first assembly missionaries to settle in Calcutta were Mr. and Mrs. John F. Smele (U.K.). He had laboured for eighteen years in the rural communities of Bihar, but in 1927 felt constrained by the tremendous spiritual need to move into the capital of Bengal. Before the commencement of World War 2, an English-speaking assembly had been established. During the war the assembly met in the Smeles' flat, and it became known to many British Servicemen, to whom the opportunity for fellowship in such a strange land proved an inestimable boon. John Smele gave himself unsparingly to open air preaching and tract distribution and was well known throughout the Christian community for the latter. He was also an ardent visitor to dockland, with its constantly changing maritime population. His was a great gift for personal work, to which he devoted himself wholeheartedly.

The Smeles were joined in 1939 by Stuart R. Stokes, who was soon active in Christian work in Calcutta. During the war, Esther R. Burnett went to Herbertpur Hospital to help during the absence of Dr. Lehmann. As already mentioned Esther married Stuart after World War II and at the invitation of Armen George, an American business man in Calcutta, they went there and were active in the area for a year until their removal to Nagpur in 1949.

Mr. and Mrs. William J. Campbell (U.K. 1939), who had also been previously in Bihar, moved to Calcutta in 1948. During their time in the city they helped Indian Christians to circulate 40,000 Gospels, New Testaments and Bibles in Bengali and Hindi, often finding active opposition. They retired in 1965. About that time, Malayalam-speaking brethren began to come up from Kerala to engage in business or to take up employment in the city. Many gathered with the assembly, which naturally became bilingual and not merely English.

While in Bihar, Ken W. Smith started a radio programme at Calcutta and in 1939 he and his wife, Bee, moved there joining Mr. and Mrs. William Campbell who left on furlough soon after. The Smiths had been particularly engaged in Emmaus Correspondence Course work and the rapid growth of this indicated that it would be advisable for it to be centred in Calcutta. Obviously larger premises were needed for meetings in view of the considerable blessing there had been in the assembly activities. One of the converts of those days was Sunil Chakraberty, who was commended to full-time service. Beside the Emmaus work, at one time the Smiths carried on an extensive literature distribution in the city and in adjoining industrial areas. There was also a live work among women and girls, college students and nurses. It has now been possible to locate the Bengali assembly which the Smiths had started, and the Emmaus work in one building in Calcutta. Sunil Chakraberty and his wife, who have been faithful co-workers are also located there. The radio work has since ceased because of rising costs.

Mr. and Mrs. Brian Hathaway (N.Z. 1967) and Ross Grant (N.Z. 1967) went to Calcutta with Gospel Literature Outreach to help Ken Smith and the assemblies, but eventually returned to New Zealand to take up secular employment.

C. T. Samuel went to Calcutta 30 years ago with a group from Madras Bible School. They slept on the floor of the assembly hall and sold thousands of tracts in the city and the surrounding villages. He subsequently set up home in a small town near the city and established a small assembly there.

N. Narayan Paul was a Hindu convert of many years. He was expelled from home by his parents on his conversion and

Tilling the land   (R. Duff)

Vegetable market   (Tear Fund)

332

Colombo   (W. T. Stunt)

Calcutta—Emmaus office (S. F. Warren)

Calcutta, 48 Ripon Street (S. F. Warren)

hitchhiked to Calcutta 700 miles north and obtained a secular job near the city. He started a Sunday school for low caste children, but eventually was commended to full-time service in Andhra Pradesh, where he settled among aborigines who had never previously been evangelized and who had no written language. He held schools for illiterate adults and children and in 1980 took ten poor village boys into his home to train them to preach to their own people.

P. V. Devasikhamoni was in the Indian Air Force and transferred to Calcutta about 30 years ago. After much witnessing for Christ around Calcutta, he was commended to full-time service in central India and labours in many cities and towns. T. A. Kurien, who is fluent in Malayalam, Hindi and English, visits Calcutta periodically for special meetings. He also conducts classes in Greek and Hebrew.

The assembly work at Durgapur was started by P. A. Koshy. Since his homecall, M. S. Jacob is working in the area. At Ajansol the assembly work began in 1963 through the efforts of M. K. Thomas and Samuel Kurien, and the latter continues at this centre. An assembly testimony was established in Bagdogra, a military centre in West Bengal in 1975 and E. M. Thomas from Kerala serves the Lord there.

About the mid-nineteenth century Messrs. Stolke, Wernicke, and Trauthler from Germany went to Darjeeling where they established a large school for the education of young unconverted nationals.

Miss M. Ramsay, commended from Australia, worked at Darjeeling from 1950 to 1954 before going on to the boarding school at Ootacamund.

George N. Patterson, who had worked in Tibet, moved to Kalimpong in 1950, where he met Bakht Singh, Jordan Khan and others, and helped in the establishment of local assemblies in various Indian centres. In 1953 he married Dr. Margaret Ingram of Ludhiana, Punjab and they continued work at Kalimpong. They later transferred to Hong Kong and then returned to U.K. in 1973.

Miss Renée M. Cooper, commended from Birmingham, went to India in 1949, having first been interested by a talk given by the late Dr. Arthur Swain, missionary to China (the father of Dr. Elizabeth R. Swain now at Kalene, Zambia). Her concern was to work among Tibetans and at first she intended to go to

China as entry to Tibet seemed possible from there but that step was prevented by the communist take-over of China. She first studied Tibetan in Ghoom and later worked for a time with Beryl Norman at Manali. She moved to Kalimpong early in 1951 which gave the opportunity to contact Tibetan traders and refugees passing through. It was not practicable to establish a permanent work among them, but it is known that some professed conversion. Later Renée worked for a time with the Prattens. Renée came home in 1959 and was prevented by ill-health from returning.

In 1943 Harold Avery went to Kalimpong, and within a year had married Mrs. Ruby J. Andrews, a widow, who was a teacher at one of the Kalimpong Cottage Homes. Because of her ill-health they returned to England in 1946, resuming their ministry in Kalimpong only for a short period (1949-1951), before retiring.

Thomas J. Pratten (U.K. 1947) went to Darjeeling to learn the Tibetan language and in 1951 moved to the village of Pedong on the Indian-Sikhian border and on the trade route to Tibet. He married Miss Barbara Hawthorne in 1953. Prior to their marriage, Barbara was working in Dr. Graham's Homes in

Kalimpong—the boys' home   (T. J. Pratten)

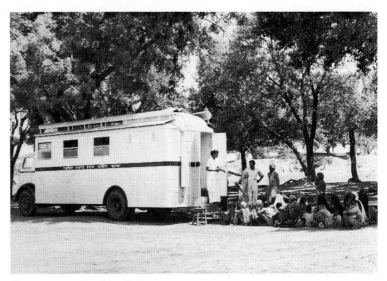

Government health clinic   (R. Duff)

Kalimpong. Not surprisingly they started a school for Tibetan boys in Pedong. They also opened a dispensary and were able to contact Tibetan muleteers and pilgrims. Because of the plight of Tibetan refugees after the Chinese invasion in 1958, they opened the Albella Boys' Home. With the help of Miss Renée Cooper, they fed and clothed refugees. In 1981 another property was acquired to accommodate needy boys. Tibetans, Indians, Nepalis and Lepchas were found in happy fellowship. Tom and Barbara eventually retired in 1981. Miss Joy Riddenhoff spent some time at Albella, and records are being made by Gospel Recordings.

The World Health Organization designated the 1980's as the 'Water Decade' and the W.H.O. magazine, *World Health,* disclosed the appalling need for safe drinking water and satisfactory sanitation. Eighty per cent of all diseases are associated with water. Not only West Bengal but India as a whole, is in desperate need of pure water and proper sanitation. Don Stanton refers to the diseases caused by water. Firstly, there are germs injested through drinking contaminated water: these cause typhoid, gastro-enteritis, cholera. Then, communicable diseases, such as scabies, and trachoma, transmission of which is favoured by chronic water shortage or poor quality of

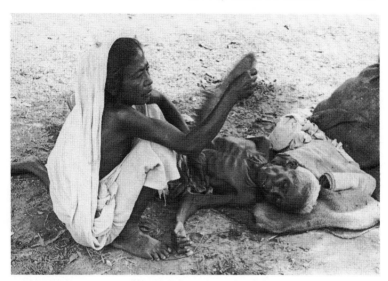

Krishnanagar—dying of cholerea   (Tear Fund)

water. Thirdly, diseases caused by parasites that inhabit water and burrow through the skin, like schistosomiosis, which is carried by snails, or dracunculinsis, carried by the guinea worm. Finally, there are the carriers (rectors) of disease which live in bodies of water. The most serious of these are mosquitoes, responsible for the current alarming upsurge of malaria and the flies which cause river blindness (onchocerciosis). The number of people in India who are suffering from these 'water diseases' runs into millions and it will increase with the rapidly increasing population.

On the other hand, India suffers periodically from serious drought. 1980, for example, opened with a severe drought for the country.

These conditions and their inevitable effect of increasing the death rate can scarcely be ignored by the Christians. Apart altogether from the practical facts and the obvious need for action, it should be evident that the presentation of the gospel in such circumstances is a matter of the highest urgency.

29

The Union Territories

In addition to the 22 states of India, there are also nine Union
Territories, each of which is administered by the President
acting through a Chief Commissioner or the equivalent, usually
assisted by an advisory committee. These are dealt with
alphabetically in this chapter.

Andaman and Nicobar Islands
(Map page 359)

The Andaman and Nicobar Islands are regarded as one entity
for administrative purposes. Their total area is only 3,202
square miles and the population is only about 188,000. The
capital is Port Blair and the common language is Bengali.

The Andaman Islands lie in the Bay of Bengal. Five large
islands are described as the Great Andamans and a smaller one
to the south is called the Little Andaman. There are also 204
islets, the two principal groups being known as the Ritchie
Archipelago and the Labyrinth Islands. The Great Andamans
are densely wooded and large quantities of wood are exported.
Coconut, coffee, rice and rubber are also cultivated. The islands
were used as a penal settlement from 1857 to 1942, but the penal
•settlement was abolished in 1945. Japanese forces occupied the
islands in 1942. From 1953 to 1967 displaced families, mostly
from Bangladesh, were settled in the Andamans, some 4,000
families benefiting in this way.

The original inhabitants live in the forests and exist by
hunting and fishing. They are of the Negritic type and it is said
that their civilization is about that of the Stone Age.

Literacy Programme (R. Duff)

The Nicobar Islands are situated to the south of the Andamans. There are nineteen islands, seven of them being uninhabited. The British first took possession of them in 1869. They were occupied by the Japanese in 1942 but repossessed in 1945. Coconut and arecanut are grown and form the main items of trade.

The Baptists, Pentecostals and other bodies have attempted to evangelize the islands for many years. Assembly work started in 1968 when M. Joseph was commended to full-time service in that area. Some have been saved and a small assembly commenced at Port Blair.

Arunachal Pradesh
(Map page 260)

Formerly the North East Frontier Agency, Arunachal Pradesh was converted into a Union Territory in 1972. It is bordered by China, Bhutan, Tibet and Burma, and its total area is 31,439 square miles. Its capital is Ziro and its population is 628,000. Assamese and Gorbhali are the languages commonly in use. Sixty per cent of the land is forest and the main industry is agriculture. Crops include rubber, coffee, coconut, arecanuts and spices.

Literacy is only five per cent and a large proportion of the people are animists, the only other religion being Buddhism.

Indian ceremony   (Indian High Commission)

Evangelistic work is prohibited and Christians are usually persecuted. Many have been beaten and have had their houses burnt and their fields destroyed. Church buildings have also been destroyed.

Chandigarh
(Map page 162)

The city of Chandigarh and the area around it was constituted a Union Territory in 1966. It is the capital of both Punjab and Haryana, although the latter state will be served by a new capital in due course. Its total area is only 44 square miles and the population about 450,000.

Assembly work started in Chandigarh in 1961 through the activities of Arthur R. Stedman. In 1963 he was joined by Lewis Samraj. Arthur had to return to New Zealand in 1969 and Lewis Samraj also had to return to Bangalore. In 1971, however, C. T. George moved to Chandigarh but he moved on to New Delhi two years later. V. T. John came from Ambala and he still continues there, helping the small assembly and reaching out to the area around.

Dadra and Nagar Haveli
(Map page 157)

The previous Portuguese possessions of Dadra and Nagar Haveli became a Union Territory in 1961. It has an area of 182 square miles and its capital is Silvassa. The population is about 104,000 and the main language used is Gujarati. Farming is the chief industry and crops include rice, ragi and pulses. Nearly 42 per cent of the area is composed of forests and there are large quantities of teak. Eighty-three per cent use the language of the Bhilodi, but Marathi, Hindi, and Gujarati are also used. Literacy is less than fifteen per cent.

Delhi
(Map page 162)

Delhi became a Union Territory in 1956. It is an enclave inside Haryana and only 573 square miles in extent and its population is just over six million. In addition to the city of Delhi, it comprises a rural area, in which are 243 inhabited and 15 deserted villages. The languages spoken are Hindi, Urdu and Punjabi. Sixty per cent of the people are Hindus, the remainder being Sikhs, Muslims, Jains, Christians and Buddhists. The literacy rate is over 60 per cent.

Old Delhi is largely Muslim. Bob Glasgow's informal description is well worth quoting. He says, *op. cit.*, p. 72, 'We saw the Red Fort and heard the story of the Persians stealing the fabulous Peacock Throne and then losing it in the Red Sea. We entered the Delhi Mosque, the largest mosque in India, where thousands each morning kneel in lines and bow in prayer. We walked across the congregational space, as large as a football field, to the distant retaining wall and looked over old Delhi – not many bullock carts but many bicycles and bicycle rickshaws and decaying secondhand stalls. The oldest Delhi was at the Qutb Minar, the Tower of Victory. It was built about the time that King John was being forced to sign the Magna Carta. It was the highest "free-standing" tower in the world. The building of the Qutb Minar marked the end of an era that would never

Delhi—Red Fort
(Indian High
Commission)

return. It flaunted the victory of the Muslim invaders over Prithviraj, the last Hindu Rajput to reign in Delhi. It became a monument to religious intolerance, built as it was with the stones of 27 Hindu and Jain temples that were demolished by the zeal of the invading Muslims.'

The modern city of Delhi is not only the largest commercial centre in northern India, but also an important industrial centre. Industries include the manufacture of razor blades, sports goods, radio parts, bicycles, footwear, etc. Some of the traditional handicrafts, for which Delhi has been famous, continue to flourish, particularly ivory carving, miniature painting, gold and silver jewellery, papier mâché work, and handwoven textiles.

Barry and Anne Mackey were commended by Canadian assemblies in 1969. Their work is the training of young Indian Christians and Barry is the Director of the Discipleship Centre.

Delhi—
Qutb Minar
(Indian High
Commission)

When they have completed their training, the young men go out to evangelise their own people. For example, an effort in 1978, called Project Tripura, led to over 1,000 turning to the Saviour. A team of men followed up the work in a unique church planting and adult literacy programme. Two other church-planting teams are working in the state of Madhya Pradesh in central India. A project called Lighthouse for the Blind is an integral part of the Discipleship Centre. It provides Hindi Braille literature and personal involvement and follow-up for the blind. Neighbourhood Bible studies are growing up and Barry and the Centre provide group Bible study materials in several vernacular languages. The Mackeys encourage a non-profit enterprise which enables handicapped people to support themselves by selling handicrafts which they have made. Anne teaches music and helps in Sunday schools and with home Bible studies.

Alan E. McKenzie (N.Z. 1934) joined G. Harold Watson at Sabathu (Himachal Pradesh) where the American Presbyterian Mission established a leper asylum in 1837, which was later handed over to brethren missionaries. Here he learned Urdu and visited markets and bazaars with the gospel. In 1936 he married Miss Myrtle Bailey (N.Z.) and in the following year they moved to Solon (Himachal Pradesh), a larger centre where they had open air meetings in the summer and worked in Delhi in the winter. Some were saved, including a number of Muslims. Alan commenced a gospel paper, *Bible Talks*, and also conducted a Sunday school in Urdu. Because of the unsettled conditions in Delhi in 1947, activities were restricted. Myrtle went to Srinagar (Yammu and Kashmir) as matron of a school. Riots continued and there was a risk of Delhi becoming a blood bath, but the unrest disappeared and the assemblies continued their testimony. The McKenzies returned to New Zealand in 1954.

A garden suburb of New Delhi is also the home of the Delhi Bhavan (or Bible Institute). This came into being in 1966 through the drive and enthusiasm of Robert Duff, now resident in the U.K., who still visits it each year. Besides basic Bible instruction the Institute offered courses in Hindi and there are study rooms and libraries and also accommodation for students. It was a project in which Sir John Laing was keenly interested. Mr. and Mrs. George Dawson and Mr. and Mrs. John Abraham

Delhi—Bible Bhavan (R. Duff)

J. Abraham, G. Dawson, S. F. Warren

were commended full-time workers at D.B.I. for many years. A number of ministering brethren have given help at the Institute from time to time. The Jorburgh assembly uses the main auditorium for their meetings. The Bhavan is also used for retreats for Christian workers.

In 1964 the Masihi Sahitya Sanstha was started, a Christian printing press to publish Christian literature in Hindi for northern India, largely the result of the enthusiasm of Dennis Clark. Roger and June Kennedy, commended from U.K. in 1955 were exercised about serving the Lord in India following an invitation from Dennis Clark, Robert Duff and Alex Smyth to go to Delhi to help in the work of M.S.S. Alex Smyth soon afterward moved to Calcutta but Dennis Havard, Arthur Stedman and Rita Salmon (N.Z. 1953) were all involved. The work started in a small way but rapidly grew in size and influence. One object of the press was to support a Christian publishing ministry in India if expatriate funds were not readily available.

Roger and June were married in Delhi in 1956 but were soon completely immersed in publishing work. They were, however, able to help in the assembly with Robert Duff and M. J. E. Pritchard, an Indian brother in government service. In 1955 S. K. Bose joined the staff of M.S.S. and eventually became its manager. In 1961 John Jones headed up the distribution side of the work being joined by Brenda, his wife, until they returned home in 1979. In 1964 Roger was able to visit Pakistan, Burma, Thailand, Kampuchea, South Vietnam, Philippines, Hong Kong and Taiwan for literature distribution workshops. June was able to use her musical training to the full in making known the gospel in other spheres in Delhi. It was clear eventually that the Indian brethren were capable of carrying on the work and in 1972 the Kennedys returned to U.K.

Miss Lorna Morrison spent two years in language study and five years' school teaching in North India and some years in South India. In 1951 she opened the Gospel Literature Depot in Delhi. Scriptures were stocked in eight languages and there were also Emmaus courses in three languages. Lorna was very proficient in Hindi and Urdu. In 1958 she transferred to Meerut, opening a small depot there for Emmaus courses and for the sale of literature. She also helped in Sunday school work, women's meetings and camps. Conditions became difficult and in 1967 several churches and homes were burnt and quantities of Bibles and other literature destroyed. In 1970 she returned to Emmaus work in order to be free to minister to women, and the following year she moved the centre of operations to Ambala and Ludhiana and helped in a number of assemblies and in the distribution of literature in streets and bazaars. Many lives have been transformed through literature.

Arthur R. Stedman joined Alan McKenzie and Alan Linton in Delhi. Following study at Landore Language School, he engaged in literature distribution. In 1955 he visited Jaipur, a large city in Rajasthan, where there was no clear gospel testimony. In 1955 he married Miss Rita L. Salmon, who had also attended Landore Language School and had worked with Mr. and Mrs. Harold McGregor. She moved to Delhi in 1954 and helped in literature distribution. Several years later the Stedmans moved to another area in Delhi where little was done of an evangelical nature. For five years they helped in special efforts with a tent at Meerut, Ambala, etc. before moving to Chandigarh.

Masihi Sahitya
Sanstha
(R. Duff)

Goa, Daman and Diu
(Map page 174)

Goa, which claims to have traded with the Egyptians and Phoenicians before the times of Solomon of Israel, was captured for Portugal by Affonso de Albuquerque in 1510 and the adjacent inland territory was added in the 18th century. Today it is virtually an enclave in Karnataka. Daman (or Damao) on the Gujarat coast was seized by the Portuguese in 1531. The island of Diu, off the south-east coast of Gujarat, was captured by the Portuguese in 1534. All three areas were occupied by India in 1961 and were incorporated into the Indian Union, becoming a Union Territory.

The territory is 1,441 square miles in size and the total population is in excess of a million. The capital is Panaji and the languages in common use are Portuguese, Konkani and Gujarati. The main occupation is agriculture and the crops produced include rice, wheat, pulses, groundnuts and coconuts. Bamboos and wild bananas grow amongst the trees. The fishing industry is quite important and fish is, in fact, the staple food of

Dennis J. and
P. Sybil Harvard
(P. A. Pritchard)

Extensive farm land   (Indian High Commission)

the people. There are, in addition, a number of small industries. Sixty two per cent of the population is Hindu, 36 per cent Christian and two per cent Muslim. Literacy is 44 per cent.

Goa was once the richest city in the east, but malaria and other diseases drove out large numbers of the people. The Spanish Francis Xavier (born 1506) became a priest at the time that Martin Luther's doctrine of justification by faith was shaking the people of Europe. He joined Ignatius Loyola, the founder of the Order of Jesuits, and was sent to the east. He worked with increasing zeal from Goa to Japan for the remaining ten years of his life. When he 'died on a small island near the present Portuguese Macau, he was waiting for an opportunity of carrying his mission into China, which, at that time, was closed to foreigners.' He was buried at Macau, but his body was later exhumed and transferred to Goa, where it is kept in a glass coffin in a silver casket at the Church of the Blessed Jesus.

For some years, Mr. and Mrs. George Turner and a team used to visit Goa in an attempt to introduce the gospel there. Then Mr. and Mrs. Gordon Ritchie, followed by Mr. and Mrs. Stuart R. Stokes endeavoured to bring the message to Portuguese and Indians. Raymond C. E. Atkinson, K. T. Savant, P. T. Patoley, Dr. S. W. Sadhu Sundar, Bill Forward and others visited the area periodically with the Scriptures and other literature. For a number of years, G. Celeste Hull and Jean Campbell did a wonderful work among women and girls.

They were particularly zealous in contacting 'world travellers' (Goa is frequently referred to as 'the hippies' paradise'). In 1963, while in the army, C. John was stationed at Goa and was able to give some help, and an assembly was started. Realizing the spiritual need he returned in 1972 as a full-time worker, together with his wife and family. They have been contacting seven different districts. Mr. and Mrs. Vay L. Vivian spent over a year in Goa, but their visa was not renewed.

At the 'feast of exposition' of the body of Francis Xavier, visitors come from many parts of India, and a large number of Scripture portions and tracts are then distributed.

Lakshadweep
(Map page 359)

The Laccadive, Minicoy and Amindivi Islands consist of a group of 27 islands, only ten of which are inhabited, off the west coast of Kerala. They became a Union Territory in 1956 but were renamed in 1973. Their total area is only twenty square miles and the population is about 40,000, nearly all of whom are Muslims. The language in Minicoy is Mahi, but in the other islands Malayalam. The staple products are coconuts and fish.

The islands do not seem to have attracted any assembly workers and there is no information regarding any Christian work there.

Mizoram
(Map page 260)

In 1972 the former Mizo Hills District of Assam was created a Union Territory. It is an area of 8,134 square miles with an elevation of 5,000 to 12,000 feet, and a population of about half a million, of whom 55 per cent are literate and 90 per cent are described as Christians. The capital is Aizawl and the languages spoken are Mizo and Lushai. Sugar cane and maize are the main products.

The first missionaries came in 1891 – Baptists in the south and Presbyterians in the north – and many were won for Christ. C. V. John has made a number of gospel tours in Mizoram, which have resulted in quite a number of professions. But there is no assembly and no resident worker. If a substantial and lasting work is to be done, it seems essential for there to be full-

Bethel, Pondicherry, 1931—L. Alphonsine Ligot

time resident workers. A Christian couple would find a useful sphere of service here.

Pondicherry
(Map page 288)

Formerly the chief French settlement in India, Pondicherry was founded in 1674. It was captured by the Dutch in 1693, but restored to the French six years later. The British captured it in 1761, but restored it in 1765, then took it again in 1778 and restored it once more in 1785, retook it a third time in 1793 and finally restored it to the French in 1814. The administration was transferred to India in 1954 and in 1962, together with Karikal, Mahé and Yanaon, became a Union Territory. It is 183 square miles in size and the population is 604,000. The population is composed of Roman Catholics, Muslims and Hindus. The principal languages employed are French, English, Tamil, Telugu and Malayalam. Rice, groundnuts, cotton and sugar-cane are produced, and there are some light industries.

A testimony was started in Pondicherry by Miss Porter in 1901 and, with the help of visiting brethren, she carried it on until 1926, and a small assembly was started as a result of her efforts. She had appealed to a number of brethren to take over the work, but her appeals met with no response. In 1926, however, Mlle. L. Alphonsine Ligot, a French sister working in

Young Indian (from *Indian Realities*)

Tirunelveli, accepted the responsibility. She carried on faithfully and almost single-handed until her death in 1942. Then, as mentioned in an earlier chapter, Mr. and Mrs. William T. Revell felt constrained to take over the work, being joined in due course by Ronald Appleby in 1949, and also by Miss Wilma G. Farringdon in 1951. Owing to the unfavourable climate the Revells eventually felt unable to continue there and, as previously mentioned, withdrew to Bangalore.

30

Country of the Demons

To the south-east of the foot of the Indian peninsula lies Sri Lanka (or Ceylon, as it was formerly called), like an emerald set in a sapphire shield. Known to the ancients as Serendib, to the Romans as Taprubane, the island was apostrophized by the Buddhist poets, according to Sir Enerson Tennent, 'as a "pearl upon the brow of India". The Chinese knew it as the "island of jewels", the Greeks as the "land of the hyacinth and the ruby", the Mohammedans, in the intensity of their delight, assigned it to the exiled parents of mankind as a new elysium to console them for the loss of Paradise, and the early navigators of Europe, as they returned, dazzled by its gems, and laden with its costly spices, propagated the fable that far to seaward the very breeze that blew from it was redolent of perfume.'

This pear-shaped island lies between five and nine degrees north of the equator and nearly midway between the tropics of Capricorn and Cancer. Its area is only 25,332 square miles or half the size of England, and it is 240 miles long and 140 miles across at its widest point. Once a part of the Indian sub-continent, it is now separated from the mainland by the shallow Palk Strait. A line of sandbanks, known as Adam's Bridge, acts as a breakwater. The island is very mountainous and the high central massif, which is the principal feature of Sri Lanka's physical structure, drops down gently by a series of steps to the coastal plains.

'From the south-western lowlands,' writes E. F. C. Ludowyk in *The Story of Ceylon,* pp. 15, 16, 'mountain ranges rise up to

Landscape   (Embassy Consulate of Sri Lanka)

8,000 feet, all along the centre of the southern half of the island. The mountain barrier, which on its south-western slopes receives both monsoons, the south-west and the north-east, makes up the south-west of Ceylon and its central mountainous core an area called its West Zone with an annual rainfall of between 100 and 200 inches. To the central plain of the north and the east, cut off by the mountains from the south-west monsoon, only the north-east monsoon brings rain. This plain, which slopes from the mountain shelf very gradually to the sea, has an annual rainfall of 60 inches and below. The north-central plain through which the largest river of Ceylon, the Mahaweli Ganga, flows to the sea near Trincomalee, was the setting of the country's ancient culture, which depended on the skill of its inhabitants in conserving the water the rains brought to the hills and the rivers carried through the land.'

The palm-fringed sandy beaches and lagoons of both west and east coasts are broken in places by the forests which run right down to the sea. Farther inland, in the undulating lowlands between the mountain ranges, rice is cultivated, and rubber trees surround the rice-fields and flourish up to 3,000 feet above sea level. Still higher, at 6,000 feet and above, are the many tea plantations. In the plains, coconut, cinnamon, orange and banana groves enclose the terraced rice-fields. Umbrageous

Palm-fringed sandy beaches (W. T. Stunt)

mango, breadfruit and tamarind trees contrast with the feathery bamboo and stately green palm. Pineapples, custard apples, pawpaws and other delicious fruit come to perfection here. In the dry zone the forests produce the valuable teak, ebony and satinwood. Even in the extreme north, in the Jaffna peninsula, where the forest gives way to scrubland, the Sinhalese farmer grows rice and tobacco.

The island is completely dependent upon agriculture for its prosperity, but the key to success lies in effective irrigation. In *Ceylon,* p. 14, Zeylanieus says that 'the islanders were master engineers, some of their giant reservoirs being thirty or forty miles in circumference. At the peak the irrigation system was unrivalled in Asia. A highly intricate web of vast artificial lakes and a maze of water-courses irrigated the arid northern plains and enabled the village communities to practise agricultural pursuits with profit to themselves and to their rulers.'

In ancient times the 'king turned his subject population into a huge labour corps, which cleared jungles, built palaces, laid out gardens, and constructed irrigation works. This period of classical glory came to an end during the thirteenth century, and thereafter the irrigation system gradually declined. The Sinhalese governments before the advent of British power were for the most part unstable and feeble. The island which passed

Colombo   (W. T. Stunt)

beneath the sway of European conquerors in the sixteenth century was an effete and decadent society, ravaged by disease, poverty and war, torn by internal dissensions, usurpations, and dynastic rivalries, virtually partitioned into kingdoms and principalities.' There seemed no strong central authority.

The construction of irrigation systems, which had deteriorated so seriously, was recommenced in more recent days and, in consequence, the agricultural industry is once more flourishing. Today, rubber, rice, tea and coconuts are grown in large quantities and are widely exported to the west. Contrary to popular imagination, spices are not grown prolifically and it is not entirely accurate to sing with the poet of 'spicy breezes' which 'blow soft o'er Ceylon's isle.' But Sri Lanka is certainly a lovely island and the climate is temperate and pleasant and owes much to the mountainous character of the country.

Centuries ago, Lanka (its old name) was on the sea trade routes from China to India and from Africa to Malaya, and merchants and seamen of every kind and of many races came to its shores. Goods of every variety naturally flowed into its warehouses and through its valleys. A number of religions also followed, but Buddhism gradually became predominant.

The Sinhalese claim that their history goes back as far as 5000 B.C., but this is undoubtedly somewhat exaggerated. There is certainly a tradition that, when Adam and Eve were expelled from the Garden of Eden (which, according to the Sinhalese, was in Lanka and not, as is usually considered, in Mesopotamia), they found a refuge in the northern part of the island. Huge boulders, straddling the Gulf of Mannar at the north-west of Sri Lanka and linking it with India, are called Adam's Bridge and are reputed to be the route taken by our first parents in their flight subsequently. Adam's Peak is alleged to be the place from which Adam took his last look at the terrestrial paradise which he had forfeited by his sin. The traditions are, of course, without Biblical or historical support, but are still firmly held. A recess on the summit of Adam's Peak is claimed to be the footprint of Adam, although the Buddhists refuse to accept this tradition and claim that it was the footprint of Buddha. The peak is a holy mountain for Roman Catholics, Buddhists and Muslims, and it is accorded reverent homage and toilsome pilgrimage.

It is even alleged that Sinbad, the Sailor of *The Arabian*

Nights fame, was actually cast adrift on the island. When Sinbad the Sailor reached Sri Lanka from Arabia in the Middle Ages, he allegedly found that the surface of the island was 'covered with emery wherewith gems are cut and fashioned, diamonds are in the rivers and pearls are in the valleys'. There is a measure of truth in this, for sapphires, rubies, emeralds and garnets are mined in pits near Ratnapura, the 'City of Gems'. Every country seems to add to its natural and historical attractions by legends and myths, which deceive no one but the ultra-credulous, and Sri Lanka has a rich store of legend and tradition. The island has so many beauties and points of interest that there is really no need to 'gild the lily', but human nature remains the same the world over.

According to tradition, Sri Lanka was originally inhabited by a race of male and female demons, called *Yakkhas* and *Yakkhinas*. These evil characters were alleged to have confused ships by flashing lights at nights to direct the unwary mariners to destruction rather than to safety. Travellers who landed on the island were also lured to their death and then devoured by the bloodthirsty demons. The stories may have had a foundation in fact, the evildoers presumably being human rather than spirit in nature.

Buddha is said to have visited Sri Lanka during the reign of King Parakrama Bahu (1153–86), when he converted the *Yakkhas*. A great impassive statue of the recumbent Buddha entering Nirvana has rested at the dead city of Polonnatuwa in the centre of the island for over seven centuries.

In the fifth century A.D. a Buddhist bhikkhu, named Mahānāma, collated the early legends and traditions in the *Mahāvaṃsa*, the Pali Chronicle of the early kings of Ceylon or Sri Lanka. This work claimed to record the history of the island from its earliest days up to the fourth century A.D. (It is not, of course, to be confused with the four thousand volumes of the Buddhist Pali of Siam). The Chronicle recorded, *inter alia*, the story of the conquest of Lanka by the Buddha (563–483 B.C.) and his restriction of the activities of the *yakkhas*, as one of the most important periods of the country's history.

Gautama Buddha was an Indian prince of the Śākya clan, who founded the religion named after him. He inaugurated a religious order known as the Saṅgha and this monastic movement, which spread to many parts of India, eventually

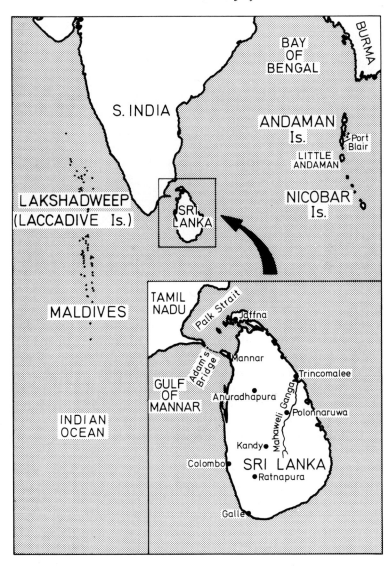

A Buddha   (W. T. Stunt)

entered Ceylon as well. Buddha's teaching (already referred to in Chapter 4) found wide acceptance in Lanka and, to this day, is woven into the fabric of Sinhalese life and thought. When Devānampiya Tissa, the ruler of Anurādhapura and his court were converted to Buddhism in the third century B.C., the great majority of his subjects followed their example, and Buddhism became more or less the official religion of the country.

Buddha was followed in Lanka by a victorious conqueror, named Vijaya, who was the leader of the first company of Sinhalese to emigrate to the island from India. They were Aryans, who claimed descent from a mythical 'lion race.' They were alleged to have originated with a princess of the Varga country in India who, as had been previously predicted, mated with a lion. Her son, whose hands and feet not unnaturally resembled the paws of a lion *(sinha)* was called Sinhabahu. According to the tradition, he escaped from the lion's lair with his mother and sister and eventually was compelled to slay the lion in order to deliver the land from the beast's ravages. Later, he and his followers moved to Lanka, the people becoming known as Sinhalese after the name of their leader. Fantastic stories are told of his prowess and miraculous doings and of the protection afforded to him by the gods, of his victory over the *yakkhas* and *yakkhinas,* and of his subsequent reign over Lanka for 38 years. There is probably some historical basis for part of the stories which are told, but they are so enveloped in the mythical that it is impossible to distinguish the real from the legendary. Sinhabahu was the first king of what has become known as the Great Dynasty.

'It is clear', says one writer, 'that the founder of the *Mahāvasa,* or the Great Dynasty, was a ruthless marauder, under whose leadership the Sinhalese royal dynasty arose in a welter of bloodshed and conspiracy. The name 'Sinhale' signified the leonine origin of the first king of Lanka. It became the name of the Sinhalese race, and they called their country Sinhaladripa, the Island of the Lion Race.' The Great Dynasty ruled from the sixth century B.C. to the fourth century A.D. Had Alexander the Great not turned back from Asia after reaching the Indus in 325 B.C., Lanka would probably have come under his sway. Later Tamil invaders secured control and established a Tamil dynasty, only to be superseded in time by Dravidian rulers from India. Of the sovereigns of the Great Dynasty, four committed suicide, six were assassinated, eleven were dethroned and murdered, thirteen were killed in battle, 22 were put to death by their successors, fifteen ruled for less than a year and 30 for less than four years.

A pagoda   (P. G. Ferry)

The capital city of Anuradhapura, first settled by Anurodha, a follower of Prince Vijaya, was really founded by Pandukhabhaya, a legendary chieftain in the fourth century B.C. His grandson Tissa (250–210 B.C.) in the third century B.C. is said to have secured from the Mauryan emperor of India all the elements needed for an Indian coronation for himself and to have become the first king of the Sinhalese to be so consecrated. His name, in consequence, was changed to Devanampiya, 'dear to the gods', and it is claimed that he was given the protection of the gods *(devas)*. The Anuradhapura kingdom retained its authority for over a millennium and was renowned throughout Asia for its architecture, sculpture and, above all, for its outstanding irrigation system. Its civilization did not cover the whole island, however. There were at that time three major territorial divisions and no single homogeneous political entity. Indeed, the three principalities of Rājarata, Ruhuṇa and Malayadesa continued until the thirteenth century A.D.

The city of Anuradhapura contains the sacred Bo tree. This tree, often referred to as Sri Mahabadhl, was allegedly grown from a branch of the tree under which Buddha was enlightened.

The dissolution of the great Mauryan empire in India led to an upsurge of Dravidians in the Deccan and to their emigration to the north of Ceylon or Lanka. The racial friction in the north that ensued is still seen as a disruptive force even today.

In 237 B.C. two young Tamil adventurers, Sena and Guttika, assassinated the reigning monarch at Anuradhapura and seized the throne for themselves, but they were murdered two decades later and the royal dynasty was restored. A decade later, however, a Chola prince named Eḷāra, who was Rajah of Madura, landed on the southern coast, captured the capital and slew the king, and proclaimed himself sovereign of Lanka. From then on there were repeated struggles for the throne. The kings of the Sulavansa, or Lesser Dynasty, claimed descent from Vijaya, but were definitely inferior to their predecessors. Sixty two kings ruled from A.D. 352 to A.D. 1100, the majority being ignoble mediocrities and totally undeserving of high estate.

The story was not an edifying one. As Ludowyk says, *ibid.,* p. 69, 'It is the story of an island torn by dynastic rivalries and civil strife. It was brought to its knees quite as much by internal dissensions as by pressure from abroad. Rival clans contested the kingship, court and army intrigues shortened the lives of kings and commanders; claimants to the throne habitually invoked the aid of their South Indian allies.' The repeated invasions from India left the country in ruins.

Chinese, Portuguese, Dutch, French and British, all played their part in invading the island. In 1796 the British took over the Dutch possessions in Ceylon and the island in due course became a crown colony. Portugal, Holland and Britain each controlled the island for about 150 years. But in 1948 she finally achieved independence. The Arabs called the island Serendit. The Portuguese renamed it Ceilao. The Dutch converted this into Zeilan, which the British transformed into Ceylon. When independence was granted, the country reverted to the old name of Sri Lanka.

William T. Stunt and Ernest H. Childs, who paid a visit to the island in 1974, said that 'inscriptions in the rock tell their tale of a glorious past, when the creed of Buddha rose like a pink coral reef, luring men to rise up and build. On that fair but frail foundation, before the eastern star led wise men to Bethlehem, and while the Druids' altar smoked with human sacrifices in Britain, a glorious kingdom was erected to endure for a while, but destined to decay and totter before the tides of evil and the storms of time. Today the broken memorials left their colossal

Colombo   (W. T. Stunt)

forms to the sunny sky in mournful ruin, solitary shrines built to an unknown God. Lofty ethic and kindly precept left the heart of man unregenerate, so that by slow degrees the moral gleam lit by Buddha was obscured by gross darkness and cruelty. Envious foes advanced to the attack. Royal cities were overrun. The capital was transferred to a rocky fortress. The years of transition were stained with oppression and blood. Men were impaled alive on pointed stakes for minor offences. Palm-crested crags looked down into a cockpit of cruelty; rivers ran red and an earthly paradise became an earthly hell.'

Today, elephants, bears, boars, hyenas, deadly snakes, crocodiles, monkeys and other wild animals have their haunts where once Oriental luxury reigned supreme. Roads and railways have been built through the jungle, but the human population is small. Beyond the ancient capitals, Anuradhapura and Polonnaruwa, the forest stretches, until nearing the Jaffna peninsula northward it becomes thin, and presently gives way to a plain dotted with stately palmyra palms.

The island is divided into nine provinces. The capital and largest town is Colombo. For centuries this was little more than a fishing village on the western coast, but it is now an important port with a population of over half a million. Thousands of tons of tea, rubber, cacao, coconuts, spices and minerals are exported through Colombo. The business section of the town has huge offices, mercantile houses and universal stores. In beautiful residential suburbs, large bungalows surrounded by palms contrast markedly with the hovels of the poor. The city presents a combination of east and west, prosperity and poverty, beauty and barrenness, gladness and gloom.

Kandy, nestling among the hills 50 miles inland and 1,500 feet above sea level, was once the royal capital. Here it was that, in the sixteenth century, the Portuguese found the dread Lord of the Island. To the Sinhalese, Kandy is still Maha Nuwara (the holy city). Today it is the centre of a planting district, the haunt of tourists, and the home of the most famous eastern relic, the Sacred Tooth of Buddha. In the Temple of the Sacred Tooth the faithful prostrate themselves before the casket containing the sacred relic. Andrew Cumming tells of a young couple lying on the floor for hours, praying that they might have a family. Outside, he says, 'the tropical night throbs and hums with countless small noises, fireflies flit silently and ghostly

Rugged escarpments, Nepal
(Tear Fund)

Dr. Paul G. Kalthoff with villagers
(Dr. R. Pross)

Thimbu valley, Bhutan   (S.G.M.)

Children of the Thunder Dragon   (B.M.M.F.)

Kandy—Temple of the Sacred Tooth   (M. Browne)

through the trees. Before a house in a clearing two altars have
been set up. Things of beauty in themselves, woven from
rushes, they are there for the Devil Dancers. On one a light
burns. Beneath the other a white cockerel lies stupefied. It will
be killed later to appease the spirits. Between the altars and the
house, the family are lined up, with the subject of the ceremony
placed centrally. She can be no more than 12 or 13 years of age,
the victim of epilepsy. She has been told that an evil spirit has
entered her body, and the two dancers, with incantations,
passes, incense and finally sacrifices, will endeavour to drive the
spirit out of her.'

For many centuries, Galle, on the south-western shore, was
the chief port, but in the latter half of the nineteenth century,
Colombo eclipsed it. Galle is a delightful, old-world town, with
well-preserved Dutch ramparts, and it has been described as a
jasper city moated by bluest sea and snowy breakers on the one
side and by a palmy savannah on the other. But its commercial
glory has departed and its spacious (but treacherous) harbour is
almost deserted. Once busy wharves are untenanted, and the
streets are no longer thronged by busy merchants and seamen.

Jaffna is the chief northern town. Here too a moated fortress,
with worm-eaten guns and stacks of cannon-balls, tells of

former perilous times when every colonist was a warrior. Hindu culture and the Tamil way of life predominate in Jaffna. The people of the area are known as Jaffna Tamils. They are progressive and are to be found in many of the professions. On the east coast is Trincomalee, with one of the most magnificent natural harbours in the world.

A. C. Rose, who was a senior executive on the Madras Railways and who gave himself unreservedly to the Lord's work, visited Sri Lanka from time to time, and his comments on the climate are worth quoting. He says that it compares favourably with that of other tropical countries but that, lying in the paths of two monsoons, it has a heavy rainfall, and that the result is a heavy humid atmosphere. The heat reaches a climax in April and May, when fortunate people flee to the hills. 'At the beginning of June, the south-west monsoon may be expected. Thick cloud-banks and welcome winds are its harbingers as it races across the ocean to break over Sri Lanka with tornado fury. For days, with slight respite, torrents of rain fall, and thunderstorms relieve the sultry air. Brief intervals of calm and sunshine alternate with furious squalls. August to early October are months of sunshine with occasional showers. During the latter part of October the north-east monsoon repeats the June experiences. During the monsoons the hill country may have eight inches of rain in twenty-four hours. Landslides interrupt railway, postal and telegraphic communication. In the low country disastrous floods result. In a tropical tornado, huge trees are torn up by the roots, palms crash down on houses, roads and railways are blocked, telegraph poles are felled and wires twisted into tangled chains.'

Sri Lanka was granted independence on the 4th February 1948, the relevant Act providing for a House of Representatives and a Senate. The United National Party acquired power but was defeated in 1956 by Solomon Bandaranaike and the People's United Front. Bandaranaike was originally a nominal Christian, who later became a Buddhist, and because he gave every encouragement to Buddhists (who formed two-thirds of the population), he became very popular. On his murder by a Buddhist monk in 1959, his widow Sirimavo took his place as leader of the party and later as Prime Minister – the first woman Prime Minister in the world. In 1961 legislation enabled her to take over from churches and missions all schools and

A brass worker   (H. N. Saunders, S.G.M.)

educational establishments which they had previously run. An
Act of 1971 also enabled her to acquire any business for the State
and the British Ceylon Corporation was accordingly national-
ized in the following year.

In 1971 appeals to the Privy Council were abolished and an
Island Court of Appeal set up instead. At the same time, the
Senate was abolished and in 1972 a Republican Constitution
came into force providing for a President and a Council of

At the Temple   (P. G. Ferry)

Ministers, responsible to a National Assembly, in which sovereignty was vested. The President holds office for four years and is appointed by the Prime Minister. The country still remains a member of the Commonwealth, however. Sri Lanka has received considerable financial help from the People's Republic of China.

Of the population of nearly fifteen million, the majority are Sinhalese. The aborigines are known as Veddalis and live in the seclusion of the jungles. They are said to represent one of the most primitive stages of human culture in the world. It has been estimated that fewer than a thousand remain, all of whom are located in the south-eastern jungle area.

The Sinhalese are a brown-skinned people of North Indian origin. Their language, Sinhala, is derived from Sanskrit and the majority of them are Buddhists. A. C. Rose opines that they are of Aryan stock who left the cradle of that race in Central Asia to drift down at last to Sri Lanka. He points out that the features of many are decidedly Semitic.

The Tamils, who are darker than the pure Sinhalese, originated in south India and they speak Tamil, a Dravidian language which is still widely used in south India: most of them are Hindus. The Indian Tamils are a distinct class and are descendants of labourers brought from India to work on the coffee and tea plantations.

The Muslims or Moors are descendants of Arab traders who came to the island during the medieval period. They have retained the Islamic faith of their ancestors. A percentage of them, however, are descendants of Indians rather than Arabs; their ancestors emigrated to Lanka at various times and, in some cases, because of persecution. Some are undoubtedly descendants of Arabs who married Indians.

The Burghers, who are of Portuguese or Dutch descent, are not very numerous. Most are nominal Christians, i.e. Roman Catholic or Reformed Presbyterians. Some of their ancestors intermarried with the Sinhalese to produce a new strain, but this is not very distinct.

There is also a fairly large group of Indians, most of whom are employed today on the tea and rubber plantations, and whose families have lived in Sri Lanka for two or three generations. These are mainly Hindus, but do include some – mostly Tamils – who are of other religions. A very small number of other races

Colombo, Bethesda Hall—Ernest H. Childs and members of the assembly   (W. T. Stunt)

(including British) may be found, but they are rapidly diminishing.

Practically everyone speaks Sinhalese – a difficult language with an alphabet of five hundred characters and also an intricate grammar. Tamil is used officially for some purposes. But English is still the second language and is virtually the *lingua franca*.

Although 67 per cent of the people are Buddhists, fifteen per cent are Hindus, over seven per cent are Christians and nearly eight per cent are Muslims. Ninety per cent of the 'Christians' are Roman Catholics – the legacy of the Portuguese invasion. Sunday is a working day and its place has been taken by a Buddhist holiday, Poya Day, which coincides with the four phases of the moon.

The country has had its full share of political, economic and social trouble since it achieved independence. As J. H. Kane points out also in *A Global View of Christian Missions*, p. 140, 'Communism is fairly strong, and more than one government has remained in power only with the reluctant co-operation of leftist political parties. Injustice and discrimination against minority groups have produced a sense of frustration. Labour unrest and corruption have adversely affected the economy.' Yet Sri Lanka is a reasonably progressive country and obviously has an important part to play (not only because of its strategic location) in the future of Central and South Asia.

As the morning mist rises up from the sea, the pink-tipped fleecy clouds tell of the advent of dawn. In a few minutes the whole sky is flooded with light. With all the spiritual nocturnal shadows which plunge Sri Lanka into darkness, there are signs of light, through the gloom. In the country's pluralistic society, each major group practises its own religion – Buddhism, Hinduism, Islām, Roman Catholicism – and the teaching of religion is compulsory in the schools. Where there are at least fifteen Christians in a class, Christianity must be taught. There is no bar to missionaries, but admission is on a quota basis, and the number of full-time Christian workers is deplorably small.

Christianity came to Sri Lanka at different times and wearing different garbs. The Portuguese brought Roman Catholicism with them. The Dutch introduced Reformed Christianity. The British presented Anglicanism. It is little wonder that the people were confused and that they found the unchanging teachings of Buddha and Muḥammad more acceptable.

The London Missionary Society was the first missionary body to enter the country, but its endeavour lasted only from 1804 to 1818. The Baptist Missionary Society, represented first by James Chater in 1812 and then by Ebenezer David, has continued to the present day, but with little to show for their labours. Thomas Coke, who had been a missionary in the West Indies, was the first to represent the Methodist Church in 1814. Since then the Church Missionary Society and other bodies have endeavoured to present the claims of Christ to the islanders, but the number of evangelical Christians is still extremely small.

The first full-time worker from assemblies was Arthur F. Witty of New Zealand, who went out in 1899 with the Poona and Indian Village Mission. While serving the Lord in Colombo in 1902 he came into fellowship in the assembly in that city. While on furlough in 1905–6 he married Miss Florence Frith, a missionary from India, and they returned to Sri Lanka with the commendation of Eden Hall, Auckland.

Ernest A. Rimmer spent a year in Sri Lanka before joining J. Herbert de Carteret at Belgaum (India) and gave help in the work around Colombo. As already mentioned Miss Amy Roper went to Sri Lanka with Mr. and Mrs. Witty, but, in the

Distributing tracts   (S.G.M.)

following year, she moved to Bengal to engage in language study. Very much later, commended from New Zealand in 1937, Miss Norah Ardrey went to Colombo, but she married Gordon Junck soon afterwards and moved to Kurianoor in India to work with him there.

For many years Mr. and Mrs. Witty held meetings in the homes of local people in Colombo and distributed literature. Mrs. Witty was also able to engage in teaching in a school. An assembly was commenced in the city in 1906. Later a Tamil assembly was also commenced and quite a number of people were saved. The Wittys also rendered valuable service by entertaining missionaries passing through. In 1908 the work demanded a larger hall and the following year they accordingly moved to another part of the city, beginning a work in the centre of a new district.

The events leading up to the move are recorded in a letter from Arthur Witty which was published in *Echoes of Service* of July 1910 and this is quoted *in extenso*. 'Three weeks after our return to Colombo, on November 1st 1906, nine of us were gathered together to remember our Lord in the breaking of bread. Since that time thirty-two others have taken their places with us, seven of these being commended from assemblies in other countries. Eight have removed from the Island, five have withdrawn from the assembly; and two have passed away to be with the Lord. Eternity alone will reveal what the work in Colombo owes under God to our late beloved brother, Mr. Anthonisz, whose hearty co-operation and fellowship we miss. Though not desirous of reckoning on numbers, yet we praise God that of those who have professed conversion we know of twenty-five who are standing true to Him. Several of these have seen the truth of believers' baptism and have obeyed.

'From the time of our return to Colombo, we have repeatedly found it necessary to "earnestly contend for the faith which was once delivered unto the saints" (Jude 3), owing to false teaching of various kinds. To our sorrow, some who withdrew from the assembly were carried away.

'For about a year the Lord tested us by keeping us in a business quarter, so that we seemed to make but little headway. Meanwhile our hearts and prayers were specially centred upon our present district and great was our joy when He opened this door for us. As the months have passed by, we have been confirmed in our conviction that this was His choice for us. Bambalapitiya is a residential quarter, rapidly growing, at the southern end of Colombo city, where the greater part of our work lies. There are eight weekly meetings in connection with the assembly; in addition to these we go twice a week to "Caxton House", which is situated some four miles distant, at the northern end of the city.

'The assembly's service of house-to-house tract distribution extends over a large area, monthly visits being paid to the homes, while the general hospital, museum and gaol are visited weekly. In this way some thousands of gospel portions and tracts in English, Sinhalese and Tamil are given to the people month by month. Our brother, Mr. Benner of Orillia, Canada, sends us 1,000 copies of the *Gospel Herald* monthly for free distribution, which are a great help to us in this work, being much appreciated by the people. We are also deeply indebted to the Scripture Gift Mission, London, for liberal supplies of English and Tamil Scripture portions.'

In 1910 they were joined by Charles J. Rolls, commended from Napier, New Zealand. He gave valuable help in the work for nine months, but then felt impelled to move to Coimbatore in India to relieve H. Handley Bird. With Charles Rolls' help, the work in the Colombo area was expanded, the Sunday school and Bible class increased in size and some believers were added to the assembly. Though suffering from ill-health, the Wittys continued after Mr. Rolls' departure to India, and engaged in extensive tract distribution and in a gospel postal ministry. Mrs. Witty died in 1917 but he continued the outreach on his own. He saw a new gospel meeting started at Willawatti in 1918 and, using a chart to present the gospel more clearly, he had good attendances. The following year Mrs. Isabel Loos, a Chinese believer, the widow of a well-to-do attorney, who had been blessed in meetings conducted by Charles Rolls, presented a section of ground and paid the cost of construction of a hall for the assembly. Bethesda Hall, Colombo, was built in 1919. Mrs. Loos was a frequent visitor to Bethesda and during the visit of Wilfred Wilcox of Clarence School she obeyed the Lord in baptism. Many gifted brethren visited Bethesda, including H. Handley Bird, A. C. Rose, Silas Fox and J. M. Davies. For some years the hall was full and many were saved, but problems arose later and the testimony was weakened. By 1920 there were two

English-speaking assemblies and two for national believers.

Mr. Witty returned to New Zealand in 1920 and continued in gospel preaching and in the exposition of the Scriptures. He married Miss R. Cooksley in 1922, but ill-health restricted his oral ministry. Mrs. Witty died in 1944 and he followed her in 1958.

Eric and Mary Phoenix, who had previously served in Mauritius and South India, were led to Colombo in 1945 and worked in the assembly and amongst servicemen stationed on the island. In 1946, however, they moved back to India.

Until the country became independent in 1948, many from U.K. assemblies, who served there as civil servants or naval officers, were able to help in the assemblies in Sri Lanka. Percival F. W. Parsons, well-known as an able minister of the Word, particularly in U.K., was one of such. These friends were gradually withdrawn from the island after 1948, however, and local difficulties arose which resulted in the closure of the assemblies other than at Bethesda Hall, Dickman's Road, Colombo. F. W. Collette, Hansard reporter to the parliament, retired early to devote his time to the Lord's work, and was ably supported by his wife. After a few years, he found himself almost the sole surviving elder, carrying the heavy burden of the assembly, and under pressure from his two sons in Australia to

Colombo, Bethesda Hall   (W. T. Stunt)

Colombo—W. T. Stunt and Maurice Herft

join them in that country. Eventually in 1971 he and his wife felt compelled to do so, leaving Fred Samuel and Maurice Herft to take on the responsibility of the assembly. Bethesda Hall is a large and well-built hall in a busy road and with considerable potential.

Peter and Peggy Ferry had hoped to work in Colombo, where Peter had held meetings on more than one occasion, but it proved impossible to obtain a visa.

Of one visit the Ferrys wrote: 'George and Shanta Nicholas took us into their home. They are Tamil and I discovered they are quite young in the faith. George is an architect and after studying in Colombo had gone on to study in Aberdeen. As he had a scholarship Shanta was able to go with him. Mr. and Mrs. Kimber who had been missionaries in South India were then living in Aberdeen and were brought into contact with George and Shanta. Shanta came to Christ through contact with a meeting for women. George was taken to the meetings by the Kimbers and it was this which was the means of their coming to Christ. Both George and Shanta had been nominal Christians but in spite of church-going and even confirmation they had not heard the gospel in Sri Lanka. They came back to Sri Lanka and against the wishes of their family were baptised at Bethesda Hall and brought into fellowship. The Lord gave them time in Aberdeen for being taught in the Scriptures; when they came to Bethesda there was very little for them and soon George himself was expected to take part in the meetings. Through their witness George had the joy of seeing his mother and sister come into fellowship. The Lord had brought them to Bethesda at a time of spiritual deadness. However, because they were really convinced that the Lord had taken them to Bethesda, they stayed there and prayed for help and revival.'

Emmaus work was started there and some have been saved through the courses, and George Nicholas has been greatly encouraged thereby. Today there is no full-time assembly worker in this attractive but needy island, with its population of nearly fifteen million. It seems incredible that no one has heard the call to serve the Lord here. Perhaps it is easier to sing of Ceylon's spicy breezes than to face the challenge of Sri Lanka's spiritual needs.

Himalayan heights
(Air India)

Happy Nepali children
(Tear Fund)

31

Closed Doors

Lying along the southern slopes of the Himalayas, Nepal is a completely landlocked country, bounded on the north by Tibet, and on the east, south and west by India. It is only 54,362 square miles in size and is one of the least developed countries of the world. Seventy five per cent of the country is covered with mountains, and it contains some of the most rugged and difficult mountains in the world. A belt of lowland in the south is the only flat land in the country. It has four physical belts. The Tarai, the low flat plain adjacent to the border of India, is the only really fertile area. The forested Churia foothills and the Inner Tarai zone, rising from the Tarai plain to the rugged Mahabharat Lakh range, is an area which has a splendid majesty of its own. Apart from the mid-mountain region, there remains only the Great Himalayan range, rising in places to over 29,000 feet. Scores of climbers have lost their lives in the attempt to scale Everest and some of the other peaks in this range.

Little is known of Nepal's early history. It is said that in 250 B.C. Ásoka, the emperor of India, visited Nepal and that his daughter settled there and founded Deopatan, near the present shrine of Pashupati. In the fifth century A.D. the country was reasonably prosperous because of the trade with India and Tibet. In A.D. 595, Amśuvarman, who founded the Thakuri dynasty, acceded to the throne. Subsequently the Rajput princes of Udaipur, who had been driven from their own country by the Muslims, moved into the Himalayan areas, and became the founders of the Gurkha dynasty in Nepal. In 1771 the great Gurkha king, Prithvi Narayan Shah, conquered the kingdom of Kathmandu and, after strong resistance, brought the whole of the country under his control. The Gurkha dynasty ruled Nepal for 180 years. The effective rule for most of this time, however, was in the hands of hereditary prime ministers, who adopted a policy of national isolation. The country's door was closed to the outside world. But in 1950 the National Congress Party were the cause of a 'palace revolt,' and, in consequence, a constitutional monarchy was restored. In 1960 king Mahendra assumed direct rule and commenced to modernize the country. In 1963 he issued a set of new laws, improving legal standards and outlawing long-established practices such as caste, bigamy and child marriage. His reforms secured acceptance despite their revolutionary character. He was succeeded on his death in 1972 by his son, Birenda, who has endeavoured to follow the same course as his father.

With its population of 13.4 million, Nepal has over seventy tribes, including the Gurung, Magar, Tamang, Newar, Limbu, Rai, Sherpa, Sunwar, Tharu and Maibili. The main language is Nepali but the multiplicity of dialects creates problems in the process of modernization. The Gurkhas of Nepal are descendants of Hindus who fled to Rajputana at the time of the Muslim invasion of India. Not only have the Gurkhas the reputation of being among the finest soldiers in the world, but their intellect and culture are also above average.

The population is a mixture of Mongoloid from the north and Aryan from the south and west, together with an admixture of the Rajputs driven out of India by the Muslims. The dominant race is the Gurkha, whose ancestors came from the north-west of India. While the hill tribes are largely animists, the remainder of the people are Buddhists and Hindus. Only three per cent of the people are literate. Ninety per cent of the people are engaged in agriculture, rice, jute, wheat and maize being the principal products. There is also a certain amount of foresting. The capital is Kathmandu, and other towns are Bhodgarn, Patan, Nepalganj, Biratnagar, Birganj, and Bhairawa.

The country was the birthplace of Gautama Buddha and his teachings naturally prevailed for some centuries. There are over 27,000 shrines in the Kathmandu valley. But today 89 per cent of the people are Hindus and only nine per cent Buddhist and a

Thimbu Dzong   (B.M.M.F. and Mrs. A. T. Burgess)

A Buddha (B.M.M.F.)

Patan—ancient
palaces and temples
(Tear Fund)

further two per cent are Muslims. The hill people still remain basically animists.

For over two centuries Nepal was sealed off from the outside world. It was impossible for missionaries to enter the country. Jesuit missionaries did attempt to introduce Christianity in the 17th century but all missionaries and Nepalese Christians were expelled in 1767. Through schools and hospitals established by Christian workers on the borders of the country, many Nepalis were brought into contact with the gospel and some were undoubtedly converted. Until 1950 foreigners were not allowed to enter the country. Even today, social, educational and medical work is permitted only if the workers pledge themselves not to engage in evangelization. The Wycliffe Bible Translators, for example, who had several members (some of them from British assemblies) working in eighteen Nepalese dialects, were asked to leave in 1976. The constitution states explicitly that 'no person shall be entitled to convert another person to his religion.' Sadhu Sundar Singh made an evangelistic trip into Nepal in the 1920's, but was unable to repeat it and there is no information as to the effectiveness of the effort.

A Roman Catholic Mission, which had been based at Patna, was the first group to secure entry into the country when the door was opened. But the Mar Thomas Church of South India established a permanent base in Nepal in 1952. The Nepal Evangelistic Band, a British faith mission, which had been engaging in dispensary work and in witnessing through this since 1936 at Nautanwa, a border town, was also able to secure entry for a number of workers. A hospital was started at Pokhara and later a leprosarium was opened. Since preaching and proselytization were officially forbidden, the leprosy and medical clinics were used as a means for the presentation of the gospel message. (See *Fires at the Foot of Fish-Tail*, by G. M. A. Turner).

An indigenous church is quietly growing and this is due to the activities of a dynamic individual named Prem Pradham. Formerly a lieutenant in the Indian army, he was converted from Hinduism to Christianity at Darjeeling through a member of the brethren assembly there. After a course at Allahabad Bible Seminary, he returned to his own country in 1959 to preach the gospel to his own people – fully aware that such activities were illegal and, if persisted in, might eventually lead

Pokhara—reading lesson   (Tear Fund)

to his death. A number of Nepalis turned to Christ and when he baptised his first nine converts, he was sentenced to imprisonment for five years. This did not silence his witness: while in prison he led 25 prisoners to Christ. Prem Pradham has spent seven periods in prison for thus violating the law. It is extremely probable that other Christians will suffer similarly for their activities. They would probably have avoided attracting undesirable attention if they had continued to meet quietly in conformity with the New Testament pattern of autonomous churches or assemblies. It is understood that Prem Pradham is also maintaining a tenuous link with Bakht Singh's followers in India, which may also give rise to difficulties at some future date.

During the undeclared war between Malaysia and Indonesia 1963–66, many Gurkha soldiers (mercenaries from Nepal) came into contact with Christians who were guides to them in the jungles of Borneo. As a result some were brought to a knowledge of the Saviour. They were subsequently posted to Hong Kong and other British bases but some returned home to Nepal with their new-found faith.

Some believers (including, it is understood, some from assemblies) have taken professional appointments in the country in order to witness to the Nepalis and to help to strengthen the Christians in Nepal, but full-time missionary activities are not practicable at present. Jeannette Hyland, from Australia, is working with the United Mission to Nepal in connection with a Government sponsored health programme.

Some believers were among the staff of Shanta-Bhavan

Paul G. Kalthoff   (R. Vetter, Wiedenest)

Nepali transport
(R. Vetter, Wiedenest)

Hospital who moved to the new Palan Hospital. A number of workers are also engaged in language study at Kathmandu.

German assemblies have taken a leading part in bringing the gospel into Nepal. Because of the difficult circumstances, it was deemed wise to work in association with other Christians in the International Nepal Fellowship from 1955. Missionaries had been working along the Indian/Nepalese border since the early 1930's, but in 1952 a group of six Europeans (a lady doctor and five nurses), together with five Nepali Christians travelled for eight days on foot from India to the Pokhara valley in Central Nepal. When they paid off their nineteen porters, they were left with total funds of fifteen rupees to carry on the work. Permission had been given to engage in medical activities and eventually the Shining Hospital was built at Pokhara – the first hospital in that area.

About the same time, doctors and nurses were able to start a medical work on similar lines in Kathmandu, Ursula Meisel, commended from Berlin, commenced service here in 1957 and, until her retirement in 1965, was engaged not only in the

Shanta-Bhavan Hospital and the leprosy hospital but also in the leprosy hospital at Anandaban in the Kathmandu valley.

In 1963 Irmgard Pitzke from Hamburg and Willy van der Wal from Rotterdam joined the work at Pokhara. Others followed but because of the restrictions on changing religion etc., they were able to come only as skilled labourers and specialists. They have, nevertheless, been able to make a valuable contribution to the work. Dr. and Mrs. William Gould went to Nepal for a time in 1964.

New centres were established at Beni and Baglung and a lepers' colony was also commenced. Later, the leprosy hospital, Green Pastures, was built, which is run by Paul and Rosewitha Kalthoff who went out in 1972. In 1973 the missionaries were given the responsibility for the far-reaching leprosy programme in the west of the country, under the leadership of Dr. Paul Gerhard Kalthoff and his wife, Rosewitha. Stations were built at Ghorai, Surkhet and Jumca, and a training programme was introduced for paramedicals at Pokhara. With the increasing need, other missionaries went out from German assemblies as nurses, doctors, medical assistants and workmen, until there are now 60 workers in the I.N.F.

In 1970 it became clear that the premises of the Shining Hospital were inadequate and that much more extensive buildings were required. At the same time, the government was contemplating building a hospital. Eventually the king decided that half of the new building should be financed by the government and half by the missionaries and that the staff should be drawn from both parties. The arrangement, in fact, worked very well. In Nepal, it is difficult to undertake service without official approval and in this case, it would be impossible without government co-operation.

In the last few years, quite a number of missionaries have been commended from German assemblies, including Jutta Weber, 1968, Patrick and Heidemarie Pares, 1972, Edith Krug, 1976, Dr. Reinhard Pross, 1977, Anne Herr, 1978, Johannes and Jutta Hlusiak, 1981, Maria Schimpf, 1981, Herbert and Martina Bedenbender 1982, Dr. Silvia Chandler, 1982, and Gertrud Immega, 1982. Over the years – and still today – a number of English and German assembly missionaries have worked with the Wycliffe Bible Translators.

Dora Bierl, commended by Swiss assemblies, is working in

Dr. Reinhard Pross
(M. Gut)

Nepal. Herbert Knuchel, also commended from Switzerland, went first to India but is now working in Nepal.

Despite the unusual circumstances and the limitations on religious liberty, it has still proved practicable to bear witness to the love of God. A report in *The Flame* for March 1983 says, 'Significant church growth is taking place in Nepal, particularly in the eastern part of the country around the capital, Kathmandu. In 1965 there were hardly twenty Christians in the land, in 1974 there were about 8,000 and now it is estimated there are about 15,000 true believers.' There are some 40 large assemblies and a number of smaller ones. In addition, there are numbers of isolated believers scattered through the country and there are Nepali Christians outside Nepal. The assemblies all form one fellowship (the Nepal Christian Fellowship) and there are no other churches or denominations.

New workers are urgently needed at the moment in all fields of service, particularly for the leprosy control programme which ranges from early diagnosis, treatment (including surgical) to rehabilitation. Whilst direct preaching of the gospel is usually impracticable, the opportunities for Christian life and witness are obvious – and have led to results.

River crossing   (Dr. R. Pross)

The Bible has been translated into Nepali and has been published in India, and copies are gradually finding their way into the country. The powerful radio stations at Manila and Seychelles are beaming gospel messages into Nepal and there are reports of blessing resulting therefrom.

In addition to Nepali Christians, there are approximately 100 Indian Christians employed in secular work in the country, and another 200 Christians attached to various secular aid missions, so that the national believers are not entirely deprived of sympathetic support. There is, of course, a constant risk of activities or personal witnessing offending the government, and prayer is needed for God's children who are living in such difficult circumstances. There is, in addition, a need for others to accept the challenge of discovering ways of introducing the gospel into this country. Some have questioned the justification for the expenditure of time, effort and finance in attempting to reach the Nepalis, and whether resources might not be better employed in some other field. Yet, as Dr. Geoffrey D. Lehmann of India says, 'the qualities of perseverance, steadfastness and continuance are emphasized in the Book.' And after all, these also were souls for whom Christ died. The church has a

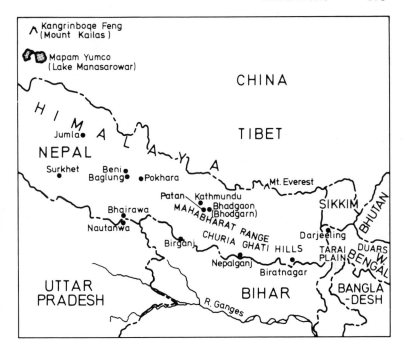

responsibility to spread the message worldwide, and the worker
dare not give up merely because of difficulties.

> 'My hand is on the plough, my faltering hand,
> But all in front of me is untilled land,
> The wilderness and solitary place,
> The lonely desert with its interspace.
> What harvest have I but this paltry grain,
> These dwindling husks, a handful of dry corn,
> These poor lean stalks? My courage is outworn.
> Keep me from turning back!
> The handles of my plough with tears are wet,
> The shares with rust are spoiled, and yet, and yet,
> My God! My God! Keep me from turning back!'

Hills and valleys
(Mrs. A. J. Burgess
and B.M.M.F.)

32

Land of the Thunder Dragon

(Map page 260)

In the Eastern Himalayas, to the east of Sikkim and bordering on Assam lies the picturesque country of Bhutan. 'Forest-clad mountains,' says McLeish, *op. cit.*, p. 138, 'stretch in every direction, and deep valleys intersect the country, carrying the rapid mountain torrents down to the Brahmaputra river. Six such rivers cut the land into distinct sections, the largest of which, the River Manas, passes Tashigang, the most easterly town of Bhutan, and hurls itself into the Brahmaputra at Goalpara in Assam. Magnificent waterfalls characterize the rivers, and crag-perched monasteries and forts the mountain heights above.' Turner says, 'The prospect between abrupt and lofty prominences is inconceivably grand; hills clothed to their very summits with trees, dark and deep glens, and the high tops of mountains lost in clouds, constitute altogether a scene of extraordinary magnificence and sublimity.' In the north the Himalayan Mountains reach a height of 24,000 feet and the northern boundary with Tibet stretches along 300 miles of snow-capped, nearly inaccessible peaks.

The climate naturally varies with the altitude. The valleys in the centre are temperate, but the plains in the south are sub-tropical. Violent storms, originating in the Himalayas, are not infrequent and these gave the country the name of the 'Land of the Thunder Dragon'.

Bhutan is a small state of 18,000 square miles and a population of just over one million. Chinese maps show part of Bhutan as within China, but various other states have also made claims upon the country. Britain, of course, annexed the Bengal and Assam Duars and by the Sinchula Treaty of 1865 agreed to pay a subsidy in recognition of the annexation of these sub-montane tracts.

In 1910 this allowance was doubled when Bhutan consented to British conduct of its foreign affairs. When Britain withdrew from India in 1947, the Indian government assumed our obligations to Bhutan and, two years later, a treaty formalized that Bhutan would have its external affairs regulated by India.

The history of the original inhabitants, the Tephus, is practically unknown. In the twelfth century the country was invaded by tribes from Assam and was completely overrun. Two centuries later, lamaistic Buddhism seems to have been introduced and to have gained a permanent hold upon the Bhutanese, but there are no details regarding the source (probably the north) from which it came. At a later date, repeated raids were made by bands of Tibetans, who seized land and possessions and settled in the country.

The country was controlled by the spiritual leaders until the sixteenth century. Then an influential and powerful lama, named Sheptoon La-Pha, from Tibet became the King of Bhutan and exercised authority over temporal matters also. His

 Tongsa Dzong (S.G.M.)

Toward the Thimbu Dzong   (Mrs. A. J. Burgess)

successor, Doopgein Sheptoon continued to exercise this dual responsibility but the next ruler confined himself to the spiritual role and appointed a minister to become the temporal authority (Deb Raja). Doopgein Sheptoon had appointed *penlops* (governors of territories) and *jungpens* (governors of forts), and the future political rulers were nominated by these governors. This inevitably led to disagreement and unrest, and during the nineteenth century, the country was plagued by a series of civil wars. Eventually, by virtue of his military prowess and statesmanship, and with Chinese assistance, a governor named Ugyen Wangchuck was recognized popularly as political leader in 1885, and in 1907 the feudalistic system of government ceased and the council of governors accepted that the occupant of the throne should be hereditary king (Druk Gyalpo) of Bhutan.

Hardy Gurkhas from Nepal, mostly members of the Rai, Gurung, and Limbu ethnic groups, began infiltrating into south-west Bhutan about 1910 and now comprise an estimated 25 per cent of the total population. Banned from settling in central Bhutan, they live along the whole length of the south of the country. Their presence may contribute to the development of the region but, as in the past, continues to fuel political discontent and instability. Discrimination against the Nepalese constitutes a major political problem for Bhutan. In an effort to

Over the river   (Mrs. A. J. Burgess)

relieve the tensions between the ethnic groups, all Nepalese
immigration was barred in 1959. It is now difficult for any
foreigner to obtain a permanent residence visa.

Lamaistic Buddhism was introduced into Bhutan by
Shabdung Rimpochi, and the Dharma Raja is deemed to
be one of his reincarnations. Relics of this religious leader are
preserved at Punakha (the summer capital), where there is an
altar and the chief lamas. Despite their alleged allegiance to
Buddhism, the people still pay homage to the spirits they see in
nature and the elements. Monasteries abound and there are over
2,000 lamas and large numbers of nuns, but the Bhutanese
Buddhism is extremely corrupt. The Nepalese minority are
Hindus.

With the exception of the Nepalese, who speak Nepali, the
language spoken is Lloka, a form of Tibetan, and the ordinary
Bhutan is described as a Llopa. The written language is also
Tibetan. It has been said that economically, socially and
morally, the people of Bhutan are the neediest in the whole
Himalayan range. The literacy rate is only five per cent.

The main industry is agriculture, although 70 per cent of the
country is covered with forest. Rice, barley, wheat, maize and
vegetables are grown, but extensive cultivation is impracticable
in many places. A small export to India of silk and cloth is

carried on, but the contact with the outside world is limited. In the densely forested area of the Duar Plain in the south, tigers, elephant and deer find their habitat.

It is estimated that 75 per cent of the people are Mahāyāna Buddhists of the Drukpa sub-sect of the Karyua school, which was first introduced from Tibet in the twelfth century.

Bhutan has been virtually closed to Christian missions. The Church of Scotland Mission has been able to establish a number of schools in the country, and other missionaries have attempted to make contact near the frontier. The Scandinavian Alliance Mission has had a school at Baksa, a village within the country, since 1892, but there seem to have been no conversions of the Bhutanese. There is no record of any assembly work here.

33

Whither Now?

Thirty years ago there were over 200 assembly missionaries in India: today there are under 50. Missionaries resident in the country today are allowed to return from furlough, but visas for new missionaries are seldom granted. The door is no longer as wide open for business and professional men, who could give their spare time to Bible teaching and preaching. The day of the foreign missionary is rapidly coming to an end. Fortunately, quite a number of able Indian Christians are taking up the work, and the complete 'indigenization' of the assembly work is inescapable. Overseas speakers, who are willing to pay their own expenses (at least, from their own land to that of India), may still be welcomed at some of the large conventions, but the concept of resident foreign workers is rapidly disappearing. Yet, although it is 35 years since independence, it is only during the last decade that a realization of the inevitable has been dawning. It does not seem to have been foreseen in the past, nor does there seem to have been any serious attempt to adjust methods to the future need.

There are well over 1,000 assemblies in India, but they are mostly in the south. Far less effort was exerted to establish assemblies in the north and, in some states, there has never been a witness of any kind to the gospel of God's grace.

It is a sub-continent with over 500,000 villages and the assembly missionary endeavour has been largely restricted to the villages. It was presumably impossible to envisage the extent of the urbanization which would take place so quickly, although it should have been evident that the industrialization so vital to

Delhi—thirst for education   (R. Duff)

the country would necessitate a shift of population. The relative neglect of the cities, and particularly of the student world, has left the Christian community in India at a grave disadvantage. Ben Watt, a leading Indian Christian puts it quite plainly in *Evangelism in India Today,* p. 3, 'By A.D. 2000 India will have about 20 cities with 20 million in each. Cities are where the action is. They are the centres of power and decision-making, which need to be influenced. For too long, most missions and missionaries have concentrated their endeavours in the rural areas, where church planting was easier. It is time now to confront the educated leaders and men of influence in government, politics, business, and the armed forces. If we saturate the large cities with the gospel, we can extend the impact to the rest of the nation.'

The task now is far more difficult because of the apparent lack of planning over the last century. Any survey of the missionary work in the sub-continent leads almost inevitably to the conclusion (whether justified or not) that the great majority of workers concentrated upon a comparatively small field and had no overall vision of the whole nation – or even a whole state. This is not to under-estimate the devotion, dedication and sacrificial labours of those who so willingly gave themselves and their talents in the Master's service. But that does not dispel the impression of a myopic vision of strategy and potentialities.

Village scenes (M. Browne)

Roland Allen's words in *Missionary Methods*, p. 3, may clarify the point. 'In a little more than ten years St. Paul established the Church in four provinces of the Empire – Galatia, Macedonia, Achaia and Asia. Before A.D. 57, St. Paul could speak as if his work there was done, and could plan extensive tours into the far West without anxiety lest the churches which he had founded might perish in his absence for want of his guidance and support. The work of the apostle during these ten years can, therefore, be treated as a unity. Whatever assistance he may have received from the preaching of others, it is unquestioned that the establishment of the churches in these provinces was really his work. In the pages of the New Testament he, and he alone, stands forth as their founder. And the work which he did was really a completed work. So far as the foundation of the churches is concerned, it is perfectly clear, that the writer of the Acts intends to represent St. Paul's work as complete. The churches were really established. Whatever disasters fell upon them in later years, whatever failure there was, whatever ruin, that failure was not due to any inefficiency or lack of care and completeness in the Apostle's teaching or organization. When he left them, he left them because his work was fully accomplished.'

The Apostle's plan of strategy in preaching was clear. He focussed on important cities, which were the key to large areas or whole provinces. He planned the evangelization of the province by establishing churches in key centres. He looked beyond provinces to countries – Italy, Spain, etc. – and to the broader horizon of the world empire itself. His was no limited vision or parochial plan: his ultimate aim was world evangelization. Here is the pattern.

One of the consequences of the methods adopted in India was that it created the missionary compound concept, with the missionary in the centre and others dependent upon him economically and socially, as well as spiritually – a concept that could conceivably negate the development of a complete trust in God for every need.

It also resulted almost automatically in the devotion of what might possibly be regarded as a disproportionate amount of time, energy and resources to educational, orphanage, medical and even industrial work. It was argued quite logically that our Lord fed the hungry and healed the sick, that it is impossible to

Bombay   (Indian High Commission)

teach the illiterate, and that it is essential to provide training if converts are to be useful. All of which is perfectly true, but perhaps Emil Brunner's comments are not entirely irrelevant. 'It is not the pressing task of the church to create, to change, to improve the social order. The task of the church lies beyond any social order, because the task is to preach the gospel of Jesus Christ, the kingdom of God which transcends all social order, the good and the bad alike.'

Whereas in one area the teaching of Anthony Norris Groves had the effect of inducing a complete faith in God, e.g. in the case of John C. Aroolappen, in another area the missionary built schools and then hired Indian teachers and paid them salaries and dictated their conditions of service. So that, in one case, a believer, appointed to run a school and to engage in preaching in the open air, was dismissed because he did not preach sufficiently often.

Village evangelism involved the missionaries in considerable travelling and physical hardship, and some, at least, of the assemblies closed down when they were deprived of the pastoral care of the missionary. Would there have been a stronger and more enduring work if the cities had been evangelized and Indian believers in the cities had assumed the responsibility for evangelizing areas from the cities.

Because the cities were left comparatively unevangelized, they have become centres for the propagation of communism, secularization, humanitarianism and syncretism. It is com-

Staff nurses seeing patients at prenatal clinic (B. D. Holt)

Student nurses class
(B. D. Holt)

Nagarjunasagar Dam, Andhra Pradesh   (Indian High Commission)

monly said in the cities that it does not matter much what is believed: the millions of gods, who satisfied the spiritual aspirations or needs of the multitudes, may still be sufficient for the purpose. Even Gandhi said that 'the soul of religion is one, but it is encased in a multitude of forms. Truth is the exclusive property of no single scripture.'

On the other hand, William Walker writes, 'The three pillars of Hinduism are: (1) the joint family system, (2) the autonomous village community system, and (3) the caste system. The Industrial Revolution in India at the present time is doing more to undermine the foundations of Hinduism than any other social or economic factor. If we do not grasp firmly the opportunities which are ours today in India, and if the gospel does not reach the darkened mind of the liberated Hindu of the future – the gospel of Karl Marx will.' That, of course, is the fear of the unregenerate politician as well.

Is it too late? If we cannot send missionaries, what can we do? It is clearly vital to give all necessary support to leading Indian workers, particularly in the realms of finance, literature and radio broadcasting. But it seems an urgent necessity for representative leaders in western countries to meet to discuss the problems and the best solutions possible and then to thrash out the whole subject with Indian leaders. But is that possible before it is too late?

Appendix I

Who are the Brethren?

Each volume contains an answer to this question by a different contributor in order to show the measure of spiritual freedom in the application of New Testament church principles.

There may be some who read this book who have had little acquaintance with the people who are commonly called 'brethren', and for whom some information about the characteristics of these people would be welcome. This appendix, therefore, is written to indicate summarily certain of their tenets and practices. Some of those which are here mentioned are features also of other communities of Christians, but others of them are rather distinctive of brethren churches.

The basic truth for which the brethren stand is
The inspiration and authority of Holy Scripture.
This involves that they believe in the utter reliability of Scripture, and oppose those trends of theological thinking which, to varying extents, question and even deny the Bible's truthfulness. Since the Lord Jesus Christ expressed Himself on this matter so forcibly (Matt.5:18; John 10:35) they hold that, as followers of Him, they should do the same. This results in their general doctrinal position being what might be expressed in the phrase 'historic orthodoxy'. They conceive of God, consequently, in trinitarian terms; Jesus Christ they hold to be both human and divine, and they regard the Holy Spirit as truly personal. They believe Christ's death to have been a substitutionary sacrifice for the sins of men; and they affirm that

His resurrection and ascension were bodily events, as will be also His second coming. They believe that salvation is imparted on the exercise of faith in Christ, and in the biblical presentation of the doctrines of justification, sanctification and glorification.

But they regard the Bible as authoritative not only for Christian doctrine in general, but for church practice in particular, with the consequence that they endeavour to constitute their local assemblies in accordance with the principles described in the New Testament. They only, therefore, receive into church membership those whom they believe to be regenerate Christians. They enjoin and practise the baptism of none but believers, and that by immersion. They celebrate with regularity the ordinance of the Lord's Supper. The government and teaching of a local church is placed in the hands of a body of elders rather than those of a single individual, for it would seem from Acts 14:23 and 20:17 that this was how it was in the New Testament Churches.

A second emphasis of brethren churches is—
Zeal in evangelism.
Not only have they been 'evangelical' (firmly standing on the truth of God's Word), but they have been also 'evangelistic' (keenly engrossed in the work of evangelism). This has been so both in the homeland, as could be illustrated in many ways, and also, as the pages of this book have demonstrated, in countries overseas. In relation to the size of the home-based movement, the extent of their missionary undertakings is quite enormous.

The Christian brethren stand also for—
The unity of believers.
It was as a Bible-prompted protest against the sectarianism of the Protestant denominations that the movement originally arose. When faithful to their principles, therefore, they receive to the ordinance of the Lord's Supper all true believers in Christ, provided that they are not living in open or flagrant sin; for they recognise the Table around which they gather as being, not theirs, but the Lord's, and hence that to which all the Lord's people have a right to come.

They stand, further, for—
The universal priesthood of believers.
In view of the fact that whenever the New Testament denotes Christians as 'priests', the reference is always to the Church in its entirety rather than to some privileged circle within the

Church, the brethren refuse to recognise a priestly 'caste' of Christians, distinguished from their fellow-believers by dress and title. They recognise, certainly, the propriety of setting aside some Christians as overseers of local churches, and indeed of releasing certain of them from secular employment, so as to devote themselves in a full-time capacity to the work of evangelism, Bible teaching and missionary enterprise overseas; but in the light of Christ's teaching in Matt.23:8-10, they discountenance any suggestion (whether by word or symbol) of the division of the Church into 'clergy' and 'laity'. At their observance of the Lord's Supper, consequently, no marked-out individual is in attendance who alone is authorised to officiate. It is commonly held in other circles that the bread and the wine need to be 'consecrated' by an 'ordained minister' for the ordinance to be valid, but this idea is alien to New Testament teaching, and finds no place, therefore, in brethren practice.

The person through whom, more than any other, the brethren movement was established in the 1820s was a dentist living in Exeter named Anthony Norris Groves; and he said in 1827 that 'it appeared to him from the Scripture that believers meeting together as disciples of Christ were free to break bread together as their Lord had admonished them, and that, in so far as the practice of the apostles could be a guide, every Lord's Day should be set aside for thus remembering the Lord's death and obeying His parting command'. The following year, he expressed himself as follows: 'This, I doubt not, is the mind of the Lord concerning us: We should come together in all simplicity as disciples, not waiting on any pulpit or ministry, but trusting that the Lord would edify us together, by ministering, as He pleased and saw good, from the midst of ourselves'. To people in the brethren movement today, these are commonplace ideas; but they were revolutionary concepts at the time when Groves expressed them.

The Christian brethren believe additionally in—
The local upraising of spiritual gift.
They view the normal way in which God supplied the spiritual needs of a local church as being His cultivation of gift from within the fellowship. Just as, in the natural creation, God made 'the fruit-tree yielding fruit after his kind *whose seed is in itself* '(Gen.I:II), so it is in the spiritual creation. God plants a church; and then from within that church He provides for that

church's development and propagation. The prevalent custom among churches generally is to rely almost exclusively on spiritual gift which is imported from elsewhere; but while this, no doubt, is the easier resort, it has the effect of quenching the upsurge of native ability, the end-result being the weakness which invariably ensues from from incessant spoon-feeding. There is indeed clear Scriptural warrant for the making of periodic visits by evangelists and Bible teachers to a church, but God's normal purpose seems to be the upbuilding of churches through the exercise of gift which has been reared locally from the church's converts. So it was among the Corinthians (I Cor.I:7); so it is among the Christian brethren.

A final matter by which the Christian brethren are characterised is—

Heart-devotion to the Lord Jesus Christ.

This is certainly not to imply that such is not the case on the part of other Christians, but simply that it is a notable feature of the brethren. Reflect, for instance, on their distinctive service, their meeting, usually on Sunday mornings, for the remembrance of Christ in the celebration of His Supper, when they spend a full hour or more in leisurely meditation on Him they love. Reflect on brethren hymnody (so little known outside their own circle), hymns, not dealing to any extent with practical or evangelistic subjects, on which much is elsewhere available, but with the adoring contemplation of Christ. It is this same devotion brethren show towards the Person of their Redeemer that has made them abnormally occupied with Second Advent teaching, the drive at the back of its having been their longing to behold Christ's face and be transformed into His likeness.

It would be unrealistic not to acknowledge the serious faults and failings characterising many brethren assemblies. One would contend, however, that these are due, not to their principles being erroneous, but to the effect of the human element, the (much to be deplored) worldliness, carnality and ungraciousness of certain of their members, not to mention those over whom, in some way, our adversary Satan has gained an advantage, so that they have fallen into sin, dishonouring the Lord and troubling His people. Such tragedies, regrettably, occur in all Christian communities, and brethren (though, one believes, with a better record than most), have not been altogether exempt from them. There is no room for complacency therefore. Those belonging to this movement need to humble themselves under the mighty hand of God, confess their waywardness and seek to rectify it; and, that done, hold their New Testament principles with increasing tenacity, meticulously translating them into practice in accordance with the needs and circumstances of the present time.

Stephen S. Short

Appendix II

Missionary Service Groups

THE ASSEMBLY CONTRIBUTION IN OVERSEAS MISSIONS

As indicated in Appendix I the nineteenth century witnessed the beginning of a number of spontaneous groups aiming, as far as possible, at maintaining the simple and flexible church order of New Testament times. The local churches which were formed became known as assemblies of brethren because of the frequent use of that term in the book of Acts.

Many of the early brethren were also impressed with the obligation to fulfil our Lord's commission to go into all the world and, as early as 1829, one of the early brethren, Anthony Norris Groves, with his wife, two sons and others renounced his lucrative practice as a dentist in Exeter to become a missionary in Baghdād.

Despite privation and sorrow (including the loss of his wife and baby daughter), Groves proved the Lord's sufficiency in every circumstance, not only in Baghdād but also in India, where he subsequently settled to serve the Lord and to which country he also took a band of missionary recruits.

Throughout his overseas service Groves followed God's leading and trusted Him to supply his needs. Others followed his example and in the last century and a half thousands of believers have gone overseas from brethren assemblies, adhering strictly to their understanding of the principles of missionary endeavour recorded in the New Testament.

Anthony Norris Groves 'was completely unfettered by tradition or precedent and regarded the principles and practices of Missionary Societies as having no validity or relevance to himself. It was to the Word of God that he turned for his guidelines' (*A. N. Groves*, by Dr. F. A. Tatford).

Groves had no doubt about the importance of prayer in overseas missionary work and on his return home from India in September 1852 it is recorded that he made a special plea for prayer at a meeting in Tottenham, London.

As a direct consequence of that plea one J. Van Sommer commenced the *Missionary Reporter* in 1853, two months after Groves' death, and this continued until about 1861. The reason for its cessation is not known.

Van Sommer clearly regarded it to be the responsibility of local churches to stimulate and maintain missionary work in their own neighbourhoods, their country and overseas (*Missionary Reporter*, August 1853, page 9). He wrote 'The Editor would prefer direct communication between churches and individuals and the Lord's servants. But where money is sent he will forward it to the persons named, if no directions are given he will apply it to the best of his judgment' (*Missionary Reporter* March 1854, page 120).

ECHOES OF SERVICE

In 1871 a circular was sent to various assemblies and individuals suggesting that a missionary periodical be started to publish letters from workers in foreign lands with the intention of stirring up intelligent prayer on their behalf. The new project was well received from its beginning.

With the first edition of *Echoes of Service* in 1872 (then called *The Missionary Echo*) the then Editors, Henry Groves and Dr. J. L. Maclean, defined their role as, 'fellowship in the gospel'. Their primary interest was those who had 'gone forth to other lands simply in His Name to preach the Word on their own responsibility to the Lord....' (*Missionary Echo*, January 1872, page 1). Those early Editors included letters from some serving with missionary societies and from some who served the Lord whilst pursuing their ordinary callings abroad.

With the subsequent rapid increase in the number of missionaries it was inevitable that priority for space in the magazine was given to those who were in full-time service.

From the first issue, those responsible for the magazine made it clear that they were willing to act, not only as Editors of the magazine, but also as treasurers of any funds received for missionaries. The Editors did not declare any Trusts to define their objects and the work of 'Echoes of Service' has continued without any formal constitution or corporate entity. Nonetheless, under the name 'Echoes of Service' it has been recognized in court as a valid charity and is registered as such by the Charity Commissioners in Great Britain under the provisions of the Charities Act, 1960.

The ministry of the Editors has grown out of their own personal exercise before God on the one hand, and the trust placed in them by overseas missionaries, and assemblies and individuals at home on the other.

'Echoes of Service' is not a Missionary Society; the Editors are content to be known as a Missionary Service Group. They do not decide whether a missionary is called of God and whether he has the requisite spiritual qualifications and character to serve the Lord in that way. This is regarded as the responsibility of the local church.

The Editors do not (and cannot) have any authority to direct missionaries as to the place or nature of their service or give any promise of support but they are willing to advise about conditions overseas, about government requirements and to put intended missionaries in touch with workers already serving in the area where they are exercised to serve the Lord.

The number of missionaries to whom the Editors of *Echoes of Service* extended their fellowship continued to grow, as is shown in the addendum to this Appendix. In the early days the Editors were in touch with some serving the Lord in many countries including the U.S.A., Australia and New Zealand. They also included in their fellowship workers with whom they were able to communicate, no matter from what country they were commended.

In 1972 it was decided that as Missionary Service Groups had become well established in the U.S.A., Canada, Australia and New Zealand, each publishing its own list of missionaries and news for prayer, the time had come for the Echoes' *Daily Prayer Guide* not to include the names of such workers unless they were married to a national from the British Isles. Since then this policy has been taken to its logical conclusion and only the names of those commended from the British Isles are now included in the *Daily Prayer Guide*.

There are two regular publications: *Echoes of Service,*

published monthly, giving extracts from missionaries' letters and missionary articles to stimulate and encourage interest and prayer; and the *Daily Prayer Guide*, published annually, giving a wealth of personal information about some of those missionaries with whom the Editors communicate.

Whilst the emphasis adopted by each Missionary Service Group differs in some respects, and all except 'Echoes of Service' are incorporated in some way, these factors are prominent in the ministry of each:

1 publishing a list of some missionaries with whom they have fellowship;
2 publishing missionary information;
3 forwarding gifts;
4 caring for the Lord's servants.

All the Missionary Service Groups send gifts for missionaries without any deduction whatever, looking to the Lord for the expenses of their ministry.

NEW ZEALAND TREASURY

When immigrants from assemblies in the British Isles settled as pioneers in New Zealand they brought with them a missionary interest which had been developed in their homeland. When Mr. James Kirk and a party of five others went in 1896 from New Zealand to Argentina and Malaya respectively, interest increased.

The *New Zealand Treasury* magazine for the ministry of the Word of God and reports of the Lord's work was commenced in 1899, the Editor being Mr. C. H. Hinman. Publication of news of the Lord's work in other lands gradually became incorporated, and this side of the journal's usefulness steadily increased as the number of workers multiplied. Owing to the difficulty experienced by Christians and assemblies in rural areas in communicating financially with missionaries overseas, Mr. Hinman was asked repeatedly to forward sums of money. This started a gratuitous service which has steadily grown in scope and usefulness. Successive Editors wisely saw the desirability of having co-treasurers so that this service might be rendered impartially and so that dependable account might be given of their stewardship and their ministry continued under the designation 'Missionary Funds (N.Z.) Incorporated'. The Treasurers have a single aim, and the office exists for the purpose of providing a channel for the remittance of funds and the dissemination of news of work and workers and matters of missionary interest. In no sense do the Treasurers comprise a Mission Board. Their calling and purpose is solely to serve, not to legislate.

A separate list of missionaries commended from New Zealand is compiled and published annually as a free supplement to *The Treasury*.

HOME AND FOREIGN MISSION FUNDS, SCOTLAND

It was in 1876 that the first two assembly missionaries were commended from Scottish assemblies and the number steadily grew. Following the departure of Frederick Stanley Arnot to Central Africa in 1881 brethren in Scotland became increasingly concerned about the care of their missionary brethren and at the suggestion of J. R. Caldwell and Thomas McLaren, 'Home and Foreign Mission Funds' was commenced.

In 1908 a Missionary Council was formed to broaden the base of the Fund, to help and advise missionary candidates from Scotland and to review problems arising on the mission field. The Council has never claimed to be a selection Board, regarding the responsibility for commendation as proper to the local assemblies.

A monthly newsletter was commenced in 1958, specifically to make known information about Scottish missionaries. It was designed to be used in conjunction with *Echoes' Daily Prayer Guide* in which missionaries commended from Scotland are named.

AUSTRALIAN MISSIONARY TIDINGS

It was in 1910 as a result of the exercise of brethren in Sydney, Australia, that a work was commenced to serve those servants of the Lord from Australia commended to work at home or overseas in a full-time capacity, but with particular emphasis on those serving overseas. The object of those brethren is stated in a foreword in the first issue of *Australian Missionary Tidings*: 'to give information month by month and extracts from letters received from those who have gone forth from Australia and are engaged in the Lord's work in the mission field'. The Editors indicated that they would 'gladly take charge of any sum that might be contributed by those who the Lord may lead ... for servants in the field, in the same way as those conducting "Echoes of Service" have done for many years'.

Since that time the title of the magazine has been shortened to *Tidings*. Like the other Missionary Service Groups, 'Australian Missionary Tidings' is not a Missionary Society in any sense and the complete freedom of missionaries, as the Lord's servants answerable only to Him and not to men, is recognized and maintained in practice.

Equally the autonomy of local assemblies is recognized and whilst the brethren responsible for 'Australian Missionary Tidings' are glad to act in co-ordinating activities of assemblies in relation to the missionary enterprise as a whole, each assembly is perfectly free to act before the Lord in deciding whether they avail themselves of the services of 'Australian Missionary Tidings' or not. Like *Echoes of Service*, *Tidings* gives extracts from missionaries' letters, as well as articles on aspects of overseas missionary work. The magazine from time to time contains a list of those missionaries who have been commended from Australia.

CHRISTIAN MISSIONS IN MANY LANDS, U.S.A.

Early this century a two-page news-sheet of missionary news began to be issued periodically by Mr. L. A. Steen. In 1904 he invited R. J. McLachlan to join him in editing it. *Voices from the Vineyard*, as it was called, was incorporated in 1936, the first president of the corporation being R. J. McLachlan, who continued to hold that office until his death in 1961.

'Christian Missions in Many Lands Ltd.' was formed and incorporated in 1921. The prime movers were Richard Hill, Charles Bellinger, and a few other brethren. The function of 'Christian Missions in Many Lands' has been the legal aspect of assembly missionary work. Governments prefer to deal with a corporation rather than with an individual missionary or assembly. 'Christian Missions in Many Lands' has enjoyed good relations with the United States Government and has assisted in obtaining passports and visas to many mission fields.

In 1925 the Missionary Fund was started by three brethren and the work was carried on by Captain John Barlow, later of Toronto. Later the membership was expanded to include Messrs. P. D. Loizeaux and Howard Gillings, and in 1939 Mr. John Reid was asked to join. The Missionary Fund functioned for 35 years until 1960.

Meanwhile, on 25th January 1938, 'The Fields Inc.' was formed by Messrs. Charles Bellinger, Richard Hill and John Bloore. The first issue of *The Fields* magazine was in February 1938. Until 1971 'Voices from the Vineyard' and 'The Fields' published periodicals and served as transmission agencies to forward gifts to missionaries. 'The Fields' also issued a list of missionaries commended by assemblies in the United States and Canada, beginning in the year 1951. It is called the *Missionary Prayer Handbook*.

Spring Lake—C.M.M.L. Centre   (S. F. Warren)

In 1971 brethren in the metropolitan area of New York City agreed to unify four missionary agencies under the name 'Christian Missions in Many Lands, Inc.' This involved bringing the two magazines, *Voices from the Vineyard* and *The Fields* under the jurisdiction of 'Christian Missions in Many Lands'. The name of 'Christian Missions in Many Lands Ltd.' was slightly changed to 'Christian Missions in Many Lands Inc.' The Julia Hasse missionary home in Union City, N.J., was also included in this new body. Fred MacKenzie, who was President of 'Fields' at the time, headed the new organization but was called home in 1981.

One magazine called *Missions* is now published ten times a year without charge.

MISSIONARY SERVICE COMMITTEE
CHRISTIAN MISSIONS IN MANY LANDS (CANADA)

At a meeting in 1940, representatives of assemblies discussed the problem of distributing support for missionaries due to wartime regulations about sending funds from Canada. The following were asked to form a Missionary Service Committee to meet this situation: George Cowan, S. K. Petersen, John Smart, S. F. Sommacal and E. G. Taylor. The facility that the committee provided proved to be so useful that it has been continued since that time, even though foreign currency control regulations no longer exist.

A sister organization, 'Christian Missions in Many Lands (Canada)' was launched in 1944. From the beginning, the membership of 'C.M.M.L. (Canada)' and the 'Missionary Service Committee' has been interlocking but not identical; both groups have one address and one office staff. 'Missionary Service Committee' accepts funds from donors, issues receipts for income tax purposes, and forwards gifts to missionaries and homeworkers. 'C.M.M.L. (Canada)' represents commended missionaries to government, assures governments both home and abroad that the person is a bona-fide missionary, assists individuals in getting passports and visas, issues Letters of Guarantee when required, and maintains an emergency repatriation fund for special occasions.

Missionaries commended from Canada are included in the *Missionary Prayer Handbook* issued by 'C.M.M.L. (U.S.A.)' and letters from Canadian missionaries are included in *Missions*, which is sent out without charge.

The Canadian groups are entirely independent of 'C.M.M.L. (U.S.A.)' but work in harmony with the American brethren. A meeting of these missionary service groups from both sides of the border is held annually for discussion of common problems.

OTHER MISSIONARY SERVICE GROUPS

In addition to the Missionary Service Groups named here, other groups have come into being in various parts of the world to support the work of assembly missionaries overseas, although not necessarily carrying out all the functions of those groups previously described in this Appendix and some are guided by somewhat different principles; among such are:

1 'Harvest Fields', Belfast;
2 'Lord's Work Trust', Kilmarnock;
3 'Scriptural Knowledge Institution', Bristol;
4 'Wiedenest Bible School', Germany;
5 'Service Missionaire Evangelique', Geneva, Switzerland.
6 'Comité de Service', Vichy, France.

Addendum to Appendix II

The Assembly Contribution Overseas
1875—1970

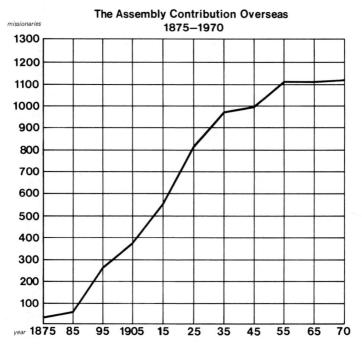

missionaries

year 1875 85 95 1905 15 25 35 45 55 65 70

1972—1982

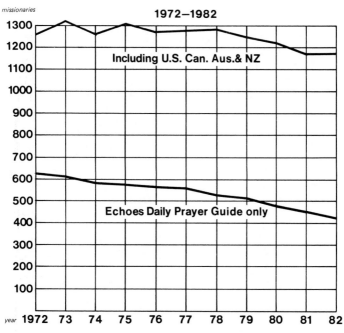

missionaries

Including U.S. Can. Aus.& NZ

Echoes Daily Prayer Guide only

year 1972 73 74 75 76 77 78 79 80 81 82

Appendix III

Record of Missionaries' Service Since 1872

(For a variety of reasons the dates given may not agree with those shown in the lists issued by missionary service groups or include the whole of an individual's service overseas)

INDIA AND SRI LANKA
Adams, D. C., 1959–1978
Adams, Mrs., 1959–1978
 (formerly Miss Smith, M. G.)
Adams, E. C., 1901–1949
Adams, Mrs., 1903–1952
Adams, Miss G. W., 1931–1969
Aiken, A. E., 1930–1934
Aldwinckle, Miss E., 1897–1907
Anderson, Miss J. F., 1936–1978
Anderson, Miss R. L., 1922–1971
Annear, D. M., 1912–1916
 (see Mrs. W. T. Revell)
Anstey, Miss L. H., 1876–1909
Appleby, R., 1949–1955
 (to Fiji) 1960–1961
Appleby, Mrs., 1952–1955
 (to Fiji) 1960–1961
Aspinall, H. G., 1962–1972
Aspinall, Mrs., 1962–1972
Aston, J. H., 1895–1924
Aston, Mrs., 1897–1924
Atkinson, R. C. E., 1926–1971
Atkinson, Mrs., 1928–1971
Austin, Miss E. A., 1892–1899
Avery, H., 1934–1946
 1949–1951
Avery, Mrs., 1944–1946
Bardsley, Miss M., 1946
Barnard, Miss I. E., 1947
Barter, Miss L. A., 1911–1912
Beale, Miss, 1898–1902
Beer, C. H., 1866–1921
Beer, Mrs., 1884–1936

Beer, J. W., 1861–1884
Beer, Mrs., 1886–1888
Bevan, Miss W., 1931–1936
Bird, Miss F. P., 1885–1950
Bird, H. H., 1888–1938
Bird, Mrs., 1888–1912
Black, Miss E., 1940–1964
Black, G. A., 1919–1946
Black, Mrs., 1921–1946
Bland, Miss O. M., 1951–1972
Bone, J. L., 1951–1970
Bone, Mrs., 1950–1970
Bounsall, Miss L. M., 1900–1906
Bowden, E. S., 1876–1924
Bowden, Mrs., 1885–1927
Bowden, Miss H., 1893–1956
Bowden, Miss L., 1890–1894
Bowden, W., 1836–1876
Bowden, Mrs., 1836–1876
Bowen, L. W., 1929–1931
Bowen, T. J., 1949–1952
Bowen, Mrs., 1950–1952
Boyd, J. M., 1911–1930
Boyd, Mrs., 1908–1935
Braden, Miss A., 1894–1920
Brayne, Miss G., 1926–1948
Brealey, Miss A. J., 1906–1960
Bresnen, Miss G. M., 1982
Bridger, Miss A. M., 1909–1928
Brohn, Miss E. A., 1959–1963
Bromley, Miss A. C., 1903–1911
Bromley, E. B., 1903–1946
Bromley, Mrs., 1905–1946
Brooks, Miss P. M., 1896–1897

Brown, F. J., 1904–1931
Brown, Mrs., 1906–1934
Brown, M., 1904–1937
Brown, Mrs., 1905–1909
Brown, Mrs., 1911–1953
Brown, T. T., 1929–1974
Brown, Mrs., 1936–1942
   (formerly Miss Treweek, J. L.)
Bryant, Miss A., 1897–1903
Bryant, Miss E., 1934–1952
Bryant, R. J., 1901–1946
Bryant, Mrs., 1902–1946
   (formerly Miss Caple, E. N.)
Buchanan, E., 1904–1952
            1962 only
Buchanan, Mrs., 1909–1923
   (formerly Miss Saunders, D. E.)
Buchanan, Mrs., 1924–1952
   (formerly Miss Murphy, C.)
Buchanan, Mrs., 1962 only
Bullock, E. F., 1953
Bullock, Mrs., 1951
Burcharot, Miss F., 1910–1915
Burnett, Miss E. R., 1935–1947
   (see Mrs. S. R. Stokes)
Burr, C. H., 1950–1955
Burr, Mrs., 1950–1955
Burt, D. B., 1936–1972
Burt, Mrs., 1929–1972
Bygrove, Miss K. E., 1902–1938
Campbell, Miss J., 1968–1975
Campbell, W. J., 1939–1965
Campbell, Mrs., 1942–1965
Cansick, P., 1906–1956
Cansick, Mrs., 1907–1956
Caple, Miss E. M., 1901–1902
   (see Mrs. Bryant)
Charters, Miss J. M., 1955–1958
Childs, Mrs. J. B., 1944–1954
Chote, A. H., 1952–1979
Chote, Mrs., 1954–1979
Churchward, Dr. R. S.,
   1939–1956
Churchward, Mrs., 1939–1960
Clark, D. E. C., 1941–1943
   (to and from Pakistan)
   1953–1960
Clark, Mrs., 1941–1943
   (to and from Pakistan)
   1953–1960

Clarke, Miss A. M., 1890–1937
Cole, Miss G., 1946
Collins, Miss E. A., 1900–1927
Conway, Miss A. L., 1919–1943
Cookson, Miss G. H., 1900–1917
Cookson, Miss J. M., 1907–1920
Cooper, Mrs. A. A., 1952–1953
   (from Fiji) 1959–1970
   (formerly Miss Dyason, A.A.)
Cooper, Miss R. M., 1949–1959
Cornelius, E., 1868–1916
Cornelius, Mrs., 1870–1909
   (formerly Mrs. Body)
Cornish, Miss I. G., 1956–1961
Cowling, Miss, 1882 only
Crawford, W., 1944–1964
   (later in Eire)
Crawford, Mrs., 1946–1964
   (later in Eire)
Darling, Miss M., 1886–1913
Darling, Dr. W. M., 1957–1968
Darling, Mrs., 1960–1968
Davies, Dr. E. G., 1956–1974
Davies, Mrs., 1956–1974
Davies, Miss I. M., 1913–1928
Davies, J. M., 1920–1962
Davies, Mrs., 1920–1962
Davis, Miss S. E., 1899–1901
Day, Miss M. A., 1890–1893
d'Bras, Miss L., 1911–1912
Dean, A. T., 1899–1940
Dean, Mrs., 1897–1940
De Carteret, J. H., 1899–1943
De Carteret, Mrs., 1899–1951
Denton, Miss M., 1912–1915
Dibben, C., 1898–1911
Dibben, Mrs., 1899–1911
Dickson, Miss M. W., 1948
Diegel, Miss K., 1913–1916
Dorling, Miss E. J., 1920–1960
Downing, W. W., 1910–1915
Draper, Dr. T., 1927–1928
Drown, D. J., 1959–1970
Drown, Mrs., 1961–1970
Duff, R., 1947–1970
Duff, Mrs., 1953–1970
Duffy, Miss C., 1922–1928
Dunn, Miss M. M., 1905–1914
   (later Mrs. A. Redwood)
Durick, Miss C., 1914–1915

Durham, W. S., 1933–1951
Durham, Mrs., 1938
Duxbury, Miss E., 1898–1899
Dyason, Miss A. A., 1924–1946
  (to Fiji as Mrs. Cooper)
Eccles, Miss M., 1946
Ekman, Miss H., 1926–1955
Edwards, Miss M., 1955–1971
Elliott, Miss A. K., 1946–1953
Evans, J., 1910–1957
Evans, Mrs., 1910–1957
Fairholm, Dr. D., 1967–1969
Fairholm, Mrs., 1967–1969
Farmer, Miss L. A., 1907–1913
Farringdon, Miss W. G., 1947–1974
Feil, Miss E. A., 1959–1980
Flack, A., 1946
Flack, Mrs., 1945
Forward, W. F., 1963–1978
Forward, Mrs., 1963–1978
Foster, D. G., 1944–1948
Fountain, Miss B. M., 1946–1970
Fountain, Miss E., 1907–1910
Fountain, G. L., 1930–1967
Fountain, Mrs., 1933–1967
Fox, S., 1917–1959
Fox, Mrs., 1917–1959
Fryer, Miss E., 1916–1922
Gander, H. T., 1907–1953
Gander, Mrs., 1906–1953
Garrard, Miss E. V., 1938
Gates, B., 1930–1955
Gates, Mrs., 1930–1955
George, Miss G. E., 1944
German, R. G., 1947
German, Mrs., 1949
Gilbert, Dr. D. J., 1938–1959
Gilbert, Mrs., 1939–1959
Godbold, F., 1898–1903
Godbold, Mrs., 1901–1903
  (formerly Miss Lloyd, E.)
Good, Miss A., 1926–1928
  (see Mrs. W. A. Morrison)
Goold, A. L., 1943–1963 (from Israel)
Goold, Mrs., 1943–1963
Gordon, Miss M., 1905–1913
Greenfield, R., 1939–1954
Greenfield, Mrs., 1939–1954
Gregory, Miss V. A., 1949–1955
Guikema, Miss F., 1974–1975

Hall, I. T., 1949–1964
Hall, Mrs., 1949–1964
Hamilton, Miss A., 1901–1902
Hampton, Miss M. E., 1924–1971
Hancox, Miss B., 1906–1909
Harding, Miss E. J., 1949
Harris, Miss M., 1906–1909
Havard, D. J., 1951–1971
Havard, Mrs., 1951–1971
Haydon, Miss W. M., 1923–1929
Heads, Miss P. M. J., 1951–1976
Hearn, W. N., 1888–1952
Hearn, Mrs., 1888–1952
Heelis, T., 1855–1901
Heelis, Mrs., 1855–1911
Henderson, Dr. G., 1908–1946
Henderson, Mrs., 1909–1946
Hendrickson, Miss V., 1948–1951
Henning, H. T., 1959–1969
Henning, Mrs., 1965–1969
Hill, D. J. H., 1949–1961
Hill, Mrs., 1949–1961
Hill, Miss E. E., 1892–1898
  (see Mrs. R. W. Rawson)
Hill, G., 1931–1968
Hill, Mrs., 1931–1968
Hill, Mrs. L. E. M., 1955–1978
Hill, R. H. C., 1920–1952
Hill, Mrs., 1920–1952
Hindman, Miss K., 1909–1921
Hipwell, Miss A. E., 1922–1923
Hitchcock, W., 1921–1923
Hitchcock, Mrs., 1921–1922
Hodgkinson, Miss P., 1965–1978
Hollands, Miss E. C., 1905–1908
Hollyer, Miss E., 1882–1889
  (to France)
Holt, Dr. B. D., 1944–1979
Holt, Miss J. E., 1952
Honeyman, E. J., 1967–1970
Honeyman, Mrs., 1967–1970
Honywill, W. G., 1892–1894
  (from and to Singapore)
Honywill, Mrs., 1892–1894
  (from and to Singapore)
Hooper, Miss N. A., 1928–1962
Horton, Miss E. N., 1951
Hosking, W. J., 1891–1899
  (visited Straits Settlement and
   Ceylon, to France)

Hosking, Mrs., 1891–1899
(visited Straits Settlement and
Ceylon, to France)
Howes, Miss J. M., 1948–1964
Hucksted, Miss A., 1894–1901
Hughes-Games, Miss G. M.,
1924–1962
Hull, Miss G. C., 1948
Humphries, G., 1895–1907
Humphries, Mrs., 1896–1934
Hunter, Miss D. G., 1913–1914
Hunter, Dr. E. V., 1905–1914
Hunter, Mrs., 1904–1914
Hunter, V. F., 1897–1910
(from W. Indies)
Hunter, Mrs., 1897–1910
(from W. Indies)
Ingram, Dr. M. A., 1948–1953
(later Mrs. G. N. Patterson)
Irvine, W. C., 1897–1946
Irvine, Mrs., 1898–1947
Jaap, Miss I. B., 1938–1978
Jahn, H. H. M., 1949–1967
Jahn, Mrs., 1946–1968
Jelleyman, Miss M. B., 1908–1909
Johnston, J. E., 1904–1946
Johnston, Mrs., 1911–1946
(formerly Miss Watts, L. H.)
Jones, Miss H. L., 1906–1915
Jones, J. N., 1961–1978
Jones, Mrs., 1973–1978
Junck, G., 1934–1960
Junck, Mrs., 1937–1955
Keen, Miss A. E., 1900–1901
(see Mrs. S. O. Peake)
Kennedy, R., 1955–1972
Kennedy, Mrs., 1955–1972
Keyse, Miss M., 1964
Kimber, H. T., 1949–1958
Kimber, Mrs., 1949–1958
Kimber, W. A., 1925–1961
Kimber, Mrs., 1925–1961
King, W. H., 1896–1952
King, Mrs., 1896–1952
King, W. R. C., 1923–1929
King, Mrs., 1923–1929
Kocher, W. A., 1906–1915
Kocher, Mrs., 1907–1916
Kuhns, Miss E., 1961
Laird, Miss M. M. B., 1940–1945

Leeser, Dr. I., 1953
Lehmann, Dr. G. D., 1934–1980
Lehmann, Mrs., 1934–1980
Liddell, Mrs. A. N., 1950–1972
Liddle, M. S., 1959–1978
Liddle, Mrs., 1959–1978
Ligot, Miss L. A., 1906–1942
Lilley, A., 1966–1979
Lilley, Mrs., 1962–1979
Lindsey, Miss M., 1942–1948
(from Malaya)
Linton, A. J., 1952–1976
Linton, Mrs., 1956–1976
Lucas, C. L., 1964–1980
Lucas, Mrs., 1964–1980
Lynn, Mrs., 1885–1911
Lynn, Miss Rachel, 1886–1900
Lynn, Miss Ruth, 1888–1945
Lloyd, Miss E., 1899–1901
Lockett, Miss E. M., 1950–1952
Long, Dr. J. E., 1920–1935
Lynn, E., 1888–1948
Lynn, Mrs., 1885–1911
Lynn, Miss Rachel, 1886–1900
Lynn, Miss Ruth, 1888–1945
Mackay, M., 1939–1960
Mackay, Mrs., 1944–1960
Mackey, B., 1969
Mackey, Mrs., 1969
Mackness, Miss E. M. A.,
1898–1902
McBride, Miss M. A., 1894–1901
McComas, Miss M., 1896–1901
(see Mrs. McGavin)
McCleary, I. E., 1958–1962
McCleary, Mrs., 1961–1962
McClelland, Miss M. P., 1941
McDonald, A., 1882–1884
McGavin, E. W., 1893–1905
(to Italy)
McGavin, Mrs., 1901–1905
(formerly Miss McComas, M.)
(to Italy)
McGregor, Miss A. M., 1956–1968
McGregor, H., 1939–1968
McGregor, Mrs., 1940–1968
McIntosh, Miss E., 1909–1911
(from and to Singapore)
McIver, J. C., 1904–1932
McIver, Mrs., 1902–1956

McKenzie, A. E., 1934–1954
McKenzie, Mrs., 1934–1954
M'Laine, F., 1901–1940
M'Laine, Mrs., 1901–1939
M'Lean, D., 1888–1895
M'Lean, Mrs., 1894–1895
McLeay, A. J., 1966–1978
McLeay, Mrs., 1966–1978
McLellan, Miss R. J., 1966–1980
McMillan, Dr. J. W., 1953–1975
McMillan, Mrs., 1955–1975
McNaught, J. S., 1949–1965
McNaught, Mrs., 1949–1965
Macrae, J. N., 1876–1925
Macrae, Mrs., 1876–1926
Mai, Miss A. B., 1913–1934
Mammen, P. E., 1899–1905
Mammen, Mrs., 1899–1905
Marshall, Miss M. J., 1900–1927
Martin, J. H., 1961–1978
Martin, Mrs., 1961–1978
Maynard, T. H., 1887–1917
Maynard, Mrs., 1894–1912
Mears, H., 1901–1926
Mears, Mrs., 1908–1926
Medland, Miss S. M., 1968–1974
Middleton, Miss M., 1919–1928
Miles, F. N., 1880–1891
Miller, Miss M. C., 1950–1968
Mills, Miss A. V., 1923–1966
Mitchell, Miss J. C., 1908–1953
Morgan, Miss E. M., 1914–1972
Morice, Miss G. E., 1924–1960
Morine, Miss A., 1920–1921
Morling, A. J., 1930–1968
Morling, Mrs., 1933–1968
Morlock, Miss E. K., 1907–1908
Morrison, W. A., 1925–1952
                    1965–1967
Morrison, Mrs., 1928–1952
   (formerly Miss Good, A.)
   (1965–1967
Morrison, Miss L., 1949–1975
Mosley, Miss M. G., 1920–1925
                    1930–1936
                    1949–1960
Mowat, Miss M. G., 1952–1964
Munce, Dr. D., 1953
Munk, Miss M. M., 1917–1919
Munnings, W. A., 1952–1969

Munnings, Mrs., 1952–1969
Munro, Miss H. M., 1922–1960
Nagel, V., 1893–1914
Nagel, Mrs., 1897–1935
Naismith, A., 1922–1958
Naismith, Mrs., 1922–1958
Napper, Miss B., 1904–1915
Newport, Miss C. R., 1904–1907
Newton, K., 1965–1974
Newton, Mrs., 1967–1974
Niblock, A. U., 1901 only
Nicoll, Miss M. G., 1931–1944
Noble, W. T., 1931–1950
Noble, Mrs., 1931–1950
Noel, E. H., 1904–1943
Noel, Mrs., 1909–1956
   (formerly Miss Shirtliff, J.)
Norman, Miss B. F., 1950
Norton, R., 1903–1946
Norton, Mrs., 1905–1946
Noscke, Miss M. A., 1921–1964
Oliver, Dr. R. M., 1946–1980
Osborne, K. H., 1946–1965
Osborne, Mrs., 1949–1965
Osborne, Miss W. M., 1950–1972
Overton, B. J., 1950–1981
Overton, Mrs., 1950–1981
Owen, Miss K. M., 1955–1956
Padfield, Miss D. P., 1952–1965
Panes, G. W., 1896–1912
Panes, Mrs., 1896–1908
Parkinson, Miss F., 1938–1944
Patient, T., 1889–1937
Patient, Mrs., 1890–1936
Patient, F., 1916–1947
Patient, W., 1907–1916
Patient, Mrs., 1900–1916
   (married 1908)
Patterson, G. N., 1950–1956
   (from China)
Patterson, Dr., 1953–1956
   (formerly Dr. Ingram, M. A.)
Payne, G. W., 1950–1966
Payne, Mrs., 1950–1966
Peake, R. S., 1939–1959
Peake, Mrs., 1939–1959
Peake, S. O., 1899–1947
Peake, Mrs., 1901–1947
   (formerly Miss Keen, A. E.)
Peebles, Miss K. L., 1927–1967

Perkins, A. C., 1904–1954
Perkins, Mrs., 1904–1954
Perry, P. E., 1903
Perry, Mrs., 1903
Phair, A. G., 1936–1967
Phair, Mrs., 1930–1967
Phillipson, Miss E. M., 1948
Phoenix, E. C., 1938–1965
  (from Mauritius)
Phoenix, Mrs., 1938–1965
  (from Mauritius)
Pitts, Miss M. E., 1950–1968
Pratten, T. J., 1948–1981
Pratten, Mrs., 1952–1981
Pring, Dr. C. E., 1909–1953
Pritchard, Miss A. A. E., 1909–1911
  (see Mrs. J. F. Smele)
Pritchard, Miss P. A., 1963–1974
Pullenger, K. R., 1957–1968
Pullenger, Mrs., 1958–1968
Pullen, Miss R. G., 1922–1925
Putwain, Miss E. S., 1940–1943
  (see Mrs. Vine, A. S. G.)
Ramage, Miss E. E., 1948
Rankin, J., 1928 only
Rawson, R. W., 1897–1939
  (to Fiji)
Rawson, Mrs., 1898–1939
  (to Fiji)
    (formerly Miss Hill, E. E.)
Rea, Dr. E., 1948–1952
Rea, Mrs., 1948–1952
Redit, Miss C. M., 1964
Redwood, A. McD., 1910–1960
Redwood, Mrs., 1914–1950
  (formerly Miss Dunn, M. M.)
Redwood, Miss G. E., 1915–1934
  (later Mrs. W. Wilcox)
Redwood, W. A., 1882–1895
Redwood, Mrs., 1881–1900
         1910–1933
Redwood, W. J. M., 1914–1960
Redwood, Mrs., 1918–1960
Rees, H., 1903–1948
Rees, Mrs., 1908–1948
  (formerly Miss Roper, A. M.)
Revell, W. T., 1905–1964
Revell, Mrs., 1909–1913
Revell, Mrs., 1916–1961
  (formerly Miss Annear, D. M.)

Revington, Miss E., 1928–1936
Rhodes, Miss J. A., 1899–1918
Rimmer, E. A., 1899–1909
Rimmer, Mrs., 1908–1909
  (formerly Miss Hollands, E. C.)
Ritchie, G., 1933–1970
Ritchie, Mrs., 1934–1970
Roberts, D. J., 1954–1970
Roberts, Mrs., 1955–1970
Robertson, Miss M., 1900–1927
Robertson, Miss H. H., 1928
Robinson, M. A., 1980–1981
Robinson, Mrs., 1980–1981
Rogers, Miss O., 1949
Rolls, C. J., 1910–1921
Roper, Miss A. M., 1906–1908
  (see Mrs. H. Rees)
Rose, F. A., 1899–1935
Rose, Mrs., 1905–1935
  (formerly Miss Wright,
   S. M. E.)
Rout, Miss A., 1940–1941
Rowat, F., 1888–1947
Rowat, Mrs., 1888–1947
Rowberry, A. J., 1945
Rowberry, Mrs., 1945
Roxburgh, A., 1910–1912
Rusted, Miss M., 1903–1910
Salmon, Miss R. L., 1953–1955
  (see Mrs. A. R. Stedman)
Sercombe, Miss E., 1923–1925
Shaw, Miss E., 1967–1974
Shirtliff, Miss J., 1907–1909
  (see Mrs. E. H. Noel)
Shirtliff, Miss P. M., 1950
Short, Dr. E. S., 1951–1976
Short, Mrs., 1951–1976
Shrimpton, Miss D., 1915–1951
Simpson, S., 1966–1969
Smele, J. F., 1909–1958
Smele, Mrs., 1911–1922
  (formerly Miss Pritchard,
   A. A. E.)
Smele, Mrs., 1926–1958
Smith, Dr. B., 1960–1971
Smith, Mrs., 1960–1971
Smith, Dr. C., 1977–1979
Smith, Mrs., 1977–1979
Smith, Miss C. V., 1958–1967
Smith, Miss H. I., 1962

Smith, K. W., 1947
Smith, Mrs., 1946
Smith, Miss M. G., 1955–1959
   (see Mrs. D. C. Adams)
Smyth, A., 1947–1968
Smyth, Mrs., 1947–1966
Soutter, A., 1920–1960
Soutter, Mrs., 1920–1960
Sparks, Miss R. M., 1923–1943
Stalley, Miss G. M., 1936–1944
Stanes, W. H., 1888–1890
Stanton, D. E., 1962–1974
Stanton, Mrs., 1962–1974
Starck, Miss E., 1904–1952
Stedman, A. R., 1952–1969
Stedman, Mrs., 1955–1969
   (formerly Miss Salmon, R. L.)
Steer, Miss R., 1885–1891
Stewart, J., 1908–1945
Stewart, Mrs., 1911–1937
Stewart, Mrs., 1935–1943
   (married 1937)
Stickley, F., 1913–1919
Stickley, Mrs., 1913–1919
Stokes, R. H., 1938–1945
   (later in Fiji)
Stokes, Mrs., 1938–1945
   (later in Fiji)
Stokes, S. R., 1935–1971
Stokes, Mrs., 1947–1971
   (formerly Miss Burnett, E. R.)
Storrie, A. E., 1899–1946
Storrie, Mrs., 1899–1946
Strachan, Miss I., 1900–1922
Stuart, Miss M. J., 1949–1971
Sturt, Miss G. E., 1951–1952
   (from China)
Sundgren, Miss C. C., 1905–1951
Talbot, Miss M. E., 1932–1960
Taylor, Miss A. T., 1885–1900
Taylor, D., 1953–1971
Taylor, Mrs., 1953–1971
Taylor, J., 1904–1913
Taylor, Mrs., 1905–1913
Taylor, Miss R. M., 1935–1978
Taylor, Miss S. R., 1924–1977
Teague, Miss M. L., 1898–1946
Tear, Miss J. A., 1896–1904
Thomas, Miss I. L., 1935–1940
Thompson, W. E., 1948–1969

Thompson, Mrs., 1948–1969
Thomson, C. W., 1910–1942
Thomson, Mrs., 1910–1942
Thomson, Miss H. P., 1968
Thomson, Miss J., 1926–1966
Thornhill, Miss J. M., 1963–1972
Thorp, Miss M. D., 1905–1906
Thynne, A. V., 1901–1910
Tilsley, C. J., 1920–1966
Tilsley, Mrs., 1922–1969
Tilsley, Miss B. J. C., 1954
Townley, Miss B., 1914–1924
   (to Malaysia as
      Mrs. E. V. Brewerton)
Treasure, Miss P. N., 1957
Treweek, Miss J., 1914–1936
   (see Mrs. T. T. Brown)
Turner, G. J., 1945–1969
Turner, Mrs., 1947–1969
Vanderlaan, Miss A. M., 1946
Vine, A. S. G., 1939–1961
Vine, Mrs., 1943–1961
   (formerly Miss Putwain, E. S.)
Vivian, V. L., 1967–1969
Vivian, Mrs., 1967–1969
Wagland, E. G., 1962
Wagner, Miss R. M., 1930–1931
Wait, C., 1880–1881
Waite, Miss S. M., 1958–1970
Walker, Miss J., 1933–1954
Walker, J. J., 1949–1970
Walker, Mrs., 1950–1969
Walker, W., 1947–1964
Walker, Mrs., 1949–1964
Wallace, Miss E. C., 1932–1980
Warburton, J. H., 1950–1978
Warburton, Mrs., 1950–1978
Ward, W., 1934–1944
Ward, Mrs., 1934–1944
Wark, M. J., 1909–1955
Wark, Mrs., 1909–1955
Warlow, Dr. P. F. M., 1954–1966
Warlow, Mrs., 1954–1966
Warner, Miss R. I., 1960
Warren, Miss R., 1973–1978
Watson, Miss A., 1919–1957
Watson, G. H., 1902–1938
Watson, Mrs., 1903–1938
Watts, Miss L. H., 1909–1911
   (see Mrs. J. E. Johnston)

Webb, J., 1921–1953
Webb, Mrs., 1932–1958
Weller, Miss B., 1898–1899
Wharton, Miss A. E., 1924–1954
Wheeler, E. G., 1920–1947
Wheeler, Mrs., 1929–1947
  (formerly Miss Williamson, I.)
Whitehouse, P. C., 1909–1965
Whitehurst, Miss A. J., 1963–1966
Wilcox, W., 1932–1951
Wilcox, Mrs., 1934–1951
  (formerly Miss Redwood, G. E.)
Williamson, E. G., 1929–1943
  (to Pakistan)
Williamson, Mrs., 1936–1943
  (to Pakistan)

Williamson, Miss I., 1926–1929
  (see Mrs. E. G. Wheeler)
Wilson, C. A., 1951–1953
Wilson, Mrs., 1951–1953
Witty, A. F., 1899–1920
Witty, Mrs., 1906–1917
Wright, Miss A. S., 1957
Wright, C. T., 1900–1949
Wright, Mrs., 1905–1949
Wright, Miss S. M. E., 1901–1905
Yates, Miss D., 1931–1968
Young, A., 1900–1940
Young, Mrs., 1909–1940
Zingers, E., 1949–1958
Zingers, Mrs., 1949–1958

Appendix IV

Comparative Statistics of Indian States

STATE	AREA (sq. miles)	POPULATION	POPULATION per sq. mile	LITERACY %
Andhra Pradesh	106,272	53,403,000	503	29.94
Assam	38,300	19,902,000	520	28.74
Bihar	67,184	69,823,000	1039	26
Gujarat	72,236	33,960,000	470	43.72
Haryana	17,561	12,850,000	732	35.79
Himachal Pradesh	21,496	4,237,000	197	40.12
Jammu and Kashmir	85,700	5,981,000	70	18.59
Karnataka	74,037	37,043,000	500	38.33
Kerala	15,002	25,403,000	1693	66.92
Madhya Pradesh	171,223	52,131,000	304	27.81
Maharashtra	118,832	62,693,000	528	47.21
Manipur	8,628	1,433,000	166	42.16
Meghalaya	8,660	1,327,000	153	33.22
Nagaland	6,368	773,000	121	38.80
Orissa	60,178	26,272,000	437	26.2
Punjab	19,445	16,669,000	857	40.74
Rajasthan	132,149	34,102,000	281	19.07
Sikkim	2,745	315,000	115	31.76
Tamil Nadu	50,333	48,297,000	960	45.75
Tripura	4,035	2,060,000	511	41.58
Uttar Pradesh	113,667	110,858,000	975	27.33
West Bengal	33,921	54,485,000	1606	40.74

Index

Principal references are in **bold** type; illustrations are indicated by page references in *italics*.

Bhopal, 241, *243*
Bhubaneswar, 264
Bhutan, 15, *366*, **395-9**
Bhutas, 279
Bhuttia language, 279
Bible and Stethoscope, 183
The Bible Student, 216
Bible Talks, 344
Bible translations, 74-5
  Bengali, 75
  Marathi, 183
  Nepali, 392
  Tamil, 71
  Telugu, 98, 131, 133
Bierl, Dora, 390
Bihar, **145-55**
Bikaner, 273, 274
Biratnagar, 382
Bird, Florence P., 159, 191, 195, 198,
  199, 200-1
Bird, H. Handley, 159, 173, 198-9, 225,
  228, 248, 251, 283, 304, *304,*
  310, 311, 376
Birenda, 382
Birganj, 382
Black, Agnes E. (*née* Moraine), 229-30
Black, George A., 228-30
Bland, Olive M., 151, *151*
Bo tree, 362
Bodhidharma, 61
Bodhisattivas, 61
Body, Mr. and Mrs. William S., 150
Bohn, Mr., 149
Bokaro, 155
Bombay, 25, 31, 34, 156, *212, 246,*
  247-8, 250-2, 254, *404*
Bone, Eileen, 161
Bone, J. Lloyd, 54, 161
Bose, S. K., 346
Bowden, Edwin, 103, 114
Bowden, Mrs. Edwin, 103
Bowden, Henrietta, 103, *103,* 127
Bowden, Lily (*later* Mrs. Thomas
  Tilsley), 103
Bowden, Martha, *99, 103*
Bowden, Mr. and Mrs. William, 91, 93,
  95-6, 98-9, 101
Bowden's Indian Balm, 96
Bowen, Leslie W., 209, 238
Boyd, Edith, *103*
Boyd, John M., *103,* 119, 123
Braden, Amelia, 197
Brahma, 48, 54
Brahma-Ātman, 51
Brahman, 48, 58

Brāhmaṇas, 49
Brahmanism, 51
Brahmaputra River, 6, 7, 138, 259, 395
Brahmins, 46, 48, 50, 76, 100, 149, 171
Brahmo Samāj, 64-5
Brammaja, 102
Brancepath, 165
Brandin, Mr. and Mrs. L., 149
Brandt, Mr. and Mrs., 149
Brayne, Grace, 177, 251
Brealey, Ada J., *103,* 105, *105,* 127
Brealey, George, 191
*Brethren Missionary Work in Mysore
  State,* 192
Brewerton, Bertha (*née* Townley), 289,
  291
Brewerton, Ernest V., 289, 291
Brice, Mr., 91, 149
Bridger, Rhoda, 106
British India, 25
Brohn, Elizabeth A. (*later* Mrs. Robert
  Hamill), 309
Bromley, Amelia C., *103*
Bromley, Anna, *103*
Bromley, Eustace B., 93, 95, *103,* 105,
  122, 124
Bromley, Mrs. Eustace B., *103,* 105, 116
Brown, Alice, *103*
Brown, David, 72, 104
Brown, Mrs. David, 104
Brown, Jessie (*née* Treweek), 289, 290
Brown, Mr. and Mrs. Joseph, 180
Brown, Matthew, *103,* 106, 116
Brown, Mrs. Matthew, 106, 116
Brown, Thomas T., 289, 290, 300, 301
Brunner, Emil, 404
Bryant, Elsie H., 103
Bryant, Mr. and Mrs. Robert J., 103
Buchanan, Catharine (*née* Murphy), 207
Buchanan, D. Elizabeth (*née* Saunders),
  197, 207
Buchanan, Mr. and Mrs. Edward, 207,
  209, 301
Buchanan, Eva (*née* Rolston), 207
Buddha, Gautama, 8, 48, 60, 319, 358,
  360, *360,* 382, 384
Buddhism and Buddhists, 10-11, 43,
  60-1, *62,* 279, 325, 340, 341,
  357, 364, 368, 371-2, 382, 396,
  398, 399
Bullock, Eric F., 209, 218, 219-20
Bullock, Ruth (*née* Kjarsgaard), 218,
  219-20
Burchardt, Frieda, 226, *227*
Burghers, 371

Moraine, Agnes E. (*later* Mrs. George
 Black), 229–30
Moran Buru, 146
Moravians, 81
Morgan, Edith M., 112, 114, 115,
 119–20, 121
Morice, Grace E., 105, 121, 127
Morling, Augustus, 285, 287
Morling, Grace, 285
Morrison, Anne (*née* Good), 115–16
Morrison, Lorna, 162–3, 323, 346
Morrison, William A., 115, 123
Morvi, 157
Mosley, M. Gertrude, 301
Motihari, 149
Moses, 63
Mother India, 39, 49
Mountbatten, Lord Louis, 26
Moving Millions, 65
Mridude, Mr. and Mrs. B. G., 255
Muguru, 192, 213
Muḥammad, 17, 18, 63
Muktsar, 268
Müller, George, 102, 199, 214, 233,
 303–4
Müller, Max, 14
Mullur, 207
Munce, Dorothy, 120
Munnings, Hilda, 287–9, 297, 299
Munnings, Wilfred A., 287–9, 297, 299
Munro, Helen M., 114, 115, 116
Murphy, Catharine (*later* Mrs. Edward
 Buchanan), 207
Murthi, R. S., 120
Muslims, 27, 43, 64, 66, 170, 221, 271,
 279, 317, 325, 341, 349, 351,
 371–3 *see also* Islām
Muttampalam, 236
Muzaffarpur, 149
Mylapore, 69, 221
Mysore, Rajah of, 16
Mysore City, 189–90, 190, 203, 211
Mysore State, 171
Mysticism, 42

Nādir Shāh, 24
Nadurajapuram, 290
Nagaland, **261–3**
Nagaland, 261
Nagar Haveli, **341**
Nagaram Islands, 102, 111–12
Nagarjunasagar Dam, 406
Nagas, 261
Nagel, Gottley, 227
Nagel, Harriet S., 227, 230

Nagel, Volbrecht, 225–7, 227, 228
Nagercoil, 281
Nagpur, 242, 251, 330
Nair, Silas C., 306
Naismith, Alice M. (*née* Cannon), 123
Naismith, Archie, 103, 112, 123–4
Nalanda, 155
Nambudripad, Dr., 270
Namgyal dynasty, 279
Nānak Dev, Guru, 54
Nandyal, 133
Nangal, 161, 267
Napper, B., 219
Napper, E., 219
Naraikkinar, 287, 290, 398
Narasapur, 93, 96, 99–101, 102, 104,
 110, 112, 114, 116–17, 118–20,
 121, 123, 126, 127, 129, 133,
 252, 306
Narbada River, 8
Nautanwa, 386
Nayagam, Samson, 155
Nehru, Pandit Jawahartal, 11, 12, 27,
 169, 223, 259, 261, 321
Neill, Stephen, 32
Nellikunnu, 232
Nepal, 2, 5, 365, **381–93**, 397–8
Nepal Christian Fellowship, 391
Nepal Evangelistic Band, 386
Nepalganj, 382
Nepali language, 279, 382, 398
Nestorians, 70, 221
New Delhi, 43
Newars, 382
Newport, Cora R., 114, 178
Newton, Kenneth J., 151, 192–3, 198
Newton, Mrs. Kenneth J., 151
Nicholas, George, 378–9
Nicholas, Shanta, 378–9
Nicholls, Bruce, 67
Nicobar Islands, 6, 27, **338, 340**
Nicoll, M. Gwen, 220
Nidadavolu, 90, 117–18, 127, 133, 309
Niddugatta, 204
Nilgiris, 286, 301
Nirvāṇa, 51, 60
Noah, 63
Nobili, Roberto de, 70
Noble, Annie (*née* Kristensen), 237–8
Noble, William T., 237–8
Noel, Edwyn H., 224, 227–8, 230, 237
Noel, Julia (*née* Shirtliff), 227, 228, 230,
 237, 239
Norman, Beryl F., 167, 335
Noschke, Minna A., 298, 298, 311

VOLUME 3

...THAT THE WORLD MAY KNOW
that Thou hast sent Me, and hast
loved them, as Thou hast loved Me.

John 17:23